Achieving Nursing Care Standards: Internal & External

Marjorie Moore Cantor

Achieving Nursing Care Standards: Internal & External

Marjorie Moore Cantor, R.N., Ph.D.

Associate Director of Nursing
Research in Nursing
University of Iowa Hospitals and Clinics
Iowa City, Iowa

with chapters by

Deborah D. McDougall, R.N., M.A. and Susan W. Kurth, R.N., M.A.

Clinical Nursing Specialists
Research in Nursing
University of Iowa Hospitals and Clinics

 **Nursing Resources, Inc.**

*Written for and dedicated to
the nursing staff of the
University of Iowa Hospitals and Clinics*

Contents

Preface

In addition to standards they set for themselves, nursing administrators are constantly confronted with the need to meet standards of nursing care developed by other agencies and organizations. Some standards are imposed by governmental agencies and carry real and specific penalties if not met—such as the conditions established for payment of Medicare or Medicaid funds. Some standards must be met because of a voluntary agreement to be evaluated, as is the case when a hospital asks to be surveyed by the Joint Commission for Accreditation of Hospitals (JCAH). Failure to comply with standards in these cases can also involve a real and specific penalty.

Compliance with governmental or accreditation standards must occur, whether or not one agrees with the philosophy behind the standards. A third type of standard is accepted entirely on a voluntary basis and failure to comply is not punished in any tangible way. These are the standards of professional organizations, such as those of the American Nurses' Association. In these cases, the extent to which one complies depends on the degree of identification one has with the organization, its philosophies and its goals as manifested by its standards.

Most problems in meeting standards stem from the tendency of individuals to view standards as restrictions or arbitrary rules that interfere with one's efficiency. This is particularly true when individuals who do not understand the purpose of a standard or the variables relevant to achieving that purpose are responsible for interpreting the standard and for directing activities designed to meet it.

Some standards are geared to meet goals unrelated to patient care outcomes. In a complex hospital setting, much of the work involves activities and people who have no direct responsibility for patient care. However, there is no reason why standards pertaining to such work should be in conflict with standards of patient care delivery. Careful examination of the various standards and the rationale behind them can help those in responsible positions to reconcile seemingly contradictory features.

The purpose of this book is to help nursing administrators examine standards—their purposes and their uses in achieving quality of care—and to suggest a method of programming that makes meeting them a natural consequence of normal nursing department function.

Part I provides a basis for examining and developing standards. Chapter 1 considers the general topic of standards, issues of accountability with regard to them, and evaluation methods to assess the degree of compliance with standards and at the same time provide the basis for programming care and improving its quality. Chapter 2 introduces a method of conceptualizing the functions and activities of nursing with a view toward programming to meet standards of quality care for patients and to engage in outcome, process, or structure evaluation.

The following sections deal with the practical use of the principles and concepts presented in part I. Part II provides material on planning for and evaluating programs for quality assurance in terms of patient results. Part III deals with process standards and includes information about developing performance standards and standards for staff education. Part IV deals with the issues involved in establishing and evaluating the structure within which nursing care is provided.

This book is intended for practitioners of nursing with administrative responsibility for nursing care delivery systems, whether in large departments or small units. It is hoped that such individuals will find some practical answers to the real and concrete questions they confront in their efforts to provide quality care to the patients for whom they are responsible.

Acknowledgments

It is impossible to acknowledge everyone who has influenced my thinking and hence has contributed in some fashion to this book. I sincerely hope that I have not in cavalier fashion presented as my own ideas some that should have been attributed to others. My apologies are extended to those who did make a contribution but who are not acknowledged below. My thanks go to a large number of individuals who helped determine the content of the book by virtue of their responses in classes and the discoveries some of them made while attempting to put certain of my ideas to work in their daily practices.

A few individuals contributed in very substantial ways that call for specific acknowledgments. In our discussions about nursing, Myrtle K. Aydelotte helped me develop and clarify some of the ideas presented. Doris Levsen gave wholehearted support to the attempts to operationalize the goal-directed model and provided invaluable assistance in the task of translating ideas into actions. Mary Fuller made it possible for some of my working time to be spent on writing this book. My sincere thanks go to Deborah McDougall and Susan Kurth for contributing two of the chapters. I also wish to thank the Contemporary Publishing staff for their excellent job of editing.

The greatest appreciation must go to Gordon N. Cantor who not only provided the usual husbandly support, but also spent hours helping to put the book in readable form.

PART I

Programming for Establishing and Maintaining High Standards of Nursing Care

CHAPTER 1 | # *Accountability, Evaluation, and Standards*

Hospital nursing is practiced in a complex setting in which restrictions and constraints are imposed at all levels. Many factors that determine the manner in which nursing is carried out are far removed from the patient's bedside. These factors may not even be recognized for the role they play when major decisions are made about nursing practice. Federal programs to improve the quality of nursing care given one type of patient can affect, for better or worse, the standards of care applicable to an entirely different patient group. A lawsuit in California can affect nursing practice in New Jersey. Consumer demands for improved quality of care, nurses' demands for more involvement in the health care decisions made in their own practice areas, new medical discoveries, changes in the economy—all affect the nature of nursing practice.

CONCEPTIONS OF THE NURSE'S ROLE

One important influence stems from the conceptions various interested parties—such as nurses themselves, patients, doctors, administrators, professional organization staff members, and educators—have about the nature of the ideal nurse and her function. The differing viewpoints generate unresolvable conflicts for the individual nurse who may find, for example, that the action she believes most suitable for a given set of cir-

cumstances is quite incompatible with that favored by the patient—the very person she is attempting to serve. The nurse may generate even more self-conflict if she tries to define her role in terms of the expressed needs and desires of the patient, because patients can be exceedingly unrealistic about their own needs and the capacity of the health delivery system to accommodate them.

Nurses have not traditionally concerned themselves with health care delivery problems and the health needs of society as a whole. They tend to think of themselves at the bedside, dealing with all the needs of the individual patient. They are not likely to weigh the cost in time and effort of administering individual patient care against the availability of health delivery resources, nor are they apt to dwell on the significance of the problem presented by the individual patient compared with the health problems of society as a whole. A nurse may set standards that could only be met by working with just one patient at a time, not recognizing that meeting the *total needs* of a single individual may entail a failure to meet the *essential* needs of other patients. She has probably been educated to believe professional nursing calls for concentrating on restricted aspects of the total enterprise and focusing on immediate particularized problems rather than on long-range consequences to the individual or to society.

3

THE NURSE'S ROLE
IN THE HOSPITAL

Over two-thirds of the nurses in this country practice in hospitals or related institutions[1]. When a new practitioner enters hospital nursing, she is confronted with some realities for which she has not been prepared[2]. Even as she adapts to her work situation, it is unlikely that she will come to comprehend every complexity of that setting or all the implications of actions taken and programs developed by her superiors or colleagues.

A good deal of the hospital's complexity stems from confusion regarding lines of authority and the location of power. Some hospital employees have responsibility without authority and others have authority without responsibility. Though the physician has supreme authority over care of the patient, the administrator has authority over the handling of materials and supplies. Nurses have a great deal of responsibility delegated to them by both physicians and administrators, but do not always have the authority needed to discharge those responsibilities satisfactorily. Furthermore, the requirements imposed by physicians and administrators may in certain respects be incompatible; the nurse in such a situation is left to sort out the essentials and to take those actions she considers most appropriate[3].

The nurse also has to integrate her activities with those of other professional groups (such as dietitians, physical therapists, social workers, and x-ray personnel). And though she may like to think of herself as the coordinator of the patient's care, she may in reality simply be a keeper of schedules who frequently has to modify her own to adapt to the requirements of other services in the hospital. In this sense, the physical therapist or the dietitian affect the way she is able to provide patient care to the same degree as the physician or administrator. In some institutions, the nurse may still engage only in those activities explicitly assigned her by the physician or administrator, plus whatever others come her way by default (when no other disciplines choose to engage in them). In such institutions, nurses rely on other professional groups to develop the systems or procedures designed to enhance the quality of patient care. Thus, the pharmacist designs the medication procedures; the administrative group develops the patient-teaching programs; the schedule for providing nursing care to individual patients is geared to physical therapy or x-ray scheduling requirements; and cleaning and linen changes are geared to housekeeping and laundry protocols.

Nurses seldom realize the extent to which they allow other disciplines or services to dictate nursing care practices, thereby setting the standards to which nursing personnel are expected to adhere. Nurses tend to abdicate their responsibilities for controlling nursing care, either by deliberately deciding the struggle is hopeless or by unknowingly relinquishing their prerogatives piece by piece in the pursuit of short-term goals. The most regrettable of all such situations is when nurses use constraints placed on them by the hospital's bureaucratic structure as justifications for permitting low standards of nursing care to exist in their institutions.

The problems involved in establishing and maintaining rigorous standards of practice are compounded if divisiveness exists within the department. If nursing administration is seen as primarily managerial, while the floor nurses regard themselves as representatives of "real nursing," efforts to achieve articulated nursing goals will probably lack cohesiveness. Nurses in the clinical areas, given their necessarily restricted perspective on the total program, might understandably regard nursing administration as the source of the frustrations they experience in their daily nursing practices, having the power to solve their problems but failing to do so.

Staff nurses who consider their supervisors and directors to be allies of hospital administration, standing against them and the nursing profession in general, may have some foundation for the belief. Some directors do function as agents, espousing the goals of hospital administration rather than of the nursing profession, thus imposing policies and methods that interfere with optimal achievement of nursing objectives. The director of nursing is in a position to set the climate for nursing practice in an institution. If she embraces the bureaucratic system instead of attempting to build an effective professional service within that system, it will be difficult if not impossible for her nursing staff to assume even a minimal amount of autonomy.

In my view, although the hospital tends to be a bureaucratic organization in which authority is frequently derived from the position held rather than from the knowledge possessed, nursing within the hospital does not have to function as a bureaucratic system, unless nurses prefer it that way. Even where nurses cannot assume complete responsibility for the care given a patient, they can organize themselves by using *the possession of knowledge* as the basis for assigning responsibilities, and for accepting accountability (together with any associated culpability).

ACCOUNTABILITY IN NURSING

"Accountability," as used here, means the individual is answerable for his own acts of commission or omission, as well as for the consequences of such acts. One who is accountable cannot claim immunity from legitimate challenges or criticisms leveled at his work. Accountability means having to explain or justify one's actions and accepting appropriate penalties or punishments for inadequate or unsatisfactory performance.

Legally, all normal adults bear responsibility for their own actions, and this of course applies to nurses and the care they provide patients. However, the nurse—even the primary nurse responsible for the overall care given a patient—cannot and should not assume responsibility for the standards of care established by her department or for the nursing care delivery system that provides the structure within which she

practices. Nor should she assume *sole* responsibility for her own actions; her superiors should in turn be accountable to their superiors for what she does. A nurse might fail to perform adequately because of her lack of knowledge, skill, or motivation, but that same failure might also be attributable to defects in a system that is not programmed to assure the provision of adequate patient care. In any case, everyone in the line of authority, from the head nurse to the director of nursing, is ethically if not legally culpable when they do not succeed in devising a system to maximize the likelihood of high-quality care and minimize the occurrence of ineffective or negligent actions by the department's nursing staff.

It is undesirable for any nurses to take on responsibility for nursing care decisions without being required by their superiors to account for those decisions. It is also undesirable to hold anyone accountable for actions or outcomes over which they have no control. The way in which nurses at all levels of authority view accountability for their own actions and for those of individuals in their charge will go a long way toward determining the kind of standards of care that are likely to be adopted and maintained.

Because the individual in authority cannot observe all the care for which she is accountable and because much of the care must be provided by individuals who are unable to take responsibility for the total system, those who do possess such overall accountability must have some way to assure themselves that their system is effective. The alternative is to rely on the commitment of others to discharge one's responsibilities—responsibilities they may not understand and toward which they feel no obligation. When the latter course is followed, much time is spent dealing with problems that could have been prevented by proper planning. For the patient in shock, it does not matter whether a nurse's failure to take appropriate preventive action resulted from willful neglect or a lack of time, knowledge, or appropriate instructions. Under any of these circumstances, the system would have to be deemed inadequate. The individuals responsible for establishing relevant aspects of the system would be culpable for *not having adequately predicted what could occur* and for *not having made plans sufficient to assure the delivery of appropriate care to the patient.*

In a system in which an individual located far from the level of implementation is accountable for such implementation, it is particularly crucial that no confusion exist about the purpose of any part of that system. In addition, it is exceedingly important that the information needed to monitor the system's functioning be readily available to and *in use* by everyone with any responsibility for the monitoring process.

The extent to which the individuals delegated the responsibility for providing direct patient care do in fact provide high-quality care will be largely determined by their superiors' ability and willingness to obtain the information by which the effectiveness of the system can be assessed. Such an assessment should determine the extent to which staff members meet the system's established standards and the extent to which adherence to those standards assures significant benefits to patients. The development of an effective evaluation system is a necessity if those responsible for nursing care are to be held fully accountable for that care.

EVALUATION

In a hospital, much of the activity that occurs is necessarily far removed from the end product—that is, some effect produced in or for a patient. Most of the time, nurses do not think about the end result of what they are doing. They establish systems, programs, and procedures, without considering the role each plays in accomplishing an ultimate goal. This situation is highly unfortunate. Hospital nursing involves a number of

subsystems which have their own particularized goals. These serve as stepping stones to an overall, ultimate goal—the well-being of patients. The complexities of this elaborate structure make evaluation mandatory. There is simply no other way to determine what will maximize the effectiveness of the system.

Evaluation in hospital nursing ought to occur, not as a means of bringing closure to a completed project, but as a basis for proposing further action, a crucial aspect of the planning stage, and as an activity with an important role to play in the implementation stage. Thus, for present purposes, evaluation will be defined as *a means of obtaining the information needed to make predictions on which to base decisions about the maintenance or revision of a system, program, or process established to achieve a specified purpose.* The decision-making aspect is crucial. The nature of the decision to be reached determines what information will be required. It is impossible to ascertain which information is relevant if one does not first know on what decision the information is to bear.

Even when the individual performing an evaluation fails to think explicitly about the decision or prediction involved, both of these are implied in whatever evaluation procedure is used. It seems doubtful that any nursing instructors stop to think about the decisions and predictions they are presumably making when they evaluate the class achievements of their students. Nonetheless, they are making decisions (such as assigning grades) based on the results of their testing procedures. These decisions carry (or at least should carry) predictive implications—the instructor's estimate of her students' potential for performing those activities the classes were designed to teach.

A beginning nursing skills class supposedly prepares students to acquire the prerequisites for more advanced skills. At the completion of the course, the teacher must predict the extent to which the student will be able to use its content to acquire advanced-level skills. The decision (expressed as a grade or qualitative evaluative statement) entails permitting the student to begin her exposure to the next level of content, requiring the student to participate in remedial sessions, or recommending that the student be dropped from the program. The grading decision will be made because the academic system requires it—grading whether a conscious prediction has been made and regardless of the adequacy of the information employed in making the decision.

In such a setting, decisions are not limited to student evaluations. The instructor (or perhaps her colleagues) will also be deciding whether the course should continue in its present form, be modified, or even discontinued. This decision will be made (implicitly or explicitly) because there is no way one can do otherwise, whether the information used in the decision-making process is sound and whether the individual explicitly recognizes the prediction she is making prior to reaching the decision.

Some people do engage in evaluation for its own sake—because performing evaluations is the order of the day. For them, the fact of having finished an evaluation satisfies whatever purpose they attach to the activity. In contrast, for those who seek some *utility* in the enterprise, the information yielded is important—not the evaluation procedure itself. To acquire the information needed to determine whether a system should continue in its current form or be modified to achieve its intended purpose, one must build in an evaluation component from the beginning. Evaluation can be (and, in my view, should be) thought of as part of the design of the system, a means of maintaining an effective activity or system designed to achieve a particular purpose.

IDENTIFYING THE PURPOSE OF EVALUATION

The first step in developing a method for achieving some particular purpose and for maintaining an effective system devoted to that end must be *a clear identification of the purpose to be achieved*. One simply cannot determine whether or not a purpose has been accomplished without knowing what that purpose is. Furthermore, to make this enterprise efficient and to assure oneself that the purpose determines the method and not vice-versa, one ought to be aware *from the start* of the nature of the purpose involved.

Returning to the previous example, the purpose of conducting a class on beginning nursing skills is presumably to provide the student with the tools needed to engage in more advanced nursing activities. To set up an effective evaluation system for such a class, it is necessary to have its purpose clearly in mind. If a group of individuals with different purposes develop a project, it is unlikely that use of a single evaluation system would assess the project adequately. In hospitals, the purposes of joint ventures can easily become obscured because each group or discipline involved has a different purpose. Sometimes, an apparent agreement reached in such situations may only be one of words—vague, imprecise words that mask what is actually a sharp disparity in purposes. Any venture is in serious trouble at the outset, unless clarification of language and a meeting of minds about purpose(s) can be achieved. For example, if a group of doctors, nurses, hospital administrators, and social workers plan to set up a clinic, clarity in defining the purposes of the clinic is essential if it is to be organized to serve patients effectively, as validated by an evaluation procedure (or, more likely, a *set* of evaluation procedures, to match the multiple purposes involved).

Clarifying the purpose entails *specifying the outcomes that will be observed if the plan is successful in achieving its purpose.*

Specifying Outcomes

The outcomes of a successful student experience in a basic nursing skills class might consist of satisfactory performances of the various skills, observed and evaluated by the nursing instructor and predictive of later facility in performing more complex tasks.

The results of an exposure to a segment of a staff development program might similarly be the skills acquired by the staff members—skills indicating potential for adequate performance of certain nursing activities at a later time. The outcomes of the operation of a given aspect of the departmental structure might be manifested by those features, stipulated in terms of the role to be played by that departmental component, which reflect smooth and effective functioning by that component. For example, the purpose of requiring the nurse to make entries in the patient's record might be to have a document that provides accurate and reliable information for planning and evaluating the nursing care of that individual patient or for groups of patients and that provides a basis for determining the need for improving a standardized program of care[4].

Appraisal of how much this purpose is being achieved would depend on how easily the record could be used to obtain the information needed to plan for the individual patient or to determine the effectiveness of the care being provided to groups of patients over some period of time. Examples of observable criteria that could be systematically used for these purposes include the following:

All lines are filled or marked off so that no charting could be inserted later than the date recorded. . . .

Mistakes in charting are indicated with one line drawn through the statement and the word "error" above. . . .

Each admission to any unit is indicated by statement of where, time accepted, and patient's condition. . . .

The time and the statement of observation or activity are clearly related. . . .

Nursing notes signed with first initial, last name and classification designation. . . [5].

Building Evaluation Into the System

An additional feature necessary for effective evaluation is *an economical and efficient method of obtaining the necessary infor-* *mation.* If evaluation is to be used as an integral part of the maintenance and enhancement of the ongoing system, the information needed for these purposes must be constantly available. Furthermore, if the evaluation system is not to take precedence over implementation of the program, the system must function economically in terms of both the time and effort expended on it. The way to achieve an efficient and economical overall program is to build in information-gathering activity systems as part of the general plan and to develop the record-keeping system, with the need for the evaluative information in mind.

Obviously, a single comprehensive evaluation program designed to assess the quality of care and the maintenance of standards within a department will not answer *all* the questions that must be answered if any specific and significant changes are to be made in the department's functioning. Each component of the complex structure must have its own built-in evaluation system, if the necessary timely and pertinent information is to be obtained when needed. Subsequent chapters will present detailed discussions of various evaluative approaches to the many different aspects of the nursing care delivery system.

In summary, a good evaluation system provides information that allows one to make predictions on the basis of which sound decisions can be made about the desirability of either maintaining or changing some aspect of the nursing department's structure or functioning. To set up such an evaluation system, it would be necessary to (1) delineate clearly the purpose of the aspect to be evaluated; (2) specify the desired end result in terms of observable outcomes; and (3) provide an economical and efficient method of obtaining the needed relevant information.

Conditions for Conducting Evaluations

These items point up the characteristics that I consider descriptive of an effective evaluation method. In addition, certain ways of arranging the specific conditions under which evaluations are to be conducted bear mentioning. It has already been argued that evaluation criteria should pertain to observable events—that is, events of which one can become immediately and directly aware by use of one or more of the five senses. When establishing the criteria (the observations to be made), it is also important to specify the conditions under which the observations will be made. Everything to be evaluated according to a given criterion must be assessed on the same basis and under the same conditions, to make comparisons meaningful.

The principle of control or standardization of procedures, conditions, and criteria of course also applies to the conduct of research, to the administration of most tests, and to many other related activities. For example, it is the usual practice to administer identical tests composed of a number of items, all of which the students answer under constant conditions involving certain physical arrangements, particular instructions, and monitoring by the test administrators.

The principle of standardizing conditions applies as well to the use of retrospective audits, at least when one follows JCAH recommendations. Thus, in suggesting how medical records ought to be used, items located, and criteria established, the commission is setting forth *the conditions under which certain observations are to be made.*

Delineating Behaviors

Once the conditions under which evaluation is to proceed are specified, one must then indicate in explicit terms *what must be observed* (behaviors or physical states, etc.) *that will constitute satisfaction of the criteria that have been adopted.* If the criteria were explicitly formulated in the planning stages, then this step would simply entail their translation into items comprising the evaluation tools to be used. One must be able to say, "yes, the results are being achieved" or "no, they are not" unequivocally. Unlike traditional classroom evaluation, there is no place in hospital nursing for such qualifiers as "almost" or "somewhat," at least when judgments are to be made about a staff

member's readiness to administer certain types of care to patients or the adequacy of a method about to be routinely used in providing such care. This kind of objectivity is essential to avoid biases resulting from fortuitously or purposefully introduced variations in evaluation conditions or from individual preconceptions or ego involvements.

Regardless of the effectiveness of the evaluation systems or how skillful staff members have become in making observations and recording pertinent data, achieving high-quality nursing care still depends on the standards established for and by the nursing department and the dedication of the entire staff in meeting and maintaining those standards.

STANDARDS FOR NURSING CARE DELIVERY

The complexities and ambiguities of the setting within which nursing practice takes place were mentioned earlier. It was also suggested that nurses might not have control over establishment of the standards by which they practice. I suspect that many nurses do not realize how standards of practice develop or the extent to which the standards they verbally espouse differ from those by which they actually practice, as shown in acts of commission and omission, acceptance of the status quo, and various other overt acts.

What is meant by such expressions as "standards of care," "standards of practice," and "standards for a delivery system"? The term *standard* here refers to *the level of performance or the nature of a condition that is considered acceptable by one having authority in the situation or by those instrumental in maintaining such performance levels or conditions.* This definition is purposely broad and is not intended to constitute the kind of technical definition proposed by Bloch[6]. In this broad usage, the term can include the level of practice a particular group actually maintains, as well as the written directives they profess to follow. The unspoken but nonetheless operative standards held by the individual practitioner are likely to have as much of an effect on her practice as those the department has adopted. The discrepancies between formally adopted standards and those actually in force can be the source of numerous difficulties hindering the achievement of departmental goals.

Enforcement of standards will not assure a high-quality product if quality is defined by different criteria. Furthermore, while it is possible to require the existence of the conditions that appear necessary for provision of high-quality care, the existence of those conditions does not, of itself, guarantee that high-quality care will in fact be provided. The groups proposing standards for nursing departments include governmental agencies (for example, the Department of Health, Education and Welfare and state licensing units), volunteer accrediting agencies (for example, the Joint Commission on Accreditation of Hospitals), and professional organizations (for example, the American Nurses' Association, the National League for Nursing). In all cases, such groups can only propose the establishment of conditions that, if satisfied, would increase the likelihood that high-quality nursing care will be provided patients. But, generally speaking, the establishment of such conditions is not sufficient. Another component is required—a commitment to the realization of the objectives that maintenance of the standards is supposed to achieve.

Commitment to Realizing the Objectives

Usually, standards bear an identifiable relationship to the achievement of other goals that go beyond or are different from the standards themselves. For example, suppose a standard calls for having a designated number of fire drills each year. Obviously, the primary purpose of such drills is to make certain that hospital personnel will function effectively to prevent patient casualties if a fire does occur. Evacuating patients, many of whom may be helpless, is a complicated process. Even in buildings with fire containment provisions built into their structures, a fire can be a disaster if appropriate measures are not taken at the first indications of trouble. Few people need to be convinced about the seriousness of a hospital fire. But fire drills are complicated and time-consuming. They interfere with the business of caring for patients.

Because fires fortunately do not occur frequently in well-constructed and well-maintained hospitals, it is not surprising that some personnel view a drill as an intrusion into their busy lives, a requirement to be dealt with just to pacify an officious committee or agency. Under such circumstances, fire drill procedures are likely to be as superficial as possible, meeting only minimally the standards that have been imposed from within or without. Using this approach, failing to emphasize that measures must be taken to assure that personnel acquire behavior patterns appropriate to a fire emergency, the exercise will be virtually meaningless and will only reinforce the staff's reluctance to participate. Even if the standard is met, fulfillment of its basic purpose cannot be guaranteed. But it is likely that, without the standard, no steps would be taken in many hospitals to assure preparation of the staff for such emergency situations.

It is unfortunate that professional groups tend not to achieve adequate standards of health care unless required to do so by some unit that can impose penalties for failures. The standards of practice traditionally accepted as part of the basic content of the various health professions have not been adequate to ensure that individual hospitals and practitioners provide safe and effective service to patients. For dedicated practitioners sincerely interested in providing the best possible care, the standards imposed by the Joint Commission, the State Health Department, or other authoritative bodies can serve as beginning bases on which to build solid structures for providing such care. Some practitioners treat these imposed standards as minimal requirements that fail to measure up to their own personal standards. Others, in contrast, who have not previously maintained high standards on their own, find the standards imposed on them difficult to achieve.

External Sources of Standards

The basis for a standard must be fully understood, so that the methods used to achieve it are not incompatible with its adoption. The sources of standards must also be recognized by those involved in organizing a nursing care delivery system. Such individuals should understand the nature of any agency or unit that directly or indirectly has a degree of control over how their department functions.

The Nurse Practice Act and the Medical Practice Act of the state serve together as the first line of control of a nursing care delivery system. These two acts together define and delineate the content of nursing from a legal standpoint[7]. The Nurse Practice Acts define nursing practice and identify those activities which are considered to fall within that province. The Medical Practice Acts are important in delineating nursing practice in that they outline the areas constituting the province of the physician and, in so doing, restrict the activities in which the nurse may engage. Neither of the two acts actually sets standards, as such, for nursing; rather, they designate the general arena of activity for the profession and establish the legal relationship of the nurse to society.

All Practice Acts, which differ from state to state, are necessarily open to a variety of interpretations. Nurses establishing standards of practice for their own departments would do well to familiarize themselves with the Medical Practice Act, as well as the Nurse Practice Act, of their state. It is also important to keep abreast of any joint statements issued by medical and nursing groups that are designed to explicate accepted practices or to interpret some of the broad statements included in the two acts.

Another legal influence on standards of practice is that area of law dealing with malpractice. Malpractice law does not define the "do's" and "don'ts" of nursing practice by statutes; rather, it is a body of precedents associated with decisions that have been made in particular law cases[8]. In regard to malpractice the law has established a measure to determine if certain actions constitute carelessness or negligence by the individual practitioner; the measure is called a "standard of care."

A standard of care in this sense simply establishes what a "reasonably prudent" person, acting under similar circumstances, would do. Part of the proceedings of a trial determines the standard against which to measure the individual act that has been questioned. Nurses are held to a prevailing standard of care as practiced by "reasonably prudent" nurses[9]. The standard employed is stipulated by the expert witnesses who express opinions regarding currently accepted nursing practice and define the action appropriate to a given situation. The term "standard of care" is used as a basis for determining liability for injury or harm to patients. Thus, a legislative process is not involved. Obviously, decisions made in various lawsuits have an effect on subsequent practice by their approval of certain procedures and the disapproval of others.

The effect of malpractice decisions can be salutary, if adverse decisions prompt nurses to examine their own practice systems to determine whether safeguards *for patients* ought to be introduced or strengthened. If, however, nurses react to such legal decisions by erecting safeguards that focus on *their* not being caught or blamed for harm to patients, their actions are likely to diminish rather than enhance benefits to patients.

States are another source of mandatory standards imposed on hospitals. However, states vary considerably in the rigor with which inspections are conducted and enforcement pursued.

The federal government also imposes standards on hospitals, through its administration of various health programs. Thus, hospitals must meet the standards set to qualify for Medicare and Medicaid payments. The Professional Standards Review Program under the Department of Health, Education, and Welfare requires that reviews be conducted of the care physicians provide patients covered by the Medicare/Medicaid and Maternal and Child Health Programs. The law requires that Professional Standards Review Organizations (PSROs) be established by local physicians to review the care provided these patients in institutions. The local organizations establish the standards and perform the reviews[10]. Nursing is not specified within the provisions of this law. Nonetheless, because such regulations do directly affect the practice of medicine (as reflected in the institution of a review system, if nothing more), nursing is also affected to the extent that nurses work closely with physicians. Standards for reimbursement by Medicare and Medicaid for the care provided in hospitals also affect nursing students indirectly.

The Joint Commission on Accreditation of Hospitals is a highly influential source of nursing standards. Because hospital personnel under the Commission's jurisdiction wish to receive its approval, they adopt its standards and submit to periodic inspections to achieve its accreditation. The hospital's nursing department is itself obliged to maintain the standards advocated by the Joint Commission.

Nursing department personnel, particularly when accreditation visits are anticipated, may spend what they consider to be inordinate amounts of time bringing the functioning of the department into compliance with the Commission's standards, as these are understood. If hospital personnel do engage in a last-minute flurry of sprucing up, writing policies, formulating and adopting nursing care plans, conducting fire drills, or moving obstructions from fire door areas, one can be fairly certain that they view the Joint Commission's standards simply as a vehicle to obtain accreditation and not as guides to establish a high-quality nursing care delivery system.

The professional organizations and the general climate of the nursing profession at any given time also influence the choice of standards established by an individual nursing department. The professional ethics and nursing care standards promulgated by such organizations, as well as the current beliefs of leaders in the field, are not forced on nursing departments. Nonetheless, such professional influences can be and typically are powerful, for two reasons. First, although the American Nurses' Association is not a member of the Joint Commission on Accreditation of Hospitals, the nurses who develop the Commission's standards are very likely to represent the current thinking of the leaders in the organization and in the profession generally. Second, many nurses need the support afforded by some authority or by group consensus to feel comfortable about programs and systems they establish within their own institutions. Many find it a good deal easier to adopt the practices considered most effective by the leadership of the profession than to determine individually the most effective procedures for their own particular situations. The latter task entails running the risk of committing errors for which such innovators would be held responsible.

It is not the purpose of this book to sort out the various influences on nurses who are planning or modifying the nursing care delivery systems in their own institutions (although a discussion of selected standards will appear in chapter 10). However, such individuals should be aware of and understand the influences determining the directions being taken in the planning of nursing care, if they are to end up with consistently effective systems.

Relevance of the Standards

Because nurses are confronted with a multitude of directives from a variety of sources, indicating what they should, must, or cannot do, it becomes essential to separate rumor from fact, the frivolous from the sound, and recommendations from requirements. It is also important to understand the purpose of a suggested standard to be certain that its method of implementation contributes to the achievement of its purpose. It is helpful to examine each standard imposed from outside the department of nursing to ascertain its meaning within the context of standards of practice that are suggested by *the needs and rights of patients*. The questions to be asked are, "Do the standards imposed from without meet those needs and honor those rights?" and, if so, "Are these the most effective and economical ways of achieving the goals involved?" If one simply adopts standards as they are recommended, one can easily find oneself in the position of trying to meet standards or practice requirements that conflict with one another. This situation is likely to deprive patients of needed services or to encourage staff members to function at less than optimal levels.

The leaders in the nursing department establish and enforce the standards of practice for that department. Individual nurses have their own standards, which may be consistent with those of the department, or may be less or more rigorous. The individual members of a department—at both the staff and supervisory levels—in fact determine the standards representing the practice of that department. The actual functioning of the department and the nursing practices of its individual members in essence determine the department's standards of care, regardless of what might be indicated to the contrary either within or outside the department.

A nursing director or supervisor can subvert the intent of or block the fulfillment of standards, simply by virtue of the amount and kind of attention she pays to their enforcement. A lack of focus on the significant standards and a failure to reinforce staff members for meeting them will inevitably lead to a diminished quality of patient care. Most important, if leaders in hospital nursing accept and adopt the standards imposed from outside their departments and view their achievement as the most desirable state they can envision for their units, the chances are good that they will *not* be maintaining a quality of care that is in reality optimal for their patients.

The nursing leaders who regard external standards as *minimal* requirements and who have developed more rigorous standards based on their knowledge of the nursing setting and what constitutes effective and efficient nursing care, will in fact be providing care of the highest quality to their patients. Such individuals will also be administering departments in which nursing practice standards are determined by knowledgeable nurses—not by doctors, hospital administrators, lawyers, or uninformed members of their own or any other profession. The purpose of this book is to discuss approaches to the development of a rational basis for establishing standards for a hospital department of nursing.

DEFINITIONS

Throughout this book, certain terms will be used in ways that may differ from other definitions. A list of these follows, together with their meanings in the context of this volume. These definitions are not intended to comprise a technical vocabulary; rather, they follow rather closely the meanings given in a general dictionary.

Accountability: The condition of being answerable for one's actions and lack of action. An individual who is accountable can be required to explain or justify his/her acts of commission and omission and their consequences.

Criterion: A measure used to establish a program or system or to judge the quality of a program, system, or performance. The plural is *criteria*.

Evaluation: A means of obtaining the information needed to make predictions on which to base decisions about the maintenance or revision of a system, program, or process established to achieve a given purpose.

Nursing Activity: All the efforts undertaken by nursing staff as part of the care given patients. It includes judgments and decisions made, monitoring, and planning, in addition to the various physical activities undertaken on the patient's behalf.

Nursing Care Plan: The plan developed for the individual patient after he/she enters the nursing unit. In determining the care requirements for the individual patient, information is obtained for the group or groups of patients to which the individual patient belongs. The nursing care plan is relevant to one patient and that patient only.

Objectives: The ends toward which planning is directed. The statements of the objectives of care, therefore, also serve as evaluation criteria for the effectiveness of the planning.

Outcome Criteria: The ends to be achieved. From one's knowledge of the usual course of events (occurring under reasonably controlled conditions) and of the factors relevant to the patient group involved, one should be able to determine the desired results that, in a given patient at the end of a program of care, indicate that the program of care was based on knowledge about the needs of this group of patients and was carried out in a fashion adequate to achieve its purpose. The extent to which the care provided the patient had the desired results can be determined by use of the outcome criteria.

Patient Group: Patients with *common* problems. To set up a system that will assure a patient receives care relevant to his particular health problems, nurses must use their knowledge about what to expect. It is possible to have the care delivery system ready for the patient *before* he comes under their care. To do this, it is necessary to group patients on the basis of the *common problems* they face and to identify both the variables relevant to appropriately planning their care and the outcomes to be achieved if the appropriate care has been provided.

Patient Program of Nursing Care: A program developed for a group of patients about whom generalizations and predictions can be made because they share certain common problems and characteristics. The program of nursing care orga-

nizes the information gained from the working experiences nurses have had with patients belonging to the group in question and makes it, and the plans based on it, available to individuals who have not already had the opportunity to acquire the same information.

Performance Standards: The quality of execution expected of staff members in performing the nursing activities necessary for the achievement of desired results.

Program: A plan which organizes the information essential to the accomplishment, the identification of, and the definition of a specific purpose; the factors to be considered in achieving the purpose, and the procedure to be followed in implementing the plan. The program may be of narrow scope (as is the case of a program of nursing care) or it may be very broad (as is the case of a program for staff development or evaluation).

Process: The action of providing care to patients or the care received by the patient[11].

Programmer: Any individual who develops a program or who obtains and organizes needed information on patient care. The programmer should be the individual most qualified to establish the standards to be followed by other staff members.

Progress Criteria: Certain signs indicating whether the patient is progressing satisfactorily and if he is free of undue discomfort, pain, and mental distress.

Standard: A level of performance or a set of conditions considered acceptable by some authority or by the individual or individuals engaged in performing or maintaining the set of conditions in question.

Structure: The conditions and mechanisms established to facilitate the provision of care to patients[12]. The components involved range from the physical and environmental to the philosophical and administrative. Included are all aspects of the nursing care delivery system that are not associated with process.

System: A combination of various parts organized to focus on a united purpose. The nursing department, a complex system, operates within the hospital, a more complex system, and contains many subsystems working together.

NOTES AND REFERENCES

1. American Nurses' Association. *Facts About Nursing a Statistical Summary*, 1970–71 edition, p. 9.

2. Kramer, M. *Reality Shock: Why Nurses Leave Nursing*. St. Louis: The C. V. Mosby Company, 1974, pp. 1–26.

3. Straus, R. "Hospital Organization from the Viewpoint of Patient-centered Goals" in *Organizational Research on Health Institutions*, B. S. Georgopoulos, (ed.), Ann Arbor, Michigan: The University of Michigan, 1972, pp. 104–205.

4. Standards for Nursing Notes in the Medical Record. *Administrative Nursing Policy and Procedure Manual*. University of Iowa Hospitals and Clinics, Department of Nursing, Iowa City, 1975.

5. Criteria for Auditing Nurses' Charting. University of Iowa Hospitals and Clinics, Department of Nursing, Iowa City, 1977.

6. Bloch, D. Criteria, standards, norms, crucial terms in quality assurance. *Journal of Nursing Administration*, 7:20–29, September 1977.

7. Hall, V. *Statutory Regulation of the Scope of Nursing Practice—a Critical Survey*. Chicago: The National Joint Practice Commission, 1975, pp. 3–5.

8. Sarner, H. *The Nurse and The Law*. Philadelphia: W. B. Saunders Company, 1968, p. 6.

9. Health Law Center and Strieff, C. J. (eds.), *Nursing and the Law* 2nd ed. Rockville, Maryland: Aspen Systems Corporation, 1975, pp. 3–6.

10. "PSRO Questions and Answers," United States Department of Health, Education, and Welfare, Office of the Assistant Secretary for Health, Office of Professional Standards Review, Rockville, Maryland, 20852, DHEW Publication No. (OS) 74-50001, 1973.

11. Term borrowed from: Donabedian, A. Quality of care problems of management, part II some issues in evaluating the quality of nursing care. *American Journal of Public Health*, 59:1833–1836, October 1969.

12. Donabedian, A. 1969.

BIBLIOGRAPHY

Georgopoulos, B. and Mann, F. *The Community General Hospital*. New York: Macmillan, 1962, pp. 1–15.

Katz, F. E. "Nurses" in *The Semi-Professions and Their Organization*, A. Etzioni, (ed.), New York: The Free Press, 1969, pp. 54–81.

Mauksch, H. O. "The Organizational Context of Nursing Practice" in *The Nursing Profession*, F. David, (ed.), New York: John Wiley and Sons, Inc., 1966, pp. 109–137.

CHAPTER 2 | # A Goal-Directed Nursing Care Delivery Model

Accountability for action and for development of a system to provide patient care was discussed in chapter 1. Accountability for use of available knowledge and the search for additional knowledge is also significant in maintaining high standards of care.

The patient entering the system makes a sizable personal investment—not just financially, but also by subjecting himself to potential discomfort, inconvenience, embarrassment, emotional upheaval, and even harm. In exchange, the patient has a right to expect that health professionals possess the knowledge, skill, and experience to arrive at an optimum solution of his problems with a minimum of trial and error and as little imposition of untested regimens of care as possible.

THE KNOWLEDGE BASE

The patient quite reasonably expects his care to be planned with attention to his particular problems. But the very *lack* of uniqueness in the patient allows health professionals to proceed with his case, because they can predict what the outcome will be, according to the particular approach to treatment and care. The intelligent use of such knowledge is the best means of effecting an adequate solution to his problem. It is essential that health professionals consider their own and others' experience and the systematic body of knowledge derived from that experience. If predictions about potential outcomes and the attendant choices of treatment are not based on such knowledge, if the professionals lack the knowledge and do not know how to obtain it, if a number of professionals claim responsibility for different aspects of the patient's care but in fact duplicate each others' knowledge and efforts, or if professionals with truly differing knowledge concentrate only on what interests them about the patient without coordinating their efforts for the patient's benefit, the patient might just as well seek help for his problems from his neighbors—such help would at least be less expensive.

Unless he is extremely affluent, the patient cannot monopolize the expertise afforded by the various professionals. He must share their services with others, but he should be able to expect that his health problems will be attended to effectively and efficiently with a minimum of cost and suffering on his part. For this to occur the professionals must know about him, his disease and its treatment, and how to provide the essentials of his care within a context that entails the provision of care to others—possibly many others—with the limited resources at hand.

In a health care agency of any complexity—and even the small community hospital is a complex organization—the knowledge relevant to the delivery of effective and efficient care encompasses more than just the pathology of the disease process, the psychosocial needs of the patient, or the various applicable treatment and care procedures.

17

However, little agreement exists as to what constitutes that body of knowledge in its most relevant form. The amorphous quality of the health care concept, as well as the elusive nature of the product involved, makes the content base difficult to identify.

In this imprecisely delineated area known as the health delivery system, nursing has a role to play and a body of knowledge and custom that gives direction to that role. Unlike almost all other health worker groups, nursing does not have a narrowly defined sphere of activity. The narrower the realm of responsibility, the more restricted the knowledge base needed for the individual to function effectively. Nursing overlaps many other services and touches all of them. Because of this broad range of activities, it can be difficult for nurses to determine the knowledge base from which they should function.

PROCESS ORIENTATION OF NURSING

Perhaps because nursing necessarily encompasses a wide range of activities requiring a broad information base, it has developed as a process-oriented discipline. Instead of developing its own scientific base, it has allowed others—notably, physicians and administrators—to interpret the facts and principles of science and thereby to determine what activities constitute nursing. Throughout the years, nurses have accepted some content from other disciplines without modification, have adapted certain content to their own use, and have developed some content for themselves. A large part of what constitutes nursing is an accumulation of directives, procedures, principles, and facts largely taken from other disciplines. If an authority in nursing states that certain methods comprise good nursing, we accept such assertions and put the methods into effect even though we do not understand the basis for their selection or have a clear idea of what goals they serve. As a result of the lack of order in the accumulation of the "knowledge" on which nursing is based, the organi-

zation of the nursing care delivery system also seems to lack order. A nursing department is often organized into self-contained compartments maintained by various rules and procedures that may or may not be relevant to the adequate delivery of nursing care. It is possible for a department to contain all the traditional units, committees, and systems (such as a staff development unit, a centralized staffing program, a patient education division, a personnel division, a quality assurance audit system, a professional standards committee, a performance evaluation system) each functioning according to standards set by its own professional staff, and working at cross-purposes when it comes to the ultimate mission for which all of them should exist—the solution of patient care problems.

For example, a staff development unit might have an abundance of outlines, lesson plans, audiovisual aids, and clinical expertise, but still devote too much time and money to teaching insignificant content because ineffective methods were used to determine the content needed to (a) meet the learning needs of new employees, and (b) maintain and upgrade the skills of veteran staff members. A central staffing program might do an excellent job from the standpoint of cost and efficient coverage but fail to enhance the quality of patient care because the planning did not focus on the program's ultimate purpose—provision of the best care possible for patients. An audit system using its own criteria might be quite effective, but have minimal impact on quality of care because it neglected to identify *significant* criteria or did not specify how to ascertain whether such criteria had been met and, if not, what action to take.

The chairperson of the quality assurance audit committee may be an outstanding practitioner thoroughly familiar with the audit system advocated by the JCAH, but nevertheless unable to extract from her practice significant indicators of the extent to which prescribed nursing activities are associated with desirable patient outcomes.

Obviously, knowledge of various systems

and methods—whether proposed by nurses, physicians, administrators, or other authorities—does not by itself give the nurse a basis for providing the most effective, efficient, and economical nursing care. The nurse who has mastered the treatment procedures appropriate to a particular group of patients, who is familiar with the current nursing literature (research and non-research), and who can fluently cite administrative policy or principles may seem extremely knowledgeable and may be asked for guidance in planning the functions of the department. But she may nevertheless be relatively uninformed about the content that is most relevant to the development of a system designed to provide effective patient care.

EVALUATING NURSING CONTENT

Certain facts and principles give some substance to the content nurses acquire while learning their profession. But often these facts and principles are mixed with the bias and the folklore of nursing so that it is difficult to separate truth from what is either thought or desired to be the truth. Such a "body of knowledge" must be subjected to some test of soundness, or it is likely to continue as a basis for planning, regardless of its merit. Unfortunately, we nurses are not known for our willingness to look for concrete evidence to support our practices. Much of our research, which should be designed to supply such evidence, is in fact geared to "proving" that what nurses want to do is good for patients. Witness the number of patient-teaching studies that use evidence of patient learning as the indicator of success, without reference to the ultimate usefulness of that learning to the patient. Or consider the numerous studies in which failure to demonstrate the effectiveness of a particular nursing practice is explained in terms of defects in the sampling procedure or of other methodological problems, not that the basic premises regarding the efficacy of the practice may be wrong.

We are surrounded by examples of our attempts to solve nursing care delivery problems by the expedient of substituting one process for another, with no attempt to determine what made one method unsuccessful and what makes its prospective replacement an improvement.

There are advocates for team nursing and for primary nursing; for the decentralized nursing department and for a strong central nursing department; for elimination of the supervisor, head nurse, assistant director, or anyone else with a niche in the administrative power structure; and for the creation of such new categories as nurse clinician, clinical nursing specialist, or nurse practitioner. In some cases, studies or demonstrations can be cited to support the various positions. But such changes tend to occur not because of evidence that they lead to better systems, but simply because they give the appearance of doing so. The reasons for such appearances may or may not be related to actual potential for success.

It is my belief that nursing suffers from four major problems that interfere with its ability to provide the kind of nursing care that affords society the most significant results at the least cost in time, money, and suffering. First, we tend neither to obtain all the information relevant to solving the existing problems nor, second, to restrict ourselves to using only the relevant information. Third, we are too quick to accept edicts handed down by individuals we consider to be experts regardless of the soundness of what they teach. We tend to seek security by shifting the responsibility to others for the rightness or wrongness of our actions. Not infrequently, the precedent for our actions consists of nothing more than tradition ("the way it has always been done") even when evidence exists that the approach is not successful. We argue against such evidence rather than give up a cherished way of operating. The fourth problem stems from our emphasis on process or method rather than on product or result. The means become all-important to us, to the extent that we forget the ends they are supposed to serve.

A NEW APPROACH

Obviously, these four problems are not independent of one another; they are interrelated and feed on one another. To resolve these problems, nursing does not need another system for nursing or another "new" method that consists of an old approach with some window-dressing, but, instead, another way to conceptualize the planning of nursing care delivery. I am not about to introduce what amounts simply to my own favorite method, to be followed religiously (and ultimately supplanted by still another "new" approach) although I am sure many will seek in this approach (as some already have) a detailed procedure which will guarantee the elimination of complaints about nursing care from doctors, administrators, and consumers. The by no means new approach I endorse simply involves *a way of thinking about the delivery of nursing care—not a method by which nursing care is to be implemented.* The approach provides only a means of organizing the knowledge relevant to *planning* the delivery of nursing care. The steps are time-honored methods for finding out what works and what does not, what constitutes reality rather than tradition, folklore, or wishful thinking.

The main characteristic of this approach is that it is *product- (result-)* instead of *process-oriented.* It is a way of establishing standards internally and of relating external standards to their ultimate goals. It is, furthermore, a way of directing the planning to maximize achievement of those goals.

In nursing, we are greatly concerned about "individualizing" care. When the patient enters our charge, we develop nursing care plans that are supposedly specific to that patient. But we have to make use of *some* generalized information to determine the nature of the patient's problem and what we need to do for him. At this point, the organization of knowledge to yield the most accurate generalizations and predictions is crucial. Although we speak of individualizing care, we must think about it in terms of valid generalizations if we are to have any basis

for sound judgments and decision making. A nurse who has been working with patients suffering from gynecological problems knows that a patient coming into her hospital with cancer of the endometrium will have surgery or radiation or a combination of both, depending on the extent of the lesion. She can predict on the basis of prior experience what the doctor will order and what procedures will be followed. She can also predict with some degree of accuracy how the patient will do as a result of the care provided.

The nurse in such a situation may think she has individualized care, but this is true only in a limited sense. She still must function on the basis of information accumulated through her own or others experience with a group of similar patients. To function effectively, the nurse has to compare the individual patient with a group of patients who share some common characteristic. For example, she may have defined the group as those receiving radium implants and who, consequently, need a set pattern of appropriate nursing procedures and care. The *outcome* of such procedures and care for the average patient then serves as a basis for establishing standards by which to judge the progress of the specific patient. The system operates according to certain prescribed patterns and even the individualization of care fits a pattern in the sense that, in every case, one recognizes that *some* kind of care must be prescribed and the patient's individual needs must never be overlooked.

Attempting to do without systems or patterns of care and standards by which to evaluate patient progress invites chaos. Since the patient must be cared for within a context that involves the care of others it is mandatory that services be systematized. The danger is that the system will take precedence over the patient—a not unlikely occurrence in a hospital. When this happens, the patient suffers from the gap between his needs and the services provided. Nevertheless, the complexity of providing multiple services to several patients where errors can be catastrophic for those patients makes systematization and standardization a must. The system must operate in such a way that the essential needs of each patient are met. This means setting up a system that gives the patient whatever care he needs, regardless of when he enters the hospital or who happens to be on the staff at the time, and that places more emphasis on *prevention* of errors than on individual accountability for them.

PLANNING PATIENT CARE BY OUTCOME

Although the system for providing care must be established before anyone in the hospital sees the individual patient, system planning can be based on projecting his probable needs, starting with consideration of a patient group (or, more likely, groups) to which the patient belongs. Examples of groups are adolescents with obesity problems, individuals requiring hip replacements, and patients suffering from problems of skin breakdown. With information at hand about the characteristics of these groups, one can arrive at some generalizations about the problems the patient is apt to present and the reactions expected of him in response to his illness, hospitalization, and treatment. Given knowledge of the problems characteristic of a particular patient group and of what can be achieved for them, one can predict what the outcomes of treatment and care *ought* to be. Such knowledge makes it possible to identify the goals to be achieved and to prescribe the nursing activities most likely to achieve those goals. This process is indicated in Figure 2–1.

The problems presented by the patient group provide the basis for determining

what results may reasonably be expected. The terms "objectives," "outcomes," and "evaluative criteria" are all included in Figure 2–1 to avoid the kind of semantic tangle that occurs when individuals use such terminology differentially. I use these terms in a highly interrelated if not synonymous fashion. Thus, the *results* that can be achieved constitute the *outcomes* of the care provided. Because these comprise what we are trying to achieve, they are the *objectives of care*. Because they are applicable to all patients in the group under consideration, they likewise are the basis by which we evaluate the maintenance of those standards—that is, the *evaluative criteria*.

THE PATIENT PROGRAM OF NURSING CARE

After identified these desirable outcomes, one can then determine and prescribe the nursing activities most apt to carry the patient's problems to their successful solution. Put in written form, the completed plan can guide the practice of all members of the nursing staff. This is not an individual nursing plan (which is more complicated); it is simply an organization of the information relevant to the care of certain patients who are grouped on the basis of common characteristic(s). Such organization of information by those having the requisite knowledge makes that knowledge available to those who lack it and who, consequently, would be unable to give effective patient care. To be useful to those requiring it, the information must be put in a specific and concise form easily available at the time the nurse is working with a patient. It should provide an easily

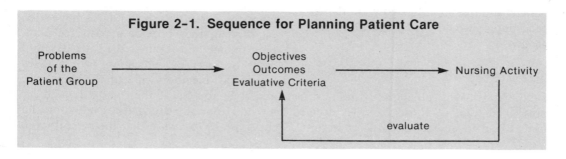

Figure 2-1. Sequence for Planning Patient Care

Problems of the Patient Group → Objectives Outcomes Evaluative Criteria → Nursing Activity

evaluate

reached and understandable reference source for the nurse who does not know all she must to provide adequate nursing care. I call this organization of content a "Patient Program of Nursing Care," usually shortened to "Program of Care."

The idea of organizing the relevant information about care of a patient group is not new. What I have in mind may be similar to what others have called a "master care plan," but a difference exists. The approach recommended involves movement from problem to outcome *and then* to nursing activity. Because the desired results are projected before the nursing activities are identified, the nursing activities are more likely to be specifically directed to the achievement of the desired outcomes. These outcomes can then be used as evaluative criteria to judge the adequacy of care given the patient. Because of the direct association of the nursing activity with the desired outcomes, failure to meet the outcome criteria and the reasons for such failure are likely to be apparent, as are the needed remediation steps. Using this approach, one has a meaningful test of the system, because it is evaluated in terms of the purpose for which it was designed.

Because the Patient Program of Nursing Care focuses so explicitly on outcome criteria, it serves as a basis for selecting the process and structural components that make both implementation of the program and achievement of the criteria possible. All Patient Programs, taken together, can serve as a basis for identifying the nursing activities to be carried out in the unit and the manner in which they must be performed to be effective. It would be cumbersome and wasteful to set up an entire system for each patient group, because many of the basic procedures would be applicable to all groups.

STANDARDS OF PERFORMANCE

On the basis of the nursing activities that are prescribed (that is, those activities deemed most likely to achieve the desired results), the *standards of performance* can be established. The performance standards are statements regarding the general level of practice required to maintain the desired quality of nursing care. The patient care results (outcomes) are the criteria for evaluating the effectiveness of the nursing activity; the performance standards are the criteria for evaluating the extent to which the activity is being performed as prescribed. The performance standards dictate the manner in which an activity will be performed to assure that all the needs and characteristics of the patients requiring the activity will be considered. For example, if the standards established to prepare a patient to return home after discharge are to be effective, they must take into account modifications required due to differences in patient characteristics, their environments, and the regimens of care that must be maintained to achieve optimal long-term results. Performance standards must be established to guide the nurse in making a variety of distinctions, including, for example, differentiations between: (1) the patient who needs to be taught a procedure versus one who must depend on others for maintenance of his regimen of care; (2) the patient who has unlimited resources for meeting dietary requirements versus one with limited financial and/or psychological resources; and (3) the patient who merely has to limit his activity for a few weeks versus one who must adapt to a new pattern of living. Building performance standards on the basis of activities that comprise a program of care makes it possible for the standards to be validated in terms of their effectiveness in achieving specified results.

As a Basis for Evaluation of Performance

Once the performance standards have been established, they provide a basis for planning the method (that is, the staff development or inservice education program) by which staff members will gain the knowledge and skills to achieve the standards, and the method (that is, performance evaluation and supervision) to assure that the performance standards are consistently maintained and met. Because the performance standards reflect the level of function required for staff members to achieve the desired quality of care, they provide the most obvious criteria for performance evaluation. The value of an individual nurse's performance lies in her ability to achieve the purpose for which she was employed. Because the performance standards reflect that purpose, they constitute highly appropriate objectives for the system. Their satisfaction assures that the nurse has been prepared to perform and is performing effectively; failure to meet them points up inadequacies that require remediation. The supervisor responsible for the quality of practice provided by the staff members in her charge can set up methods to assure that good care is given by identifying the components most likely to constitute such care and by seeing that these are implemented.

The quality of a staff nurse's performance can be effectively evaluated by using the performance standards. Because the supervisor has responsibility for maintaining these standards, she must determine under what conditions the standards will be met and use that information in building her program of supervision. The test of a successful supervisor is the extent to which she has established a system to ensure that her staff members consistently maintain and meet standards. The performance standards provide the supervisor with objectives for her program of supervision and evaluative criteria by which to measure her success in developing an adequate system. Similarly, the performance standards can and should serve as both the long-term objectives and the ultimate evaluative criteria for the staff development or inservice education program.

As a Basis for Staff Development

It is sometimes difficult for nurses to realize that the ultimate purpose of staff development is not to correctly answer questions in class or to hand in a project. The staff development instructor's concern is (or should be)

the learner's ability to put acquired knowledge to work in the actual nursing situation. Although instructors must identify short-term objectives to use in planning and evaluating specific content offerings, these objectives (evaluative criteria) must be predictive of the learner's ability to meet performance standards in her on-the-job functioning. The performance standards should comprise a basic component in structuring a staff development program.

Being intimately acquainted with her trainees' records on both performance standards and the evaluative criteria is critical for the staff development instructor. Although she may not be held accountable for the quality of care her trainees provide, she must certainly share culpability for any deficiencies in patient care that characterize the work of those individuals in the areas covered by her teaching.

In sum, providing staff members the necessary knowledge and skills, and seeing them retained, should derive directly from the system that is used to organize information about patients to plan their care.

Evaluating Process

Whereas the program of care is directed to product or outcome, the performance standards pertain to the *process* of nursing practice. Performance standards provide a basis for making meaningful assessments of the quality of staff performance, but not of the quality of care from the standpoint of the patient's well-being. Establishing that a blood pressure was taken every 15 minutes until stable does not in itself constitute evidence that the patient benefited from the activity. Nonetheless, quality of process is a necessary ingredient of an effective nursing care system. Figure 2–2 extends the diagram to include the process factor.

STRUCTURE COMPONENTS

The performance standards are used to evaluate process. The mechanisms by which the performance standards are met—the

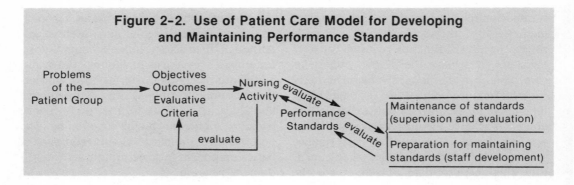

Figure 2-2. Use of Patient Care Model for Developing and Maintaining Performance Standards

staff development unit and the systems for performance supervision and evaluation— could also be considered structure components. Structure components include the various environmental conditions, the organizational framework, the material and resource supply system, and the administrative activities required to facilitate the performance of nursing activities. Thus, the structure aspect of the total enterprise encompasses all the programs and subsystems necessary for the appropriate nursing actions to take place; these include such diverse items as maternity leave policy and medication administration procedures. The present discussion has emphasized staff development, supervisory, personnel evaluation, programming, and evaluation systems, in order to focus as strongly as possible on the outcome and process features of the total system.

The mark of success for a structure component should be the degree to which it contributes to the facilitation of professional service. Any structure component should be (but seldom is) planned with the same focus on purpose that characterizes the planning of any other aspect of the care delivery system. Its purpose should be to facilitate the provision of high-quality nursing care to patients. Its relation to the conceptual framework under discussion is illustrated by the further extension of the diagram shown in Figure 2–3.

Planning New Structure Components

Evidence that nursing activity is being carried out as prescribed is the ultimate evaluative measure of a structure component. However, attempting to correct deficiencies in the system on the basis of information about inadequate nursing performance can only be fruitful if the conditions necessary for adequate functioning have been identified.

When planning a new structure component—such as a new system of patient

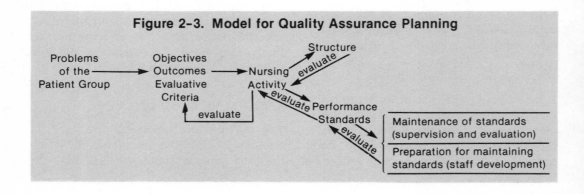

Figure 2-3. Model for Quality Assurance Planning

care assignments—it is important to determine essential features by considering the purpose of the addition and the factors likely to affect achievement of that purpose. Unfortunately, the end product of the system is not always easy to identify. Most individuals can designate objectives for a program or plan they are developing, but such objectives tend to include vague, general concepts; they need to be defined in concrete terms to make the objective clear. Objectives for a program of patient care assignments might include such phrases as "to maintain the continuity of care," "to establish accountability for care," and "to individualize patient care." Frequently, such phraseology is included because of the demands of tradition and is subsequently ignored in the actual development and implementation of the program.

Not infrequently, the program or system to be developed (including the form it is to take) has already been decided before the objectives have been formulated. A decision to institute primary nursing care or team nursing, for example, is made and *then* information is organized to support the decision. Staunch advocates of team, primary, or functional nursing might find that each method of organizing a patient care unit would serve equally well, if only each was developed through careful consideration of the problems to be solved in the achievement of certain nursing care objectives, and the relation of the expected results to the overall mission of the health care delivery system. For example, suppose one defines continuity of care in terms of certain activities that must be carried out to achieve specific outcomes. One may find the organization of nursing care assignments is not critical in this case, rather, the amount of relevant information obtained and used by the staff, the amount of responsibility assumed for achieving the designated outcomes, and the availability of certain resources. If continuity of care is defined in terms of people, one may have to assume that primary care constitutes the only avenue for achieving the objectives. But a patient who is provided continuous care by a nurse is not in an enviable position if that nurse is ineffectual or incompetent. On the other hand, if continuity of care is defined in terms of efficiency and effectiveness in achieving certain patient outcomes, team or functional nursing (if appropriately planned) may do as well.

Crucial to the development of a "structure" component is the use of nursing care activity requirements that can serve as evaluative criteria and objectives. The same situation applies here as in the case of process planning. If evaluative criteria or objectives are employed as a basis for planning, then the structural components of the program (the staff development program, the personnel evaluation system, the supervisory program, or the supply system) are more likely to be derived from the purpose than vice versa. All components of the system will be more completely discussed in the following chapters.

Adapting Structure Components

Obviously, no one starts planning from scratch. No nursing department could discard all existing routines and procedures and start completely anew in developing programs of care. Any new system must evolve from what is already known, however imprecise such knowledge. Current routines and procedures form part of the knowledge base that must be drawn on for effective and efficient planning.

Developing programs for effective functioning requires the ability to determine what information is relevant to a situation, what can be accomplished in that situation, and what methods are available to achieve the desired goals. Possession of such ability does not guarantee the job will get done. Those with the necessary experience and knowledge may be so steeped in tradition and habit that they are unable to objectively evaluate their beliefs and predictions. But neither would it make sense to assign a student or a novice nurse to the task of developing a program of care, a staff development program, or any other major aspect of the nursing care delivery system. They might realert oldtimers to facts long since forgotten, but they lack the background, experience, and knowledge needed to evaluate their own ideas and judgments.

Some may have difficulty with planning that moves from a problem to an outcome as a means of determining an action. It can be difficult to understand a planning method that starts at one end (the problem), skips to the other end (the outcome), and then works back to the middle (the activity), when in actual practice one cannot deal with the results until the action has been performed. If one thinks only in terms of process, it is difficult to appreciate the difference between the organization of thinking for the purpose of planning on the one hand and the organization of activities for the purpose of implementation on the other. One needs an ability to perceive a relationship between a problem and an outcome, and then to perceive a connection between this relationship and a method; this is no simple task. And this is not the only approach.

It is possible to start with a process approach and end up with a product-oriented system or program by making certain that the process bears a valid relationship to the problem and to the desired outcome. One can begin the planning by listing the activities required for a given group of patients. As the complex of activities is identified, it can be checked for appropriateness by determining what problem it is supposed to solve and what patient outcome should eventuate. If one is performing a procedure—for example, taking a sleep history or interviewing a patient about his usual eating pattern—and is unable to identify a *specific and significant* problem this activity is supposed to solve or cannot specify a beneficial effect of the activity for the

patient, then the activity is clearly not essential for that patient group. Those activities which *are* essential should be identifiable by reference to the problems their use will solve and the favorable patient outcomes which can be expected.

The same middle-to-end check can be applied when one starts with a total system as opposed to a particular method. If a system or program is developed first, as frequently occurs, then a careful check of the relationship of the system to the problems and the desired outcomes can be made, with a view toward modifying or abandoning the system if it cannot be justified.

Regardless of which way the planning is pursued, relevant information must be applied in the process. It is not easy to be objective about activities to which we have an emotional commitment. If we have been told by experts that interviewing all patients about their sleep histories or eating patterns is the thing to do, we may need to invent a problem for which such action is supposed to provide a solution. If the problem is conceptualized in vague, general terms and with no concern about linking the problem to the action, then the patient is unlikely to derive any benefit from the activity. It is beside the point that the expert may have developed the plan of action on the basis of a well-defined problem presented by a particular group of patients. If others who wish to use the procedure or program do not assess its applicability to the problems and outcomes of a particular group of patients, then the probability of the activity having value for those patients is low. In the long run, the success of such an enterprise depends on the extent to which the individual doing the planning makes appropriate use of the information that is pertinent to her own situation.

PART II

Standards of Patient Welfare

Patient Programs of Nursing Care: The Basic Planning Unit

CHAPTER 3

The patient program of nursing care differs from the nursing care plan. The program of nursing care is developed for a *group** of patients about whom certain generalizations and predictions can be made because the members of the group have common problems and characteristics. The program of care organizes available information about the group and makes that information, and the plans based on it, available to individuals who have not learned about such patients from their own experiences or learned all the facts relevant to their care. It provides a means by which the essentials of care are identified and systematically assured of being carried out. The *program of nursing care* is not specific to an individual. It organizes the information needed to plan his care.

The *nursing care plan,* on the other hand, gives specific directions regarding the care provided an individual patient. The nursing care plan is relevant to one particular patient only, and is developed after the patient comes into the patient care unit. In contrast, the program of nursing care has already been developed prior to anyone seeing that patient. The program of care provides the basic information on which the individual nursing care plan can be developed. The

nursing care plan can be effective only if it is based on a valid program of care.

A program of nursing care will be valid only if its development includes an analysis of all the information needed to identify the essential features of the care to be given the selected group of patients. This analysis must explicitly identify the activities required to achieve specified results in those patients and the observations that must be carried out to monitor the care.

The program of nursing care sets the standards held by the department of nursing. If the program is to become a basis for providing the highest quality of care possible, then only those who know what can be achieved and how best to do so are qualified to develop it. The importance of the information that is obtained, the wisdom with which it is interpreted, and the skill with which it is applied cannot be overemphasized. It is no small feat to translate factual information into standards that are both optimal and achievable and into directions for practice that can be implemented by individuals who know a good deal less than those who develop the program. Drawing up lists of categorized items—such as a column labeled "problems" and a column labeled "outcomes"— is not sufficient. The ability to list problems for each patient group is not the skill to be cultivated. Merely labeling or categorizing information does not produce a meaningful program of care. Such categorizing will prove useful only when it provides a basis

---

*Some may prefer the term patient *population* to patient *group.* I use these terms synonymously. Some individuals who are new to this concept have difficulty understanding a definition of *population* that restricts the aggregation to a limited number of characteristics.

for accurately predicting the outcomes of specific activities and for determining the appropriate actions to take under specified circumstances.

To guarantee optimal care for every patient regardless of when he enters the institution or who provides the care, some arrangement must assure that expert knowledge is available every hour of the day. A relatively inexperienced nurse can begin putting an individual nursing care plan into effect if she has access to and understands nursing care programs that provide a basis for assessing the patient, for using the assessment to select appropriate actions, and for evaluating those actions in terms of the effects achieved in the patient. If a nurse is to maintain the standards of the unit and department, those standards and the means for achieving them must be made clear to her. A program of nursing care that can be implemented only by a clinical nursing specialist hardly constitutes a tool that can assure high-quality care in a practice setting where nurses possess various levels of skill. The best nursing care programs are those prepared by individuals who are not only knowledgeable, but also can translate their knowledge into terms that are meaningful to others.

A useful patient program of nursing care can serve as a convenient reference to be put to immediate use while the practitioner is at work in the clinical service area. Scientific content will be used as a basis for developing a good program. Such content provides a rationale for the choice of problems to attack, actions to follow, and criteria for judging the effectiveness of those actions. The scientific content should be available to the nursing staff, but as a supplement to the program of nursing care, presented separately in a more concise, outlined form. The supplemental content should be available to help the practitioner understand the care she is to provide, but the program of care should be complete enough to allow the nurse to provide the necessary care without it. If necessary information is not immediately available, it probably will not be sought by the individual already at work on a busy nursing service area.

DETERMINING THE PATIENT GROUP

The first step in developing the patient program of nursing care is to identify the patient group. The members of the patient group all have one or more common problems for which accurate projections can be made. All the characteristics of various members of the group are irrelevant to the development of the program. Rather, the focus should be on those characteristics shared by all members of the group and for which common goals can be projected and similar actions prescribed. The program does not describe an actual group of patients, but a hypothetical group whose characteristics are limited only to those known to be present in all its members. Lest this procedure raise concerns that the treatment of the patient will be depersonalized and become mechanistic, I reiterate that the program of care is simply a way to organize information. It does not replace individual patient planning.

A group of patients who have had cholecystectomies, for example, will all present certain treatment problems associated with their surgery. But there will also be a variety of other problems not shared by all— for example, difficulties in oral hygiene, nutritional deficiencies, or sensory impairments. No single program of care could cover all the combinations of problems such individual patients might present. Despite the fact that these individual problems exist and call for special attention, it remains useful to think in terms of a hypothetical patient group with no characteristics other than those associated with the focal nursing problems presented by all members of that group. Individual patients should, of course, expect to have all of their nursing care needs appropriately attended, but through the use of information provided by *several* programs of nursing care.

Nursing care programs may encompass the full range of treatments to be given a group of patients in a given diagnostic category or they may focus on a single problem that has a complex treatment requirement. One way to group patients for programs of care is by medical diagnosis, such as myocardial infarction. Another way is by treatment, such as appendectomy. (See chapter 5 for a program of care for the group of patients undergoing a femoropopliteal bypass graft.) Or programs can be built by age—for example, a program of care for toddlers or for elderly patients. Any one of these approaches is appropriate, as long as sufficient evidence exists that valid decisions can be made on the basis of the group's common characteristics. As one finds certain consistent characteristics that provide a reliable basis for predicting what is likely to occur in a specific group, a basis has been identified for building a program of care around that particular grouping.

Physicians group patients according to medical diagnosis or treatment, categorizations that can also be helpful in planning nursing activities. But nursing deals with other types of problems. For example, planning focused on problems presented by the nursing needs of the elderly or the terminally ill patient would not be appropriate using a medical diagnosis or treatment approach. But because terminally ill patients share certain problems and certain nursing care needs, their grouping can provide a basis for a program of nursing care. Nurses may have difficulty obtaining and organizing information pertaining to topics that have not already been fully developed by other professional disciplines, but such information nonetheless does frequently exist. It is quite possible for nurses to organize the information that is pertinent to their practice and to ensure that it is made available to everyone who could make good use of it.

If the program is to facilitate efficient functioning, it is important that the group be defined with knowledge that its shared characteristics can be used to make accurate predictions about treatment outcomes. If the group is too loosely defined, one will be faced with frequent exceptions to whatever rules are being applied. If the group is too restrictive, a lack of generality would be the outcome. In the latter case, one would be faced with the necessity of developing a separate program of care for each new patient. For example, a category including all cancer patients is overly broad and loose. It would require an attempt to provide directions for coping with all the problems associated with the different surgical, radiation, and chemotherapeutic treatments. A more useful group might be limited to cancer patients who have undergone surgery of a particular type. At the other extreme, categorizing patients receiving radiation treatment by the specific locations of their lesions would represent overly restrictive groupings. A more effective approach might use body region categories, for example, patients who are receiving radiation treatment in the regions of the head and neck.

Grouping patients to identify common problems, determining the treatments to be used to cope with those problems, and their likely outcomes are not easy tasks. Patients who on cursory inspection seem to fit together may prove to have quite different problems or outcome expectations. Experience with the development of programs of care and with evaluation by audit provides a good basis for evolving more precisely defined groups. Grouping by medical diagnosis is a good way for nurses to begin their organization of content, because much of the relevant information has already been identified. Increased experience with medical diagnostic categories may make it easier to organize around broad problem groups such as the terminally ill.

Experience also can help determine how to streamline programs and, in the process, reduce both the amount of duplication among programs and the effort expended in developing them. For example, nurses at the University of Iowa Hospitals and Clinics were developing programs of care for patients grouped according to surgical treatment. They discovered that all such groups share some common problems and care requirements stemming from surgical trauma and the administration of general anesthetics (see chapter 5). A program of care dealing with just these aspects of the care of surgical patients was developed. Use of the program permits the grouping of patients who happen to be in the operating room, in the recovery room, or in intensive care, regardless of other problems they face by virtue of being in these areas and regardless of their individual diagnoses. They are not operating room, recovery room, or intensive care patients, but rather patients with common problems requiring the services that can be provided in the short-term, intensive patient care areas. Although the period of responsibility for these patients is short, nurses still need information relevant to and organized around the patient's problems to provide the nursing care essential to their well-being.

Some programs of care developed within the operating room, recovery room, or intensive care area may be uniquely associated with the patient's stay in that area and may deal only with the problems brought on by the treatment provided within that area. However, it is more likely the programs of care used in developing nursing care plans for the short-term treatment area will also be applicable to areas providing longer-term care, under the assumption that some types of treatments are administered in both kinds of areas. Such programs of care, together with those having a broader perspective, can be developed for many kinds of problems common to patients who do not necessarily have the same medical diagnosis.

The question of how patients should be grouped for a program becomes easier to answer if one remembers that the rationale for the grouping is to make planning more effective, to provide information that will contribute to improvement of nursing care, and to make such information available to nurses who do not already possess it. If it turns out to be necessary that detailed directions for modification of procedures be built into a program of care, then the grouping involved and the program of care developed for that group will not be as effective as would be desirable. The same may be said if one cannot stipulate the desired outcomes or

if the nursing unit has a large number of different programs, each of which applies only to a few patients.

As problems are identified, optimal outcomes selected, and the program developed, the group, as conceptualized to that point, may need to be enlarged or restructured to provide the most useful tool for planning patient care. For example, ñurses on a urological nursing service at Iowa developed a program of care around a particular treatment group—ileal conduit. They found that the individuals thus organized fell into two different groups, those who were given ileal conduits for cancer of the bladder and those who had neurological problems affecting the bladder. The nurses considered whether it was more efficient to organize the information into two programs of care, each including the aspects of care involving the ileal conduit (and thus abandoning a separate program dealing just with ileal conduit), or to develop three programs of care. In the latter case, two programs would be based on diagnosis (cancer of the bladder and neuropathic bladder) and the third would involve the fundamentals of care associated with management of the ileal conduit. The final choice was to retain the separate ileal-conduit program. Such a decision is justifiable if other programs of care deal with the potential patient problems that are not simply associated with the ileal-conduit procedure and if the individual nursing care plan incorporates information from other relevant programs of nursing care. If the program of care had been developed primarily for one of the diagnostic groups and the problems associated with the other group put aside, or if the individual care plans had been built around problems connected with the surgical procedure with no attention to the medical diagnosis, the method of grouping would interfere with rather than ensure the provision of high-quality nursing care.

The major portion of care is provided according to the treatment, but grouping by treatment modality does run the risk of missing problems that differ across diagnostic groups. Some treatment groupings work well because they have a common diagnostic origin. For example, a program of care built around patients who are to have a gastric bypass is efficient and effective because these patients also share a common diagnostic problem, morbid obesity. When the treatment is specific to the diagnosis, developing a program of nursing care on the basis of treatment presents no difficulties. If patients share a common diagnosis but require different medical treatments, it is preferable to group by treatment. Even modifications of the same basic treatment form could involve quite different problems and prospective outcomes for patients, for example, when patients are grouped on the basis of being given chemotherapy, but where the different drugs have radically different effects and the patients' prognoses differ widely.

Any number of ways exist to group patients for programming. If using programs of care for organizing information is to succeed with maximum efficiency achieved in the process, the groupings should be as large as possible while limiting membership to those sharing common problems.

PROBLEM IDENTIFICATION

After a general category has been selected, a more precise definition can be formulated by identifying the group's major characteristics, its presenting problems, and additional problems likely to manifest during treatment. It is important to remember that the problems and characteristics of concern should be those which are relevant to planning nursing activities. Possibly, certain patients assigned to a given category do not possess some of the traits or even present some of the problems that characterize the group as a whole. Nonetheless, if most group members do possess similar traits and do manifest similar problems and if these characteristics are relevant to nursing care planning, they should be part of the data used in program planning. For example, not all patients with chronic obstructive lung disease are unreformed smokers, but this nevertheless constitutes both a characteristic of and a problem for a large number of the

group's members. As such, it must be dealt with in programming nursing care for such patients. In contrast, the old "fair, fat, and forty" epithet frequently attached to the patient with cholecystitis, whether applicable to the group's members or not, has no significance for the planning of nursing care for the members of that group.

Problems, actual or potential, may be conceptualized in three categories. The first involves problems that result or could result from the disease or dysfunction itself, such as pain of arthritis; the second includes those which can result from the treatment, such as radiation sickness; and the third involves problems that result or can result from the environmental or psychological restrictions imposed on an individual who is hospitalized, such as subjugation to the control of medical personnel, or the older person confused by unfamiliar surroundings. In all three categories, potential problems exist for any patient group.

To find the most effective nursing activity to solve an existing problem, the specific anatomical, physiological, or psychological factors that underlie that problem must be analyzed. Designation of a problem merely as "ineffective oxygen exchange" is obviously not specific enough to provide a basis for action that will benefit the patient. Planning for effective action would require knowledge of the cause of the interference— edema in response to surgery on nearby tissue, depressed respiratory functioning associated with a drug reaction, or whatever. Unless the particular dynamics of a given condition in a particular patient group are known, it is difficult to determine whether a prescribed activity is in fact most likely to correct the situation.

For each problem identified as relevant to a particular patient group, information should be available to support the contention that the problem is significant enough to the patient to warrant spending the time and effort to deal with it. It is commonly believed that a woman scheduled for breast surgery is going to experience problems pertaining to her feelings about her femininity and that an elderly man scheduled for a transurethral resection of the prostate will be troubled about his sexuality. One should be able to document the bases for such beliefs and to cite evidence that those activities incorporated into a program of nursing care have in the past solved or significantly alleviated such problems. The nursing activities and their projected outcomes must be stipulated in very specific terms if they are to be helpful to an uninformed nurse. The patient obtains little benefit from the sympathy of a nurse who can identify problems and regret their existence, but who lacks the knowledge to handle them effectively.

Determining what problems are significant enough to warrant planning is not a task to be taken lightly; simply translating traditionally recognized needs into statements of "problems" does not provide the kind of direction required for planning effective care. Every significant problem identified should have a projected resolution and every projected result should be based on a problem that is predictably characteristic of a particular patient group. The problems presented by the patient group and the results that *can* be attained with that group should set the boundaries for planning.

Evidence of problem solution may be considered long-term nursing care goals or objectives. Because such objectives are also used to evaluate the quality of care given the patient, one can refer to them as "criteria". Thus, one speaks of *"outcome"* or *"discharge"* criteria. These terms are familiar to those who have engaged in retrospective auditing using the JCAH system.

The use of evaluative criteria as a basis for planning nursing care may be less familiar. But if one is to evaluate the effectiveness of nursing activities by referring to certain criteria, those same criteria ought to be used to direct the planning of nursing care. It is necessary to know what one is trying to achieve to determine the most effective means of achieving it. Outcome or discharge criteria, because they stipulate what particular nursing activities to accomplish, provide a useful basis for planning those activities.

However, some problems must be resolved well before the patient is ready for discharge. For example, a patient entering a unit with a high fever would probably be afebrile at the time of discharge. However, a focus on this criterion by itself ignores the possibility that discharge was delayed and patient suffering was unnecessarily prolonged because inadequate nursing care permitted the high fever to persist for an unduly long time. Good nursing care would produce beneficial effects much sooner—effects that are measurable and can serve as useful objectives in planning the nursing care for such a patient. In this case, the criterion for effective nursing care would obviously not be applied at the end of the patient's stay in the hospital.

Much of what the nurse does is geared to increasing comfort and decreasing fear and anxiety in the patient. By using criteria other than discharge criteria to assess the extent to which these goals are being met, one has a basis for planning specific, day-by-day care activities and for evaluating aspects of care that might otherwise be ignored in quality evaluation. These criteria also provide the nursing staff with indicators along the way that reveal how well the patient is moving toward the ultimate resolution of his problems. To the extent that this movement appears to be retarded, modifications in nursing care activities may well be desirable. Because such criteria reflect the progress the patient is making, they shall be referred to as "progress criteria."

A modification of the planning diagram includes the progress criteria, as illustrated in Figure 3-1.

Figure 3-1. Modification of Planning Diagram

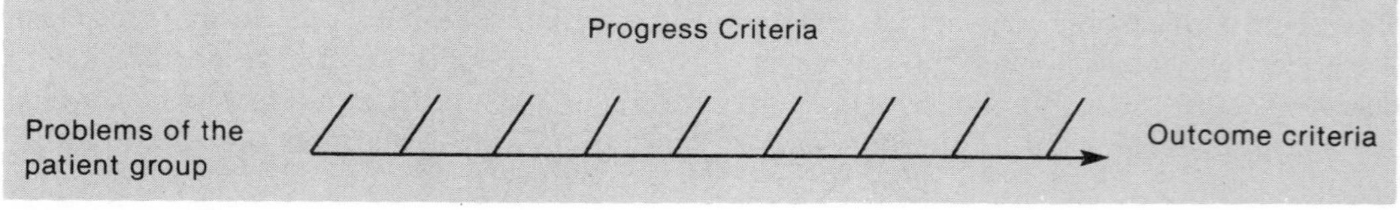

Progress Criteria

Problems of the patient group → Outcome criteria

DEVELOPING USEFUL CRITERIA

Criteria selection and definition are crucial to a quality assurance program. Criteria make explicit the standards of a particular unit or department. Further, because they are also used to evaluate the patient care provided by that unit or department, the criteria may determine whether information essential to the maintenance or improvement of care can be obtained.

Because the criteria deal with the effects of care as manifested in the patient, they must be couched in patient-result terms. In the JCAH evaluation system, the audit requires an orientation to the responses of the patient rather than to the care provided him. For those who have been focusing on the nursing process (that is, nursing activities), shifting emphasis to result criteria may be difficult. In such a shift, it is a mistake to assume that, by changing some wording to identify the patient as the beneficiary of the activity, one is changing from a process to an outcome evaluation. Changing a phrase such as "Gives supportive care to the patient" to "Patient receives supportive care" does not change the meaning; both phrases describe actions taken by the nurse. Another example—"Patient had blood pressure taken every 15 minutes until pressure was stable"—does not constitute a patient-result criterion. One might argue that these measures are designed to assure that early signs of difficulty are noted and that steps are taken to prevent a potential problem. But, it is a nursing action to take the patient's blood pressure, make a judgment about his condition, and decide whether some intervention by the nurse or doctor is required. The outcome of this nursing activity is manifested by the maintenance of the pressure within a specified range, or above or below a particular level, or at a given level for a given time period (for example, "Within three hours of surgery, blood pressure has remained within 10 ml. of mercury for four consecutive readings taken at 30-minute intervals").

Thus, criteria emphasize patient results. A second requirement for criteria for programming is that they be stated with clarity. They must be spelled out in terms that refer to observable phenomena (biological or behavioral), making it possible for independent observers to agree that a given criterion either has or has not been met. Thus, a criterion such as "patient feels supported" would not be satisfactory, even though it is couched in patient-outcome terms. The criterion, as stated, may mean different things to different observers. This defect can be remedied by stating explicitly what patient behavior(s) would signify "feelings of being supported" and under what circumstances the relevant observations are to be made.

Clarity requires that if one is setting up objectives, the observer know how to determine whether they have been attained. (Clarity, by itself, is not sufficient, because clear criteria may not necessarily be useful. But a criterion cannot be useful if it lacks clarity.) Clearly defined criteria allow the nurse to know by what standards she is to evaluate the effects of her own nursing care efforts and to determine whether the patient is making satisfactory progress.

Conditions For Making Observations

In evaluating patient care effects, nurse performance, structural systems, and other program components, it is necessary to specify the circumstances under which an observation is to be made. For example, when one wishes to ascertain that the patient is afebrile, measurement with a fever thermometer using a previously established set of procedures and a previously established standard or criterion (such as under 37.8 °C) makes it possible to determine whether the desired condition (lack of fever) is present. Because procedures for ascertaining that the patient is free of fever are already established, the criterion in this case needs only to specify what constitutes "lack of fever"—that is, "under 37.8 °C."

In contrast, many patient conditions exist for which we have no previously established conditions under which observations are to be made, or for which no precise measuring instrument exists, or both. In such cases, all aspects of the criterion must be as explicit as possible to make certain that everyone is applying the same standard. One might decide that the only reliable way to measure a patient's comfort is by obtaining his verbal report. The evaluative criterion would be, "The patient states that he is comfortable."

Of course, the occurrence or nonoccurrence of such a statement can be noted, but the conditions under which he makes or fails to make the statement must be established. Just as one takes specific steps to observe the reading on a thermometer, one also needs to take deliberate and specific steps to obtain a verbal report from a patient. One cannot reliably put such a criterion to work by waiting for the patient to make the statement spontaneously, nor should the nurse assume that absence of a patient statement indicates he is comfortable. It may be necessary, therefore, to state the criterion in such a way as to include the conditions under which the patient's statement will be elicited—for example, "Twenty minutes after pain medication has been given, patient is asleep or states that his pain has been relieved."

The necessity of specifying the conditions under which an observation is to be made pertains directly to the requirement that criteria be clearly defined. It also relates to a third requirement—the significance (validity, utility) of a criterion.

Validity of a Criterion

We may have succeeded in establishing clear, explicit criteria stated in patient-oriented terms. But the quality of care based on those criteria could still be questioned if meeting those objectives signifies less in the way of benefits to the patient than a more ambitious program of care might achieve. One might, for example, decide that the purpose of teaching a patient about his illness is achieved if the patient can repeat the information and demonstrate the ability to perform a particular procedure. The diabetic who can explain the food exchange system, administer his own insulin shots, and test his urine could be said to have learned what he has been taught, but he might nevertheless be ill-prepared to deal with his diabetes within the context of his daily life.

A nurse who believes she has discharged her duty by seeing that a patient has acquired knowledge and ability in selected areas, has made a decision about the extent to which she will extend herself on behalf of that patient. If this nurse develops the program of care that will be used by all staff nurses, her beliefs will become standards of nursing practice for the unit. The quality of nursing care will be defined in terms of these criteria and the limits of the staff's nursing activities in caring for that patient will be set. Within some nursing settings, given the resources and information available, making certain that the patient has been provided with certain information may be all the nurses can accomplish. The programmer might reason that, although she cannot be certain the patient will translate newly acquired knowledge into practice, she can be confident he at least has the needed knowledge.

Another nurse in the same situation might not be able to develop a teaching program that satisfied her until she had gathered information about the relationship between a patient's status at the time of discharge and his ability to maintain satisfactory self-care over a period of time in his own environment. She might set as goals those conditions she believes most likely to contribute to the patient's long-term control of his diabetic condition and she might continue to seek more effective methods of achieving those goals. Her program of care would reflect a different set of standards and would probably change as new information became available.

Some programmers will select criteria that fit whatever they are already achieving as a means of defending long-standing practices. Others will choose criteria on the basis of the optimal results they wish to achieve and as a means of helping them determine what nursing practices must be revised to achieve optimal effects. By such choices, these individuals are indicating the extent of their concern, the effort they are willing to expend on the patient's behalf, and the standard of quality they wish to pursue.

Those who select criteria that reflect satisfaction with current practices and a desire to defend themselves against evidence of inadequate functioning will have an easy time of making such choices. In contrast, those who are concerned about the effectiveness of their practice and who desire to achieve the greatest possible benefits for the patient will have a more difficult time. It is not difficult to specify criteria for auditing purposes if one has mastered the art of communicating in clear, patient-oriented terms. In contrast, it is difficult to establish clear, patient-oriented criteria that are significant, in the sense that they can be used as a basis for identifying and correcting existing deficiencies.

No rules exist by which to judge the quality of an outcome or progress criterion. No lists of criteria have been developed that could serve as dependable guides for nursing activity in every nursing care situation. One might adopt the criteria already developed by other nurses, but these must be assessed for their appropriateness in light of the nurse's particular patient population, the resources available to her, and the level of her nursing skills. What might constitute appropriate criteria for a patient group in a large medical center might involve totally unachievable goals in a small community hospital.

If one starts with a well-defined, significant problem and obtains information about what has been achieved with patients presenting that problem under various conditions, then the criteria that will help solve or alleviate the problem have already been suggested. If one defined the problem adequately, it was necessary to gather information relevant to the dynamics involved. To determine what can be done about the problem, it would also be necessary to answer a number of questions. What therapeutic programs are usually chosen by physicians? What are the effects of various kinds of treatments on the patient? Do these effects call for alterations in the management regimens usually employed with such a patient? What resources and time are required to achieve specified levels of improvement? How much time and what material and human resources are available within the setting in which the program of care will be implemented? In most cases, some information about the problems encountered is available to the nurse who must program the nursing care for such patients. This information should provide assistance in selecting the criteria that, when satisfied, will have the greatest beneficial impact on the patient in the long run. The nurse must process that information in terms of its applicability to her own setting to develop the most realistic program of care.

Pain is a symptom that is characteristic of many disease conditions. It is a problem that falls within all nurses' realm of concern. A body of information about pain exists. It does not provide rules to follow or a foolproof solution to the problem. The information should be processed carefully to identify which components constitute scientifically based knowledge, which indicate how the scientific findings can be applied, and which point up any values that may have been incorporated into recommendations for action. If this body of information is processed wisely, it ought to provide helpful clues to the nurse who is attempting to select criteria to be applied in the program of nursing care she is developing. Such knowledge cannot be translated into all-purpose criteria.

What can be achieved in pain relief will differ considerably from patient to patient. The patient group entering the hospital with a diagnosis of acute appendicitis can expect to be completely free of pain in a relatively short time. In contrast, patients with severe arthritis can only hope to keep their pain within certain bounds until science finds a cure for the condition. Knowledge of pain—how it differs in cause and in its response to efforts to alleviate it—is necessary for the nurse who wants to build a program that will result in optimal comfort for the patient and who wants to know what level of comfort she can assure the patient.

Pain is one of several problem areas that can provide a basis for identifying significant criteria to be met with various patient groups. Certainly, freedom from pain is a condition desired by any group of patients. Other general problem areas also provide a body of content from which to develop specific criteria. The Department of Nursing at the University of Iowa Hospitals and Clinics has built these areas into its departmental objectives, which serve as guidelines to those developing more specific criteria for some particular patient group. The patient-care–related objectives include, among others, the following statements:

The patient is free of preventable complications.

The patient's pain and discomfort are minimized.

The patient's fear and anxiety related to illness and hospitalization are reduced.

The patient is prepared or arrangements are made for continuation of the necessary regimen of care posthospitalization[1].

Because these statements are, in effect, promises of what all patients can expect, they are also guidelines for the programmers of nursing care in tailoring criteria to particular patient groups. These statements point to general areas of significance and identify topical areas from which information can be gathered to formulate significant criteria.

Outcome criteria, for the most part, indicate conditions established in or for the patient that make it possible for him to be discharged from the direct supervision of the professional staff. Such criteria should be predictive of the patient's future status with reference to the particular problems that brought him under care in the first place. Thus, one way to validate outcome criteria is to ascertain the extent to which they are in fact predictive of long-term benefits to the patient.

In this regard, one might question criteria built around the family-centered concept of maternity care, because there is little evidence to support the contention that specific nursing actions taken during the mother's hospitalization have identifiable effects on family relationships. A couple's expressions of pleasure over special considerations afforded the father or over a candlelight dinner provided by the hospital may constitute appropriate criteria by which the hospital administrator evaluates his own activities, but they hardly indicate the extent to which the nursing needs of the patient have been met. In contrast, criteria related to the mother's ability to meet her baby's needs when she no longer has the direct support of the professional staff pertain to outcomes of obvious significance that can be documented through available evidence.

The family-centered maternity care concept might have spawned criteria such as "Baby is held and fed by father prior to discharge from the hospital," the apparent assumption that such an event will contribute to the healthy development of family relationships. Although there is no evidence that he should not do so, neither is there evidence that the father's holding and feeding of the baby will have any effect, other than perhaps giving some momentary pleasure to the parents.

Consider, in contrast, a criterion that requires the parent to demonstrate an ability to bathe and diaper the baby with skill sufficient to maintain adequate physical care of the infant. There is ample evidence that this criterion is predictive of the individual's ability to engage in the behaviors involved later on; hence, it is a significant criterion that should be applied in the case of every newborn baby. Even though the first criterion might be retained because it involves an easily implemented service to the parents, it ought to be eliminated as a basis for evaluating the quality of care given the mother and infant. Furthermore, if it ever became necessary to choose between implementing one criteria or the other the pleasant, popular service for patients should give way to the criterion concerned with the essentials of care.

Useful criteria can be identified by the following characteristics: (1) they are stated in terms of effects on patients; (2) they deal with observable aspects of physical or psychological functioning; (3) they are realistic, given the setting in which they must be satisfied; and (4) their significance to the patient can be documented by evidence indicating the undesirable effects when they are not satisfied.

DETERMINING NURSING ACTIVITY

Once the significant nursing problems and their solutions have been determined, guidelines for obtaining those solutions can be established. Obviously, no aspect of the programming function is performed in isolation. One cannot process the problems without referring to possible outcomes and the means of achieving them. One does not start from scratch in prescribing nursing actions designed to achieve the adopted criteria. The nursing activities traditionally associated with the problem are typically the first items that come to mind. This knowledge about customary ways can serve as both an aid and a hindrance in developing an effective program of care. Knowledge of methods currently being used forms part of the basic information needed; such methods have been tested for effectiveness on at least some dimension. Because they have been applied over a period of time, they provide information that can be used as a check against the criteria that are being proposed. However, one can be so comfortable with customary methods that one fails to recognize their deficiencies.

A difficult task for the nurse who is new to programming for patient care is to differentiate between nursing actions prescribed to solve a problem for a particular patient and those which form part of a system set up to ensure that all programs of care can be implemented. To overcome this difficulty the programmer makes certain that every nursing activity prescribed for a patient group is bounded on one side by a clear statement of the problem to be solved and on the other by an explicit stipulation of the progress or outcome criterion to be met. It also may help to remind oneself periodically that establishing a basis for

evaluating every single aspect of a system (that is, all the care to be given to an individual patient or all the components in the functioning of a nursing care unit) is not what is at stake.

For example, obtaining a urine specimen on admission would not be a prescribed nursing activity forming part of a program of care, because it is performed routinely with all patients. Elimination of such a direction to the nurse in a program of care would not indicate the activity is not to be performed, but rather that it does not relate to a significant problem for which one wishes to develop a specific solution. Certain patients will, of course, manifest a problem for which information obtained from a urine sample is needed to determine the extent of the problem or the appropriate treatment. In such cases, directions to the nurse should incorporate the observations to be made and the method by which such specimens should be obtained. The directions should clarify that this activity in this case is not a routine procedure, but one of special significance for the patient group involved.

How specific should one be in providing directions for obtaining a special urine sample or for any procedure or nursing activity included in a program of care? No simple rule exists. However, one principle is likely to be helpful: include as much in the program of care as is needed to assure that the individual using the program can achieve its objectives as well as could the developer of the program. For activities that involve a previously established procedure, it is necessary only to name the procedure; there is no need to include directions for administering an enema, performing a catheterization, or starting an intravenous infusion. All such activities have been clearly spelled out in the procedure book used in any well-regulated nursing department. In contrast, most departments of nursing do not include procedures for dealing with psychological or sociological problems.

For example, a major problem in a program of care designed for patients facing devastating surgery (say, radical neck resection) is the patient's anxiety level. It is necessary to spell out specifically the behavioral and physical signs that signify that the objective of reducing patient anxiety has been realized. Similarly, it is essential that the steps to be taken and the methods to be used by the nurse be spelled out in detail. Such admonitions as "Relieve the patient's anxiety," "Let the patient ventilate," or "Give the patient supportive care" are too general and vague to assure communality of meaning or effective action.

Even when all nurses must meet the same criteria, they may not use methods that will achieve the desired results. The approach chosen by the programmer should have been tested to determine that it does in fact achieve those results, and then steps must be taken to ensure that everyone employs that approach.

On occasion, skilled nurses can achieve desirable results with patients but are unable to outline their steps in that process. They simply cannot program the nursing activities so that others can duplicate their efforts and achieve the same outcomes. If patients are to be assured competent care in such circumstances, then somehow it must be made certain that someone with appropriate knowledge and skill is always available to them. If such a person is not on duty in a given unit when the need arises, then some means for obtaining her assistance should be built into the program of care. In the meantime, it would behoove those who do possess the skills to analyze their own activities to arrive at a program that others can understand and follow.

In many hospitals, there are personnel who provide certain services but who do not have ultimate responsibility for the patient's 24-hour care. When such individuals are not part of the unit nursing staff, the nurses in that unit do not have control over the activities even when such activities are of concern to the nurses. The program of nursing care could not be considered an instrument to guide personnel who are not under the nursing administrator's jurisdiction. In such circumstances, nurses must determine their

responsibilities in securing and supporting such functions. For example, the nutrition department may assume responsibility for teaching the diabetic patient how to manage his condition. In some cases, the nutrition department might have sufficient staff to guarantee every diabetic patient's mastery of such skills. But in other cases, the number of dieticians available may be limited and nurses might have to assume the teaching on an irregular basis.

If nurses do not assume responsibility for outcomes achieved primarily through the activities of other groups, programs of care do not have to be concerned with those activities. But if nurses have a concern for the extent to which the patient reaches all objectives, they are obliged to specify those objectives and their own responsibility for seeing that they are achieved. I assume most nurses feel some commitment to the diabetic's acquisition of the abilities and knowledge needed to maintain a therapeutic regimen at home. If so, the program of care must include not only the criteria to be met, but also the directions to the *nurse* (not the other professionals involved) for evaluating the individual patient's progress in meeting the criteria. The program of care also should make explicit the nurse's activities in securing or supplementing the services of the other professionals *and* any modification in care that might be indicated should other personnel not meet the objectives at a level the nurse considers acceptable.

Returning to the previous example, a program of care could direct that the diabetic patient's status in learning about his diet should be ascertained at given periods during his hospital stay, regardless of who is responsible to teach him. If the nurse discovers the patient has fallen short of meeting certain criteria, she has several options, depending on the interdepartmental structure of the hospital. She could refer the problem back to the nutrition department or, if hospital protocol made it appropriate, to the doctor responsible for the patient's care; she could provide the original teaching herself if the patient could not be taught in the usual fashion; or she could supplement the teaching provided by others.

In any case in which the nurse believed a discrepancy existed between her standards and those accepted by other professional personnel, it is assumed the nurse will first validate her criteria, gathering evidence that such criteria are both optimal and realistic. Having done so, the nursing department would have to identify the action most likely to achieve the desired results. Because we are dealing with patient criteria and because it is rare that only one professional group is totally responsible for providing patient care, it is difficult to determine exactly how one professional group's actions relate to the total effort to meet the adopted criteria. If the quality of nursing action is going to have any effect on a patient outcome, it is necessary to determine precisely how given nursing activities relate to outcomes and what will make them maximally effective.

The physician must be accountable for the patient who "goes bad" on the operating room table. Does the nurse have any responsibility for preventive actions in such a case? Do any nursing activities exist that, if performed routinely, would have prevented even one patient from experiencing difficulties or dying on the operating room table? Are these completely unforeseeable circumstances over which we have no control or are there occasions when we could have made use of available information to predict the possible existence of unusual problems? If prediction is a possibility, can we identify measures the nurse might take that would detect the presence of such problems or ameliorate the situation?

The activities nurses prescribe for themselves in such areas define their standards of quality even more than do the criteria they select. We can justify our failures to meet criteria if the situations in which the failures occur involve areas deemed outside our realm of responsibility and for which, consequently, we have not prescribed any nursing activities. For example, we may believe that the preoperative monitoring of certain types of patients for signs of excessive anxiety, unusual reactions to preoperative medication, or other known indicators of potential problems is not a nurse's responsibility. If this case, the nurse need feel no culpability for problems that occur on the operating room table—problems that might have been prevented, in certain instances.

In contrast, if we do include directions for preoperative monitoring in programs designed for patients facing extensive or frightening surgery, we have indicated our belief that nurses do carry some responsibility to see that the patient survives the surgery and its aftermath.

The problems identified as being of concern, the results the nurse projects as objectives of care, and the methods she chooses to attain those results—all taken together define the standard of excellence she holds for nursing care. A useful and significant program of nursing care can be developed only by one who can recognize the interrelations of these parts. Criteria are significant only if they identify outcomes related to significant problems; criteria can be met only if the prescribed nursing activities are the appropriate means for solving such problems and are comprehensible to those who administer the care.

A FORM FOR USE

When a comprehensive and complete set of nursing care programs is available on the patient care unit, the nurses have access to the basic information needed to develop individual nursing care plans. (See example of use for developing nursing care plan in chapter 5.) The finished programs of care will be most useful to the staff if they are arranged in a format that provides information quickly and succinctly. The form that best satisfies this criterion for those who develop individual nursing care plans is the form of choice for that particular clinical unit. If the department of nursing wishes to establish a standard form to be used in all patient care units, such a form may be helpful if it is not overused in the development of individual programs of care.

The usefulness of the whole concept of programming as a basis for planning care can be negated if more emphasis is placed on the existence and form of the program than on the qualitative aspects of the program and its uses. Different nursing staffs might find that they can use one type of format better than another. Most individuals who have been actively engaged in developing and *using* programs of care believe that a straight narrative form is too cumbersome for ready use in the clinical area. ("Using" is emphasized here because there are always some people who develop and evaluate programs of care by a set of criteria unrelated to the realm of practical application.) Some like an outline form, but most prefer a column approach that highlights the essential elements. If the columns are ordered in the way that planning takes place (the method I propose), the format would conform to the following sequence.

Problem	Outcome Criteria	Progress Criteria	Nursing Action

Those using the plan, however, might find it more useful if the program were arranged in the sequence in which it is to be implemented:

Problem	Nursing Action	Progress Criteria	Outcome Criteria

Some nurses prefer to segregate the outcome criteria from the rest of the pro-gram of care, either putting them together in a list or by using each one as a heading to introduce a particular area of concern. Thus, the working program might take the following format:

Problem:

Outcome Criterion:

Progress Criteria	Nursing Action

When it is possible to identify circumscribed stages of progress (for example, with surgical patients), a chronological ordering may be superimposed on the column format. It might be much easier for a staff nurse to follow a program that divides the care into stages labeled "preoperative," "immediate postoperative," and "convalescent." The same columns would be used, but these would be repeated across the different stages of care.

Even more important than the form the program takes and its applicability to possible problems is the system established to assure its use and to evaluate its validity—that is, the extent to which it makes available to the nursing staff information that they use and that helps assure the provision of high-quality care to patients.

Subsequent chapters will deal with the systems set up to evaluate the effectiveness of the programs of nursing care and for establishing and evaluating the methods designed to facilitate their development and use.

REFERENCE

1. Department of Nursing Objectives. *Administrative Nursing Policy and Procedure Manual.* Department of Nursing, University of Iowa Hospitals and Clinics, Iowa City, 1974.

BIBLIOGRAPHY

Brodbeck, M. "Logic and Scientific Method in Research on Teaching" in *Handbook of Research on Teaching,* N. L. Gage, (ed.), Chicago: Rand McNally and Company, 1963, pp. 44–93.

Mager, R. *Goal Analysis.* Belmont California: Fearon Publishers, Lear Siegler Inc., 1972.

Thorndike, R. L. and Hagen, E. *Measurement and Evaluation in Psychology and Education* 3d ed. New York: John Wiley and Sons, Inc., 1969.

CHAPTER 4

Evaluating the Effectiveness of Patient Programs of Nursing Care

Nurses' concerns about the quality of the care they provide did not suddenly develop in the 1970s, although the emphasis on evaluation by outcome criteria has been much more pronounced recently. To some extent, nurses have always been concerned about the quality of the care they have provided patients. According to the literature, by the 1950s individuals were attempting to develop standards of quality for the profession and to find ways to systematically evaluate the effectiveness of nursing activities[1–6].

The idea of formally evaluating the concept of nursing care arose from the need to have nursing care criterion measures for research purposes. Research projects studying methods for influencing the total quality of care required measures that would encompass the overall effects of care. In the early attempts to measure the effectiveness of nursing care, the measures chosen (with a few exceptions) focused on the judgments of individuals about the quality of *nursing actions* taken rather than on the *results* achieved.

One notable exception was the use made of patient welfare indices in Aydelotte and Tener's study of the relation between nursing activity and patient welfare[7]. Patient welfare was defined in terms of effects on the patient. The investigator's concern was to measure changes in patient condition; the focus was on patient improvement, not on numbers of patients manifesting conditions

indicating some absolute level of excellence. Although this study did attempt to identify patient conditions as a basis for judging the effects of nursing care intervention, it shared with other approaches certain problems that limited its utility.

First, an attempt was made to develop one set of criteria to evaluate the care of a variety of conditions; such an approach necessarily reduces the sensitivity and efficiency of a measurement tool that is used to evaluate the planning and solving of individual problems. Second, as is true in most cases, the methods used for gathering data require an investment in additional time, effort, and personnel; although such an investment may be justifiable for completing particular research projects, it would not be practicable in maintaining and controlling the quality of nursing care given on a day-by-day basis. The nursing audit approach developed by Phaneuf provides a more efficient method of gathering data, given its use of the patient's medical record and of routine recording[8]. But the method described by Phaneuf, although intended to serve as a quality control device, suffers from the problem of questionable criterion validity; the criteria that are recommended involve statements pertaining to *nursing actions* or to *services* provided the patient.

When Phaneuf's approach was introduced, other methods entailing direct observation of the care given in nursing service areas were also being described in the

43

literature[9–12]. Unfortunately, however, these also tend to focus on nonclinical indicators that pertain more to the presence or absence of certain nursing activities than to the effectiveness of such activities in producing specific signs of patient progress. These activities might involve multiple sources for gathering data (such as incorporating observations of the patient's environment with examination of nursing care plans and other records), but they all are directed at the question of whether the *nursing process* is being pursued, rather than whether *patient progress* is observable. Furthermore, most of these approaches involve attempts to identify general criteria that would apply to all patients, regardless of diagnosis or the particular problems presented by the individual condition.

In 1972, the *Procedure for Retrospective Medical Care Audit in Hospitals* was published by the Joint Commission on Accreditation of Hospitals. The original audit system was designed for use by physicians and was geared to auditing by patient outcome criteria through retrospective examination of medical records[13]. The system requires that patients be grouped for purposes of predicting desired outcomes. When the requirement for audit by clinical outcome criteria was extended to nursing staffs as well, nurses had to plan in terms of patient groups and patient outcomes—new concepts for a traditionally process-oriented profession. Because the audit has become a requirement for JCAH accreditation, nurses who practice in hospitals have generally concentrated on learning and implementing the Joint Commission's evaluation system—a desirable turn of events, from my viewpoint.

Despite the Joint Commission's focus on organizing evaluation around diagnostic and patient outcome criteria, there are still nursing groups that are trying to develop criteria that apply generally to all patients or that deal with the occurrence or nonoccurrence of prescribed activities rather than with patient outcomes[14,15]. The Joint Commission recognizes that the method of retrospective record audit by itself, even when based on outcome criteria, cannot replace all other methods of evaluation of quality of care[16]. But they insist that at least one form of evaluation use patient outcome criteria and that the information obtained be used to improve patient care. These requirements cannot be met by a process- or structure-oriented evaluation system.

It should be clear that meeting the Joint Commission's standard for retrospective audit does not guarantee the information obtained will be useful in attempts to improve care or to maintain a high standard of care. No evaluation system can guarantee that its application will result in the provision of high-quality care. No evaluation system can do more than provide a vehicle for obtaining information. If that information is not what is needed to make appropriate decisions, or if the decision makers do not know how to interpret the information, then the evaluation project ends up as just another activity that distracts nurses from more meaningful and useful functions. Before any evaluation system can be used to improve the quality of a nursing care program, it is essential that one specify what sorts of decisions are to be made, the kinds of information needed to make those decisions, and how an evaluation system can be used to facilitate the gathering of that information.

Assuming the purpose of a program of nursing care evaluation is *not* simply to meet standards imposed by an external agency, it is imperative that the basic rationale for such a time-consuming activity be clearly identified. Presumably, the focus would be on the need to maintain a nursing care delivery system that will help solve the problems of individual patients as quickly as possible and with the least amount of suffering on their part. Achievement of these goals would entail an initial formulation of plans, a mechanism for monitoring the patient's responses to the care provided, and a means of altering the care when changes are necessary. Both the decision to maintain an existing regimen and to alter that care should be based on information that indicates whether the desired patient outcomes are being achieved.

To ensure that this whole enterprise works, we need to know the following: (1) how the patient is responding to each aspect of the care being given him (the bedside evaluation); (2) whether the patient is actually receiving the care that has been prescribed and in the fashion that has been specified (medical record as the tool for evaluation); and (3) whether the prescribed activities are consistently effective from patient to patient (evaluation by concurrent or restrospective chart audit). In sum, information is needed to manage the individual patient's prescribed care plan and also to determine whether the programming has been an effective and appropriate basis for planning for future patients. These aspects of planning nursing care require different information and therefore different evaluative approaches.

THE BEDSIDE EVALUATION

Obviously, a retrospective audit of an individual patient's record can provide no assistance in preventing problems or in enhancing the quality of his care. The information required for successful daily management of a patient can only be obtained at his bedside. Nurses have always (in one fashion or another) monitored patients for their day-by-day progress and their responses to prescribed treatments.

If nurses were told to develop a standardized or structured system for bedside evaluation, they might think this meant a system separate from their daily activities— one that would require raters armed with patient interview forms or checklists. Although such a method *might* provide some useful information, it is not likely to be an efficient means of correcting a deficiency in care before that defect causes discomfort or other problems for the patient. Therefore, the assessment of the patient must be ongoing and built into the daily procedures. This does not rule out the use of structured and standardized tools. Such devices can

help the individual who is accountable for patient care on a particular unit to determine whether the system is functioning adequately or changes in procedures are needed.

If the evaluation system is made an effective and efficient part of the daily nursing routines, it will be accepted just as is the morning report or the assignment of staff members. But the bedside evaluation must not be confused with the methods used to supervise the activities of the nursing staff. Bedside evaluations can provide information about nursing staff activity, but it is basically the patient's responses to the nursing activities that are to be assessed—not the way the individual nurse is performing.

The bedside evaluation system has two aspects that make use of the criteria developed in the programs of care. One part of the system involves the activities of the nurse responsible for the patients within a given unit or category. The second involves the nurse responsible for implementing the care of individual patients for a given period of time. The system is very simple, meant to obtain information to be used only in the area at a particular time and does not require processing data for summarization and future activity.

Because decision making follows immediately after the relevant observations have been made, any recording that is done involves notations on individual patient records and nursing care plans. The major components of this evaluation system include the progress and outcome criteria for individual patients, which are made available by transferring the Program of Care to the nursing care plan, and a standard requiring that: (1) reports and recordings include statements about patients' progress and the achievement of desired goals as measured by progress and outcome criteria; and (2) nurses responsible for care on a given day or work shift make patient rounds, using individual patient criteria to assess the patient's current condition.

Whether the system would involve checklists (or even specific statements of all the criteria relevant to a given patient) would depend on the style of administration prevailing in the particular department or unit, on the nursing staff's knowledge and experience, and on the depth of commitment on the part of staff members to the concept of evaluation as a means of assuring high-quality nursing care. In an area in which the patients share common problems and the nurses are experienced, the criteria could be sufficiently well known that listing them all on individual nursing care plans would be unnecessary. The nurses in such cases would be so accustomed to assessing patient conditions against the criteria that the process would be virtually automatic.

An indication that the nurse has made an evaluative check would be entered as a notation in the patient's record. In an area in which the staff is not as experienced or the diversity of the patient group precludes much routinization of care, using the individual nursing care kardex form for recording evaluative reactions may provide the only way of assuring each nurse knows the goals of the care she is providing.

The value of the bedside evaluation system depends on the extent to which it is incorporated into the daily routine as an integral part of patient care. If staff see it as additional work or if the information obtained is not put to immediate use in planning and modifying patient care, the system is not likely to be maintained.

If the programs of care are used as a base for planning, making bedside evaluations becomes relatively simple, because the job is essentially completed with the development of the programs of care. Necessary criteria for checking the patient are available and, should the patient present special problems (as indicated in the program of care), directions for modifying the usual procedures will be available in one program of care or another. Not only does a means of checking to see if the patient is responding adequately therefore exist, but the possible source of any discrepancy (that is, a failure to meet a criterion) is likely to be apparent because of the direct association the program of care makes between the criteria and the methods for achieving them.

If the criteria—both progress and outcome—have been used for individual care evaluation and the evaluative statements have been included in the medical record, the basis for evaluation by means of chart audit has been established.

Bedside evaluation for a nurse responsible for the care of a group of patients might take the form of patient rounds. The nurse, armed with the nursing care plan kardex or with criterion lists, might systematically check each patient for his progress in the correction or prevention of problems specific to him. A nurse on an obstetrical unit might check the patient's breast, perineum, state of comfort, and ability to handle her baby against the standards held for the maternity patient. Modifications would be made in the care plans of those patients who were not progressing satisfactorily to assure that they would be able to meet the criteria for discharge within the projected time.

The nurse caring for the patient on a given day would evaluate the patient's progress in the same way, checking to see that the patient was progressing in accordance with the projected criteria. She might be working with a patient who was having difficulty in getting her baby to feed. The nurse would evaluate the effectiveness of the methods she was using to assist the mother and record in the medical record the patient's response to her efforts. If the patient responded satisfactorily, the approach would be included as a part of the care plan. Other nurses would use the information to continue the approach that proved helpful or to try different methods if the first had not been successful.

MEDICAL RECORD AS THE TOOL FOR EVALUATION

The quality assurance auditing recommended by the Joint Commission on Accreditation of Hospitals entails the use of the patient's medical record as the means of obtaining information about the quality of patient care. The usefulness of the medical record for evaluating care lies in its very purpose in the treatment system. The medical record organizes information about the patient—information to be used in planning his medical regimen, a record of what has been done on his behalf, and an indication of how he has thus far responded to treatment.

If the record serves its role adequately, the information needed to evaluate the individual patient's care will be available. By grouping various patients' records, information can be developed about the function of the whole delivery system or the effectiveness of programming and planning for patient groups. The individual records provide valuable information for teaching purposes and can support or refute testimony in court when questions arise about the needs or care of a patient. These functions, however, are secondary to the main role of the medical record—to serve as a history of the progress of individual patients and as a basis for planning their future care.

If the standards for recording on medical records develop out of a concern to make them accurate, reliable documentations of patients' treatment and care histories, then the secondary purposes mentioned above can be adequately served, as well. But if concerns about research, education, or litigation predominate as the basis for recording standards, the reliability, accuracy, and completeness of such documents may be jeopardized.

Some nursing records contain more information about nurses than about patients. They include statements indicating the actions taken by the nurse, but reveal little about how the patient responded or whether the nursing care regimen should be maintained or modified. In some instances, such documents will contain descriptive information about the patient, but no rationale for its inclusion. Evaluating the quality of nursing care given patients from these sorts of records is an impossible task. Furthermore, although nurses may in such instances believe that the problem is solely one of poor documentation and that its solution lies in more charting about specific items, the truth may be that substandard nursing care and not simply inadequate documentation is the problem.

Nurses' Approaches to Record Keeping

The source of the problem may be the nurses' attitude about their function in and responsibility for the evaluative aspect of patient care. Many individuals regard nursing notes simply as records of (a) nursing activities carried out under the physician's direction and (b) observations of the patient made by the nurse for someone else's use. Traditionally, nurses have been taught charting as one of the functions they perform as part of a set of procedural rules. One of the rules that was taught to many nurses over the years (and may still be taught in schools today) enjoins nurses to chart only what they see—they should not interpret or diagnose.

As a result, their notes are frequently cautious in the extreme (for example, "patient *appears* to be bleeding") or trivial ("ate half of his meat, all of his fruit and vegetables, and took 250 cc. of fluid"). In both examples, the nurse is avoiding responsibility entailed in 1) potentially making an incorrect judgment, and 2) deciding what constitutes trivial information. The latter is more serious. Indiscriminate recording of the patient's behavior indicates a lack of understanding of his problems and of the meaning of signs or symptoms associated with his condition and probable prognosis. Lack of knowledge about what constitutes significant information cannot be remedied by increasing the number of rules for charting.

Nurses have also been encouraged to engage in defensive charting by the increasingly prevalent concern about malpractice suits. They frequently seem to believe they have fulfilled their obligation to the patient if a notation in the record demonstrates that they did in fact carry out a particular activity with or for the patient. Performance of the activity (however well or poorly done) is the crucial factor. If the activity was carried out, then the nurse is immune to charges of negligence. Charting is done to "cover" oneself.

The attitude implied in this approach to charting suggests that the nurse is more concerned with preparing a defense for herself than with establishing a system that will prevent mistakes from occurring. Unfortunately, the legal protection afforded by charting is sometimes more compelling than is the fact that charting can be used to help assure the patient of high-quality nursing care. If the quality of care is good and the charting is accurate, the records will of course provide a valuable protection for the nurse. But if the quality of care is poor, inaccurate or incomplete, charting will not protect the nurse indefinitely. A lawsuit may be avoided or even won through the use of such records, but sooner or later the fact that the nurse is providing poor care is bound to become known.

The availability of time and the efficiency with which procedures are carried out must be considered in any nursing care situation. They undoubtedly influence nurses' approaches to record keeping. When nurses are extremely busy, they do not regard charting as a top priority activity. Evaluative statements may seem superfluous in the absence of any indication of problems. It may seem much less time-consuming to cover the whole situation with such notations as "no complaints," rather than enumerating all the indications that the patient is progressing satisfactorily.

Nursing supervisors who ignore the question of efficiency and require arbitrary standards of charting may find that, when time is at a premium, the charting tends to be routine, tailored to meet the standards, with significant information about the patient omitted. The danger of inadequate reporting always exists when the standards make charting an activity unto itself, rather than one that contributes crucial information about the care given the patient.

Role of Program of Care

Nurses may have to be taught to write significant nursing notes on the patient's medical record. But to teach nurses in a class on charting how to identify and record significant information would be a formidable task. An alternative would be to use programs of care, which can provide directions for making significant observations and notations about the patient.

Rather than expecting the inexperienced nurse to personally select what is significant, one can place the burden on the expert nurse who, in preparing programs of care, will have organized information pertaining to the patient group. This material would presumably include a specification of the significant and essential information to be entered in the patient's nursing record. Of course, the expert should be discriminating in what she selects to include. It would be unrealistic and prohibitive to try to record even those procedures deemed essential in the care of a given patient group. To enforce charting requirements and practices, one must be able to justify the time involved by providing evidence for the significance of the content that is to be recorded. This means one has to be explicit regarding how the information will be *used*. In my view, that use must center on *planning for and providing the care needed by the individual patient*, and it must attempt to improve the system within which that care is given.

The kinds of decisions that must be made and the information required to make them will determine what is to be recorded and when. The individual developing the program of nursing care can use her knowledge of the patient group and of the patient care setting to determine the *minimum* amount of charting needed. That minimum should be sufficient to assure that the necessary activities are carried out and their quality can be assessed. The most difficult aspect of the enterprise is likely to involve keeping the requirements to a minimum while maintaining the necessary quality control. When one is immersed in developing a single program of care, it may be difficult to avoid the tendency to regard virtually everything as essential.

Selecting items to be recorded will be determined by analyzing the problems and prognoses associated with the particular patient group. Decisions about the frequency of recordings can be based on predictions of when significant positive or negative indicators are likely to appear. If the nurse is monitoring a patient in unstable condition, she will have to record detailed observations fairly frequently, depending on estimates about the speed with which changes are likely to occur. The nurse would certainly want to detect the first indicators of an unfavorable reaction—for example, the immediately postoperative patient's vital signs must be checked to pick up the first indications of a drop in blood pressure so that treatment to prevent shock may be instituted.

Other situations may not entail making immediate decisions or the changes involved might be much more gradual. In these cases, even though the program of care might call for frequent observations, the charting could be restricted to summary evaluative statements that avoid frequent repetition of the same detailed information. For example, nurses working with patients receiving radiation treatment to the head and neck were able to provide information needed to evaluate patient progress by recording the patient's weight and the condition of his facial and neck skin and his oral mucous membrane every five days.

This standard required the nurse to consider the total effect of the treatment—a consideration that might have been neglected had each treatment episode been viewed as a separate experience.

As another example, consider a patient receiving frequent medication to control intractable pain over an extended time. In such a case, it might be more appropriate that a summary describing the patient's response to the medication be required at the end of the day, rather than every two hours. A quick method of assuring that the medication is being given on schedule can be devised, while at the same time limiting the evaluative statements to the once-a-day regimen.

A program of nursing care built around the concept of pain could provide meaningful directions for record keeping and also stipulate the measures taken when the patient is not responding well to treatment.

Charting directions included in the programs of care can serve in ways that standards of charting developed in isolation cannot; they can help assure that the specific information required for the provision of comprehensive care will be available when and in the form it is needed. Such directions can teach staff members that standards of charting are closely associated with standards of care. By specifying what needs to be charted for a particular patient group, one can identify the information that is critical to decision making regarding patients' nursing care.

When a patient is admitted to a nursing unit, information is needed so that a nursing care plan can be developed for him. Some decisions must be made immediately and therefore acquisition of the necessary information should form an integral part of the admission procedures. Rather than setting up a standard for admission notes that requires a statement about every aspect of the patient's condition, the patient would be served far more effectively if the program of care indicated just which information is critical for the patient group involved, to be recorded upon admission, either because of its immediate applicability, or because it will be needed for later assessments of the patient's progress. This becomes especially crucial in cases in which only amelioration (and not a cure) of the patient's condition is a possibility. The patient's record will constitute the most dependable repository for such information. In the program of care, the categories of information that are critical to planning for the patient can be identified and explicit directions can be included indicating how and when the information is to be recorded.

By using the program of care to make explicit what is to be recorded, the way is prepared for auditing the patient's medical record to evaluate the quality of his care. Several audit approaches exist. In addition to the required retrospective outcome audits, the JCAH, under certain circumstances, also recommends process audits, conducted either by concurrent or retrospective procedures. By using progress criteria in programming for patients, the concurrent audit can be employed to evaluate the quality of care while it is being provided.

EVALUATION BY CONCURRENT CHART AUDIT

The bedside evaluation can provide information that will indicate both whether the patient is progressing satisfactorily and if any immediate modifications in care ought to be instituted. But its highly individualized character can obscure the view of the total system within which the bedside evaluation is performed. Knowledge about the progress of one individual patient does not provide a head nurse with the information needed to decide whether the total system is functioning adequately for all the patients for whom she is responsible. Nor does it indicate whether modifications called for in the care given one patient would be applicable in other cases. Furthermore, if the bedside evaluation reveals problems in the functioning of a particular employee, the question remains—is the difficulty an individual one or a problem of the entire staff?

To differentiate problems associated with the entire system from those peculiar to a particular patient or to one isolated circumstance, the head nurse must have an overview of the total enterprise in her unit. The information that comprises such a view should be available to her as she goes about her daily work, so she will be in a position to institute modifications as they become needed. She should be able to obtain information about those aspects of care which pertain to all patients in her unit so that she can assure herself that the system is working effectively and patients are receiving the care prescribed for them.

Such information can be obtained by conducting interviews, checking nursing care plans, having staff members keep logs or checklists, and having periodic ratings made by trained observers. But the most efficient and effective method, in my opinion, is the concurrent audit approach that uses the nursing notes in the patient's medical record, already collected as part of the process of dispensing care. The concurrent audit also provides a useful follow-up after a retrospective outcome audit has been completed. It can supply information which would clarify problems the retrospective auditors were unable to resolve during their auditing activities.

In addition to providing nurses with valuable information, the concurrent audit has the merit of reducing the time lag between the decision to gather the data and the availability of the data to those who can use it. The concurrent audit is a valuable tool for head nurses and supervisors in identifying problems in the system before those problems become entrenched. The supervisor responsible for several patient care units could obtain a great deal of information in a short period by sampling records from various areas and auditing them on the basis of some predetermined progress of process criteria.

The method is simple enough. It requires that the records of current patients be examined with specific criteria in mind. For example, a supervisor might be interested in the effects of a staff development program concerned with bladder infection control. She might want to check by referring to two kinds of indicators—the quality of care progress criteria (which specify what conditions indicate that the patient is free of precursor signs of bladder infection) and statements by the nurse indicating her control of the situation (that she is monitoring the patient, knows what symptoms of infection to look for, and knows what to do should such symptoms appear).

A mixture of both progress and process criteria can provide a great deal of information indicating whether the nurse is functioning as she should and how her activities are affecting the patient. Included in this regard might be *patient* criteria indicating how the urine should appear at various intervals, the amount of fluid the patient should be ingesting, the ratio of output to intake that should exist, and what the condition of meatus and the surrounding area ought to be.

Also included might be *nurse* criteria that specify what nursing actions should be recorded when the patient criteria are not met. For example, one criterion might state that the patient's oral liquid intake should never fall below 1500 cc. for any 24-hour interval without the nurse increasing the patient's intake. In this case, both progress (patient) and process (nurse) criteria are combined for easy and quick processing by a supervisor or head nurse. The significant criteria can be quickly identified by examining the program of care, which includes both the patient criteria and the criteria pertaining to the nurse's activities.

If the concurrent audit is to be used as a follow-up to a retrospective audit or if it is intended for some purpose other than providing the supervisor or head nurse immediate information applicable to an existing problem, the system may have to be highly structured and formal (following suggestions in the Joint Commission recommendation). However, whatever its purpose, the concurrent audit must be set up by individuals who know its use. Otherwise, the audit will not contribute to the quality of care provided patients.

Strangely, some nurses will conduct concurrent audits and then consider their work finished once the data have been summarized and reported. An audit seldom signifies the end of a job. If an audit is performed for any useful purpose, its results usually signify the need for further action. An exception is an audit performed simply to validate the success of a measure taken to remedy an already recognized defect. But even in the latter case, action will be needed to ensure the continuation of any modified procedure that has been shown successful.

Although it is gratifying when a repeat audit shows a reduction in the gap between patient care goals and what is actually achieved, if discrepancies remain, the system is not adequate. The nurse who has gathered the information needed to help her decide what to do next is not likely to view the audit as a final process. But the individual who is simply complying with directions in conducting a follow-up concurrent audit may not recognize any relationship between the audit procedure and positive modifications in the nursing care system.

If a retrospective audit is viewed simply as a task that meets certain requirements, it is highly likely that a follow-up concurrent audit will be perceived in the same fashion. Also, a well-designed retrospective audit procedure may, by its very design and the reasons for its inception, encourage nurses to view it as complete in itself, as separate from other aspects of their activities, and as necessary simply because it is required. But the standards of the Joint Commission are believed to be instrumental *in leading to* the provision of high-quality nursing care. The Commission does *not* imply that their standards are *synonymous* with high-quality care. The retrospective audit procedure simply provides one means of obtaining high-quality patient care. The audit procedure does not in and of itself define high-quality care.

THE RETROSPECTIVE AUDIT AS A MEANS OF ACHIEVING HIGH-QUALITY CARE

The retrospective audit developed by the Joint Commission Quality Review Center is a method of evaluating the *effects* of care by examining the medical record for information about the patient. It was designed originally for use by physicians as a performance evaluation procedure for auditing and improving patient care. The nursing system recommended by the Joint Commission is a shortened version of the physician audit.

No consideration is given to any special needs nurses might have, nor are any formal acknowledgments made of differences between the roles of physicians and nurses in the health delivery system. To whatever extent these differences are recognized, such acknowledgment is expressed in the criteria themselves and in the levels of responsibility attributed to nurses for patients' problems.

The Joint Commission system is not mandatory. Any procedure that fulfills their criteria for audit is considered satisfactory. Although the system it outlines has limitations for nursing use, its recommendations can be rather easily adapted to facilitate the gathering of some kinds of information of concern to nurses. Thus, if used along with the programs of care, the Commission's system can be a tool for evaluating programs of care and also provide a means of meeting the Joint Commission's standards. Such adaptations would not require a change in the mechanics of the format used, but rather in the nature of the knowledge and understanding applied in the use of the system.

The retrospective audit system, which uses records of discharged patients, is not as effective as the bedside audit for controlling individual patient care, nor is it as useful as the concurrent audit for monitoring the current nursing care system for various reasons. First, the lag between the time of an infraction and its identification is so great that the nurse has considerable opportunity to become accustomed to engaging in "inappropriate functioning." Second, if the turnover rate in the hospital is substantial, the nurses on whom the information has been obtained may no longer work there. Third, because the audit covers one group of patients over several clinical units, the sampling of a given nurse's behavior is not very large. Fourth and most important, although the accountability for the practice of the individual physician can usually be pinpointed, the practice of the individual nurse is enmeshed with that of other nurses working on the same unit. Under this circumstance, it is often difficult or even impossible to relate patient outcomes to the practice of one individual nurse.

A nursing audit considers not so much what the individual nurse has done (or failed to do), but whether the *system* of nursing practice has led to the achievement of high-quality nursing care. As pointed out in chapter 1, no *individual* nurse is accountable for the care given a particular patient. The meaningful information provided by the retrospective audit reflects the nursing *system*. Among other things, the audit provides a picture of the effectiveness of the program of care and of the overall effectiveness of various nursing activities prescribed for a given unit—its information covers a relatively large group of patients for whom available information is quite complete.

If one finds, despite the fact that patients are receiving the nursing care prescribed in the programs of care, that a sizable percentage are not meeting the outcome criteria, then the activities as they have been prescribed must be examined. By looking at large numbers of charts, one can likely specify the variables that affected individual cases of inadequate progress and identify previously unconsidered variables that may be relevant to the care of the total patient group. But if the audit is to yield this kind of information, its approach must focus on the system of providing nursing care and on programming for a group of patients.

For those who are not familiar with the Joint Commission PEP procedure for evaluating quality of care, the material presented here will follow the format of the system, with only a few additions or modifications suggested along the way.

The steps of the system are, in brief: (1) the selection of the patient group to be audited and the development of criteria by the audit committee; (2) review of the patient group's records by assistants as an initial screening procedure; (3) analysis by the audit committee of those records containing discrepancies (that is, the failure of prescribed activities to achieve desired results); (4) analysis of the causes of discrepancies and recommendations for corrective action; (5) development of a plan for follow-up monitoring; (6) administrative reports made to individuals.

The Audit Committee

The selection of audit committee members is important in determining the quality of the audits. Several factors should be considered before deciding the size and composition of the committee. The committee for totally patient care oriented audits should be composed of health professionals involved in dispensing the services provided for that patient group. In some institutions, an interdisciplinary audit committee would provide the information required to alleviate problems in the system.

There are dangers as well as advantages inherent in a combined audit—physicians might dominate the audits and subjugate nursing interests to their own. If members of the nursing group are strong in their commitments to obtaining information that will improve their practice and if they are resolute in their convictions about what constitutes relevant information for their purposes, they should be able to participate in a combined audit in a manner that would produce beneficial results for themselves. A necessary ingredient would be their ability and willingness to speak up in the presence of physicians; again, the strength of their commitments and convictions would go a long way toward determining how effectively they assert themselves. It is safe to say that most combined audit committees are composed mainly of physicians, with a token nurse or two to provide an appearance of joint effort. It is a rare nurse who can withstand the pressures generated in this kind of situation, particularly when the focus is on domains traditionally considered to belong to the physician.

Nurses may find that they prefer to do their own audits, under the assumption that they can then be certain that the focus will be on information that pertains to activities in which they can fully expect to participate. It is hoped that a time will come when, in all areas of care, the nurse, the physician, and other members of the health team can actually *function* as a team and guarantee each others' rights to make decisions bearing on their own contributions to the health endeavor. But until nurses have developed their own skills and knowledge to a degree that makes them feel secure about their own abilities, they would be better served by performing nursing audits on committees made up solely of nurses. 'f the situation requires participation in combined audits with physi-

cians, they might conduct additional audits of their own pertaining to those topics directly relevant to nurses. This could provide valuable experience in determining for themselves what constitute critical types of information and significant criteria for assessing the effectiveness of nursing activities.

The number and composition of nursing audit committees will depend on the size and complexity of the institution involved, as well as on the talent available within the nursing department. If the hospital is small and if the care provided is of the usual basic sort, one committee should perform all auditing tasks adequately. In a large, complex institution in which clinical services are separated, several committees organized by areas of clinical knowledge might be useful.

The membership of the committees will determine the level at which standards are set. If a committee is to promote improved care rather than simply maintain the status quo, its members should be those who are most knowledgeable about the relevant nursing procedures and how those procedures can be improved. Equal representation from all staff levels is not necessary, because its focus is narrower than general policy matters that would carry implications for all staff members—it concentrates on specific factual questions regarding how well various procedures work in achieving specified patient outcome goals. Opinions or feelings about what individuals would *like* to do (or would like to see others do) are irrelevant.

Whether a committee should include staff nurses, head nurses, clinical specialists, supervisors, staff development coordinators, patient care coordinators, or any others depends on the knowledge at the command of the person in question. It would be a mistake to assume that a staff member, just because she happens to carry a particular designation in the hierarchy of the nursing department, is therefore qualified to assess the quality of care given to particular patients. The main characteristic needed to conduct an objective audit is an interest in obtaining information that will make it possible to improve patient care. Seeking information that will help defend procedures already in use should not play a role in the committee's functioning.

Selection of the Topic and Development of Criteria

This discussion assumes that an all-nurse audit committee is being considered. Its first job is to select the topic for audit study and the criteria to be employed. The topic being audited by nurses will probably be dealt with by a committee of physicians, as well. In fact, the Joint Commission may require that audits be combined or at least that the same group of patients be audited by both physicians and nurses, a heavy restriction on nurses working in settings where adaptation to the desires of physicians is constantly demanded. The patient group that presents the most compelling problems for nurses may not be one the physicians wish to audit.

Thus, because of the need to conform to standards imposed by an accrediting agency or by the hospital, nurses may find themselves auditing patient groups that do not yield the information most useful to them. In such cases, nurses might want to institute additional audits directed at groups that will provide more pertinent information. Nurse audit committees may find they are encouraged by their superiors, who want only to show up well on the audit, to audit the patient group that tends to be the most compliant, that presents the fewest complications, or that is represented by the greatest number of members.

If the purpose of an audit is to *appear* to be giving good care, then giving in to such pressures would make sense. But much more compelling reasons exist for performing audits. Suppose, for example, a nursing department has specialists—nurse clinicians or clinical nursing specialists—who work only with one type of patient. Somewhere along the way, it should be determined whether improvement in care is sufficient to warrant the extra cost of such specialized care. If the patient group requires complex care and one is not certain that the care given

is actually the best that can be provided, an audit might be very informative. Of most crucial importance would be the nature and frequency of discrepancies between desired and actual patient outcomes.

When a nurse knows she is having difficulty working with a particular patient or group of patients, she ought to be ready to use information that stems from an audit analysis of the care given a large number of similar patients. A basic premise in a successful audit is that information pointing to problem areas is more useful than information that only protects an already existing system.

Criteria for Evaluation

If the audit is based on already developed programs of care, then criteria included in those programs can meet that function in the audit. The task then remains of selecting the particular criteria to be used and, if individuals from outside of nursing are to conduct the search of the records, of translating the criteria into charting terms those individuals can understand.

The audit procedure, as it has been taught by personnel from the Quality Review Center of the Joint Commission on Accreditation of Hospitals, uses only outcome criteria. No provision has been made for progress criteria. The introduction of progress criteria requires no basic change in the system—only the inclusion of progress criteria in the same fashion that outcome criteria are included. Trained medical record evaluators can locate progress criteria as easily as outcome criteria if their directions are explicit. If an audit is developed for a patient group for which no program of care exists, it may be difficult to identify the most appropriate criteria—that is, criteria that are significant, realistic, clearly stipulated, and directly relevant to quality of care. When no program of care exists and the criteria must therefore be developed by the audit committee, it becomes even more crucial to have individuals on the committee who know a great deal about the patient group being audited.

Many nurses seem to be plagued by problems in formulating criteria, even after they have had experience in developing audit materials. Restricting oneself to a few critical items and couching these in patient outcome terms seem to be the most difficult aspects of the task. Nurses do many things for their patients, the results of which may be summed up in just a few statements pertaining to the benefits that accrue to those patients. It is difficult to comprehend that, in order to evaluate the effectiveness of patient care, it is not always necessary to document every aspect of a prescribed regimen. The difficulty of separating process and result elements is likely to persist for quite some time, even for nurses who base their audits on programs of care. In fact, more difficulty may be entailed when programs of care are used, since they spell out the requisite nursing activities in detail, whereas only the results of those activities are dealt with in the audit.

The nurse may feel that all the work invested in helping the patient achieve a given level of improvement is being dismissed with a few statements taking up a few lines in the nursing notes. Under these circumstances, the audit committee may want to include process indicators to demonstrate the nursing contribution. This is understandable, considering that nurses might have been required to chart extensively on a given patient (for example, one in an unstable condition), and yet only those record keeping items that reflect the end results are used in the audit. In a *process* audit, one might want to verify that a statement relating to some particular aspect of the patient's condition was entered in the record regularly (say, every 15 or 30 minutes). But, in a quality assurance retrospective audit based on patient results, one might only be interested in determining if the patient's condition stabilized within a specified period.

It is conceivable that one program of care might become the basis for a whole audit. But if the audit concerns a patient group defined in terms of a particular medical diagnosis and if the program of care deals with only part of the nursing care needed by the members of the group (such as the patient requiring an ileal conduit in chapter 3) then more than one program of care must be processed to find useful criteria for gathering information. If the program of care focuses on the ileal conduit and if other separate programs have been developed for the cancer patient and the patient with neurogenic bladder problems, then the audit should be restricted to a single diagnostic group and the two programs of care used—the ileal conduit program and the program appropriate to whichever group has been chosen to be audited. For the surgical patient having an operation under anesthesia, the general surgical program of care would have to be combined with the program related to that particular kind of surgery. In this way, one can be more certain that complete information pertaining to this patient is being assembled.

If the program of care included charting directions for the nurse, the appropriate information was probably recorded in the nursing notes when any given nursing activity took place. An advantage exists in having non-nursing personnel do the initial processing of charts to determine if the criteria had been satisfied. Because they are not nurses, and because it is necessary to spell out explicitly what to look for in the records, the criteria used and the bases for deciding if they have been met become more standardized, with a consequent uniformity in decision making, regardless of the patient or the assessor involved. In contrast, nurses performing the audit might accept far less explicit directions. Those who develop the criteria will want to preserve their right to define good nursing care and to require unvarying adherence to their standards. Such adherence requires explicit directions to the auditor about what kinds of statements can be regarded as evidence that acceptable nursing procedures were followed.

Wording Criteria

One mistake audit committee members tend to make is to couch directions concerning record searching in terms of the occurrence of a given item. For example, "A statement is included in the nursing discharge summary pertaining to the condition of the wound." Such a direction implies that any condition of the wound will be regarded as acceptable, as long as a note about it appears in the discharge summary. In an adequate program of care, the nurse would be directed to describe the condition of the wound. The objective would be that, by the time of the patient's discharge from the hospital, the wound would be healing adequately with no signs of infection. In any event, a statement making it clear that the wound was healing satisfactorily would have to be present in the record for the auditor to conclude that a criterion pertaining to the state of the wound had been met.

The audit committee decides what types of statements are acceptable indicators that a criterion has been met and what types require further study. How specific must such statements be to be considered acceptable? For example, are general observations such as "wound is healed" or "condition of wound is satisfactory" sufficient, or should the statements be more specific (such as "wound is clean" or "incision is approximated")? If the available evidence strongly suggests that a systematic evaluation was performed and that attention was paid to appropriate criteria pertaining to the condition of the wound, then a general statement might be quite acceptable. If the record contains no information indicating how the nurse performed her task, a general statement might well be considered unreliable.

Criteria Regarding Patient Teaching

One ought to be especially careful about criteria that have to do with patient teaching by the nurse and the patient's understanding of such information. Is a statement simply asserting that the patient understands the directions for carrying out his regimen of home care sufficient? Or should the nurse specify in detail the patient responses that indicate his understanding and readiness?

Such a decision should be based on an assessment of what is reasonable to expect in the way of charting and what additional information is available to help evaluate any general statements entered on the record.

If the nurse was functioning in a program of care that included directions for teaching and evaluating the outcome of such teaching, the committee might feel assured that the nurse's use of the term "understands" was justified—that is, that she quizzed the patient sufficiently to ascertain that he was prepared to assume responsibility for his own care, as indicated by his answers to questions stipulated in the program. On the other hand, if the record included nothing to indicate that the patient did more than simply respond "yes" when asked if he understood, it would be appropriate for the committee to strongly recommend that such record keeping be improved as soon as possible. A judgment would have to be made regarding the minimum acceptable amount of charting and the nature of a statement to assure the committee that the teaching activity was effective. A balance needs to be struck so that unrealistic demands regarding the amount of detail needed are avoided, while at the same time a degree of specificity is required to document that adequate care was given.

The Exception Category

In an audit, it is customary to consider the conditions under which failures to satisfy a criterion might be "excused." These exceptions are omitted from consideration in the final evaluation. This "exception" category can be a source of serious difficulty, because its misuse can provide a basis for excusing poor nursing care. If a committee is concerned lest every record brought back to it will signify a black mark against the nursing department, it may make excessive use of the exception category as a way of minimizing the number of discrepancies discovered. The category could also be used as a means of rationalizing a failure to satisfy a criterion when in fact a modification in the care being given is called for.

It is helpful to recall what the various aspects of the audit process mean when considering whether to excuse a failure to meet a criterion. When a committee allows an exception, it is refraining from examining discrepancies between stated goals and achieved outcomes, presumably under the assumption that the prospective gains in improvement of patient care would not outweigh the loss involved in devoting time and attention to such discrepancies. In effect, the committee members are indicating they do not wish to look at the record because they have already judged that the discrepancy is justifiable.

For example, if the committee decides that patients should be free of decubiti, except patients with urinary incontinence because they have a greater tendency than others to develop decubiti, the committee members are absolving nurses of any responsibility for modifying nursing care procedures to adapt to the individual needs of these patients. They are blaming the patient for a failure to meet a nursing care objective. Furthermore, they are exhibiting a belief that they would learn nothing by studying the records.

An audit committee will realize that a certain percentage of the patients in a given group will not meet the criteria set for them because of unforeseeable circumstances. For example, some confused and debilitated elderly patients may be in an acute care setting to solve certain specific medical problems. It might be completely unrealistic to expect such individuals to understand their illnesses or manage their regimen of care. Discharge to an extended care center or nursing home might be indicated in such cases, because these individuals could not possibly meet the criteria set for their group. Such exceptions in particular audit criteria would be reasonable if, at the same time, it could be documented that those taking over the care of the patient were clearly informed about the nursing care procedures that worked well with those patients. The exception might read, "Discharged to a nursing care facility; referral information sent indicating the nursing care requirements of the patient and directions for implementing such care."

Occasions will arise when criteria will not be met, despite the best efforts of nurses; nevertheless, the decision to allow exceptions must be considered as carefully as decisions about setting up criteria. Expending this kind of effort is essential if the requirements for maintaining a high-quality system of nursing care delivery are to be determined. It would probably be much more useful if committee members, rather than trying to presuppose all possible exceptions, spent most of their time analyzing the records that come to them because of discrepancies.

Complications, Prevention, and Critical Management

The sections in the audit devoted to complications (0 percent achievement standard), prevention, and critical management have similar built-in dangers. It is easy to ignore a complication if the nurse did carry out the prescribed activity, even though it was not successful.

The preventive and critical management sections in the audit are stated in process terms. Thus, one might decide to overlook a complication involving urinary infection, as long as the nurse involved notified the attending physician or took a urine sample for examination. Similarly, one might overlook postoperative pneumonia because the nurses caring for the patient did follow the prescribed procedures (for example, turning, coughing, and deep breathing the patient every two hours). Because she performed the prescribed activity, the nurse is not considered negligent by the auditors.

Unfortunately, the nursing profession does not have a well-developed body of demonstrated relationships between nursing practices and patient outcomes. Without such a body of knowledge, the use of process criteria in place of outcome criteria is not valid. The failure of one method to prevent a complication does not prove there is no nursing practice to prevent it. Perhaps, in some cases, prevention is impossible. But an examination of the records of cases in which complications have occurred might suggest alternative ways of dealing with the problem.

At the University of Iowa Hospitals and Clinics, the nursing audits seldom allow exceptions for complications. They also require that any member of the committee who wishes to justify a complication discuss it with the whole committee. Excusing a complication is not a trivial matter.

On occasion, nurses have identified certain events as nursing complications when the physicians would not. Nurses have found it useful to focus on complications to obtain information about certain problems that are difficult to conceptualize in progress criteria form. Complications and criteria can be viewed as opposite sides of the same coin. If criteria were defined explicitly enough, a category labeled "complications" would be unnecessary. But it is difficult to deal with something in terms of its absence, the consequence being that we typically resort to discussing it in such negative terms as "complication." Nonetheless, each complication identified in an audit should have a positive criterion on the opposite side of the coin.

Frequently, the complication category of an audit includes items that are also covered in the outcome and progress criteria sections. If the patient has a wound infection as a complication, the criterion describing the expected condition of the wound will obviously not have been met. One might not have what the physicians would term a complication, and yet not meet the nurse's criterion. The focal criteria in an audit should spell out what is optimal for the patient. Their satisfaction should reflect a high quality of care. In contrast, the complication category represents the undesirable extreme and, accordingly, should be seen only rarely in an institution that ostensibly provides high-quality care. The important consideration for nurses is that they recognize their own role in preventing avoidable complications. Also crucial is their responsibility to react immediately at the earliest sign to minimize the extent of unavoidable complications. And the nurse must also incorporate these considerations in any auditing activity in which she participates.

Review of Records

The next step for nurses in the audit procedure is the review of the records brought to the committee after the initial screening. At this stage, the committee members can identify situations which make achieving certain criteria unrealistic. It is also a time to examine the appropriateness of the criteria and to compare the effects of different patient care procedures which had not previously been differentiated (because their application to substantial numbers of patients had either not yet occurred or had not previously been subject for inquiry). If judgments are made only after careful consideration of the evidence available in the records, any possible bias—that is, putting the nurse's actions in the most favorable light—will be minimized, if not eliminated.

Using the Audit to Correct the System

The next crucial audit step involves examining the records containing unjustifiable discrepancies to locate the sources of problems and to recommend remedial action and determine whether improvement in nursing care is necessary. When departments first start to perform audits, they will probably encounter many discrepancies that will be categorized under the heading "no documentation." Without the use of programs of care, the recording of information revealing whether a criterion has been met is apt to be sparse.

The first recommendation audit committees are likely to make is for improvements in charting. A myth prevails in some audit circles that any problems one may meet involve simple inadequacies in documentation. The auditors assume that the care was excellent; it was just not documented sufficiently. Often, however, individuals fail to record information because they do not know what information is significant and, more important, because the activities called for by a patient's condition were not performed or were performed without a genuine focus on the patient and his welfare. Few indications in the nursing notes that patients were comfortable after receiving pain medications probably means a lack of systematic checking to make certain the treatments were effective. The absence of any follow-up information about symptoms that had been mentioned once in the notes might indicate that some nurses are not aware of the significance of such symptoms. A class on charting probably will have no appreciable effect on the quality of care, although it may have a temporary effect on the quality of the record keeping.

Attempts to correct deficiencies by dealing with individual nurses are inappropriate, in my view. If an individual nurse is responsible for the deficiencies disclosed by an audit, her inadequacies are a product of a system that allows her to function ineffectively. It is the system or at least parts of the system that should be examined. A head nurse might need to be replaced because her unit has consistently been shown inadequate in a succession of audits. But if the system that made possible her appointment and subsequent inadequate functioning is not altered, there is no guarantee that an equally inept individual will not be hired to replace her.

The information yielded by the audit would have to be assessed in the light of the total system before formulating permanent corrective measures. If programs of care are available, one can determine if they are being used and can examine them to assess their adequacy. If existing programs appear to be relevant to the care of a given patient group and yet are not being employed in planning the nursing care for that group, one should determine why they are not in use. Perhaps the nurses involved do not know how to use a program of care or the head nurses responsible for those units are unable or unwilling to evaluate the quality of care on the basis of the criteria in the programs of care. Or perhaps head nurses are unable to provide leadership in striving for high-quality care because they are busy with other activities deemed more important by their superiors.

It may very well be that no program of care exists, which is reflected by a lack of nurses' awareness of various nursing care problems and how best to cope with them. If the staff development program exists it may be inadequate for teaching the kinds of content that nurses must master to provide high-quality care.

Numerous factors could account for the discrepancies uncovered by an audit. This is partly why it is important that those on the nursing audit committee know most about how to meet the needs of the patient groups, about the overall system as it exists when the audit committee is formed, and about the role each part of the total structure plays in achieving the nursing department's goals. An easy, superficial answer may solve a given problem temporarily, but a major impact on the quality of care will most probably come only from a change in the system. Effecting such a change is not an easy task. If the audit is looked on simply as an exercise that provides some kind of evidence for the Joint Commission on Accreditation, the audit committee and the department in general will most probably settle for superficial answers. But if the expectation is that a department's retrospective audits will have a real impact on the quality of care, everyone in the nursing department must apply the audit information in upgrading her own functioning. Furthermore, it is crucial that any changes in the system suggested by the audits be instituted and given widespread support.

Some changes will make the audit procedures function more smoothly and subsequent audit results appear more favorable. But most crucial are the changes that come as a result of in-depth investigation of the entire system and those parts of it which are most relevant to the practice of the nursing staff. The follow-up step that ascertains whether needed modifications have been made and how they are working constitutes a natural outcome of any serious effort to use the audit to improve the system.

If the follow-up efforts consist simply of making certain that a suggested change has been effected for a brief time or that one process audit is performed as a way of going through some expected motions, the whole audit enterprise will probably not have any meaningful impact on the quality of care. Under such circumstances, existing problems may be cleared up for the moment, but they will invariably reappear somewhere in the system. On the other hand, if genuine modifications are made in the system, the beneficial effects of these changes should appear in subsequent audits involving different patient groups and conducted over substantial periods of time.

REFERENCES

1. Abdellah, F. G. and Levine, E. Developing a measure of patient and personnel satisfaction with nursing care. *Nursing Research,* 5:100–108, February 1957.
2. Aydelotte, M. K. and Tener, M. E. *An Investigation of the Relation Between Nursing Activity and Patient Welfare.* Nurse Utilization Project, Research Grant GN 4786 United States Public Health Service and University of Iowa, Iowa City, 1960.
3. Bailey, J. T. The critical incident technique in identifying behavioral criteria of professional nursing effectiveness. *Nursing Research*, 5:52–64, October 1956.
4. Reiter, F. and Kakosh, M. E. *Quality of Nursing Care, a Report of a Field-Study to Establish Criteria.* Conducted at Division of Nursing Education, Teachers College, Columbia University, 1950–1954, Graduate School of Nursing, New York Medical College, New York, New York, 1963.
5. Holman, B. L. An evaluation of nursing care on an obstetrical service. *Nursing Research*, 9:125–136, Summer 1960.
6. Safford, B. J. and Schlotfeldt, R. M. Nursing service staffing and quality of nursing care. *Nursing Research,* 9:149–154, Summer 1960.
7. Aydelotte, M. K. and Tener, M. E. 1960.
8. Phaneuf, M. C. *The Nursing Audit Profile for Excellence.* New York: Appleton-Century Crofts, 1972.
9. Langford, T. The evaluation of nursing: necessary and possible. *Supervisor Nurse,* 2:11:65–73, November 1971.
10. McGuire, R. L. Bedside nursing audit. *American Journal of Nursing,* 68:2146, October 1968.
11. Routhier, R. W. Tool for the evaluation of patient care. *Supervisor Nurse,* 3:1:15:8–27, January 1972.
12. Stevens, B. J. Analysis of trends in nursing care management. *Journal of Nursing Administration,* 2:12–17, November–December 1972.
13. Jacobs, N. D. and Jacobs, C. M. *The Pep Primer: Performance Evaluation Procedure for Auditing and Improving Patient Care.* Quality Review Center, Joint Commission on Accreditation of Hospitals, Second Edition, PEP acknowledgements, 1975.
14. Haussmann, R. K., Hegyvary, S. T. and Newman, J. F. *Monitoring Quality of Nursing Care Part II Assessment and Study of Correlates.* U. S. Department of Health, Education and Welfare, Public Health Services, Health Resources Administration Bureau of Health Manpower, Division of Nursing, Bethesda, Maryland, 1976, pp. 71–101.
15. Phaneuf, M. C. and Wandelt, M. A. Quality assurance in nursing. *Nursing Forum,* 13:4:328–345, 1974.
16. Smith, A. P. *PEP Workbook for Nurses.* Quality Review Center, Accreditation of Hospitals, Second Edition, 1975, p. 3.

CHAPTER 5

Two Programs of Nursing Care: Their Use and Evaluation

Deborah D. McDougall

To illustrate the principles discussed in the other chapters, two programs of care are presented. They guide the development of a nursing care plan for a specific patient anticipating a femoropopliteal bypass graft. A retrospective audit plan outlines the method to evaluate that patient's care.

PROGRAM OF CARE FOR PATIENTS UNDERGOING GENERAL ANESTHESIA

A surgical procedure that entails administration of a general anesthetic exposes the patient to many insults, the consequences of which are difficult to trace to any one etiological factor. Most events during the preoperative, operative, and postoperative periods exert both individual and interactional metabolic effects on the patient. This narrative examines those effects which are attributed in some way to undergoing general anesthesia, and uses that body of knowledge as a basis for a program of care.

At present, a unified theory of anesthesia does not exist, although many have been proposed[1,2]. However, even though the exact means and site of anesthesia production are undefined, understanding the sensory pathways to the cerebral cortex helps explain the general neuropharmacological basis of anesthesia.

Two afferent (sensory) systems carry stimuli to the cerebral cortex. With the long or lateral ascending pathways, a single stimulus projects to a specific cortical location. The ascending reticular pathways in the core of the brainstem are nonspecific; they regulate consciousness and integrate central nervous system activities. General anesthesia affects cortical response mainly through its action on this ascending brainstem reticular structure. Differing agents and dosages most likely impair different parts of the reticular activating system, from the peripheral afferents to the cortex. Other portions of the central nervous system, such as primary ascending pathways, can also be affected by general anesthesia. In addition, the areas affected are depressed in what seems to be the order of phylogenetic development, the newer structures being influenced first[3–5].

Patients receiving a general anesthetic are also administered other agents that have their own effects and actions (preoperative analgesics and sedatives, operative muscle relaxants). Considering all the demands placed on the patient in terms of medications received in each operative period and surgical trauma inflicted, the group of patients receiving general anesthesia share certain potential problems—such as respiratory, cardiovascular, and gastrointestinal function, and fluid and electrolyte homeostasis. Each identifiable problem is preventable through certain nursing actions and has a set of criteria available for evaluation of care.

Most general anesthetic agents act as central nervous system depressants, upsetting respiratory homeostatic mechanisms. As a result of respiratory depression, tidal volume and respiratory rate decrease the patient may respond inappropriately to hypoxia or carbon dioxide accumulation. In addition, the peripheral neuromuscular system is disturbed. Muscle-relaxant drugs prohibit nerve to muscle transmission, thereby adding to respiratory depression[6–8].

The involuntary protective mechanisms that assist in maintaining a patent airway (such as yawning, coughing, or deep breathing) are also depressed. Respiratory ciliary action is inhibited and mucosal glands are affected. As a response to anesthetic agents and instrumentation irritation, the bronchiolar musculature may become thickened or constricted and secretions may increase. If secretions are allowed to be retained in the bronchial tree, atelectasis may result[9–12].

The cardiovascular system is also challenged by general anesthesia. As a result of interference with the autonomic nervous system's control of vein walls, venous dilatation and peripheral pooling of blood may occur. Cardiac depression and maldistribution of blood also contribute to circulatory inadequacy. Most anesthetic agents are cardiovascular depressants, the effect on heart rate being primarily related to effects on the autonomic nervous system. However, it is difficult to make broad generalizations about specific action because agents have both common and unique effects.

Halothane, through autonomic inhibition, ganglionic blockage, and norepinephrine suppression, contributes to decreased total peripheral resistance, arterial blood pressure, myocardial contractile force, and heart rate. The additional effects of arteriolar and venous dilatation lead to peripheral pooling, decreased venous return, and ultimately decreased cardiac output. Nitrous oxide also depresses blood pressure, heart rate, and myocardial contractile force.

Cyclopropane, in contrast, enhances both facets of the autonomic nervous system, the sympathetic nervous system being predominant. Therefore, catecholamines are released and sympathetic tone and peripheral vascular resistance are increased. Myocardial contractile force tends to be maintained. Ether has similar effects on the sympathetic nervous system. Because of such challenges to the cardiovascular system during anesthesia, knowledgeable assessment and action are mandatory until homeostasis returns[13–17].

The changes produced in the gastrointestinal tract by general anesthesia have been discussed less frequently than the other body systems. The etiology of most decreased peristalsis is probably caused by a combination of humoral, metabolic, and neural factors. The humoral factors responsible for inhibiting peristalsis are unknown at present; however, electrolyte imbalances, such as hypokalemia, are known to contribute to decreased peristalsis through ionic movement disturbances. Distention of the bowel or surrounding organs can also decrease motility. Nitrous oxide is believed to diffuse into body cavities until equilibrium with the blood partial pressure of the gas is reached. Diminished smooth muscle tone and peristalsis is seen in most surgical patients, especially where some degree of ischemia is involved. If peristalsis is not enhanced, intestinal obstruction could result[18,19].

Renal function alteration occurs with all general inhalation anesthetics. The hemodynamic effects include decreased renal plasma flow and glomerular filtration rate and increased renal vascular resistance. These changes are associated with decreased cardiac output, renal vessel tone change, catecholamine action, and increased sympathetic nervous activity.

Water and electrolyte excretion effects that result primarily from the liberation of antidiuretic hormone during anesthesia include a decreased urine volume, an increased urine osmolality and reabsorption of fluid in excess of solute, and a decreased excretion of sodium and potassium (possibly caused by hormonal factors and a decrease in glomerular filtration rate). Preoperative narcotics, barbiturates, and phenothiazines also accentuate some of these effects. As a whole the antidiuresis resulting from anesthesia, trauma, and narcotics may lead to postoperative oliguria and fluid retention. Even though these homeostatic disruptions are most often transitory in nature, careful assessment and action are mandatory[20–24].

Such effects provide the basis for the development of a program of care for patients undergoing general anesthesia (see Table 5–1). It lays the groundwork for the problem areas identified, the nursing actions suggested as standards for care, and the criteria set forth for evaluation.

Table 5–1. Program of Care for Patients Undergoing General Anesthesia
Preoperative Period

Patient Problem	Outcome Criterion
1. Lack of knowledge and understanding about the importance of postoperative turning, coughing, and deep breathing.	

Progress Criteria	Nursing Action	Recording Information
On preoperative evening is able to demonstrate correct turn, cough, and deep breathing regimen and relate reason for and frequency of process.	On admission assess patient for history or presence of dyspnea, chest pain, cough, expectoration, hemoptysis, respiratory disease, and smoking habits (teaching is especially valuable for these patients). Assess respiratory rate and depth, blood pressure, pulse. If respiratory problems are pronounced, notify physician and/or respiratory therapy.	Record history or presence of respiratory problems and respiratory rate and depth, blood pressure, pulse. Record any action taken.
	On preoperative afternoon or evening:	Record preoperative instruction completed on Turn-cough-deep-breathing.
	1. Instruct patient on means of turning from side to side every 2 hours for the first 24 hours postoperative (using side rail and legs to assist in turning, assuming Sims' lateral position). Assure patient that nurse will assist as needed.	
	2. Demonstrate to patient deep breathing exercises—head of bed elevated or sit on side of bed, inhale until upper abdomen expands, exhale slowly by tightening abdominal muscles. Instruct patient to repeat 5 times every hour for the first 24 hours postoperative.	
	3. Instruct patient to cough every 2 hours until lungs are free from secretions—inhale and exhale twice, then expire forcefully. Instruct to repeat 2 to 3 times each session, have head of bed up or sit on side of bed, use pillows for support. Assure patient nurse will assist as needed.	

Table 5-1. *cont.*
Preoperative

Progress Criteria	Nursing Action	Recording Information
	4. Relate to patient why TCDB is necessary —irritation of anesthetic can cause mucus to be produced. If mucus pools in lungs and is not coughed up, pneumonia could develop.	Record patient is able to state reason for TCDB.
	5. Supervise return demonstration of TCDB and assess patient's understanding of frequency.	Record patient is able to demonstrate TCDB and state frequency.
	Repeat reinforcement for patient if return demonstration or understanding is inappropriate.	

Patient Problem	Outcome Criterion
2. Lack of knowledge and understanding concerning the importance of post-operative leg exercises.	

Progress Criteria	Nursing Action	Recording Information
On preoperative evening is able to correctly demonstrate leg exercises and state reason for and frequency of regimen.	On admission assess patient for history or presence of peripheral vascular disturbances —arterial, venous, lymphatic (teaching especially valuable for these patients). Assess leg circumferences, peripheral pulses, blood pressure, extremity temperature and color, capillary filling time, orientation level.	Record history or presence of peripheral vascular disturbances. Record assessment of leg circumferences, pulses, blood pressure, extremity temperature and color, capillary filling time, orientation level.
	On preoperative afternoon or evening:	Record preoperative instruction completed on leg exercises.
	1. Demonstrate leg exercises to patient— flexion of ankle, knee, and hip joints and movement of foot in a circle. Instruct to repeat 5 times every 2 hours until ambulating (unaffected leg only for patients having peripheral vascular surgery).	
	2. Relate to patient why leg exercises are necessary—to prevent pooling of blood and clot formation in lower extremities.	Record patient is able to state reason for leg exercises.
	3. Supervise return demonstration of leg exercises and assess patient's understanding of frequency.	Record patient is able to demonstrate leg exercises and state frequency.
	Repeat reinforcement for patient if return demonstration or understanding is inappropriate.	Record action taken if patient is unable to return demonstration or state rationale.

Table 5-1. *cont.*
Postoperative Period

Patient Problem	Outcome Criterion
3. Depression of respiratory system by anesthetic agents and medications received pre- and postoperative, leading to potential pulmonary congestion, atelectasis, pneumonia.	Patient's lungs are fully expanded and clear on percussion and auscultation.

Progress Criteria	Nursing Action	Recording Information
At 24 hours post-operative: Oral temperature is below 38°C. Cough is productive and secretions are loose enough to be expectorated. Lungs are free of rales, but scattered decreased areas of breath sounds may be present. Respiratory rate is below 30 per minute. Lower lobes are expanding with deep breathing.	Assist patient in deep breathing exercises 5 times per hour (reminding patient/family to carry out regimen when staff not at bedside). Assist patient in coughing every 2 hours (if secretions are tenacious consult physician concerning humidification). Assist patient in turning every 2 hours, alternating positions after coughing. Assist patient in dangling and ambulating as ordered, encouraging deep breathing simultaneously. Notify physician concerning nasotracheal stimulation if patient cannot raise secretions. Assure patency of nasogastric tube to prevent gastric distention and inhibition of deep breathing. Medicate patient prior to coughing regimen to prevent excessive pain, which interferes with coughing ability. Assess patient's temperature and respiratory rate every 4 hours and increase frequency of assessment if temperature is above 38°C. or respiratory rate is above 30 per minute.	Record every 8 hours: Frequency and adequacy of deep breathing. Frequency and productivity of cough. Frequency, type of activity, and toleration level. Action taken if unable to raise secretions. Status of nasogastric tube patency and measures taken. Record medication received, rationale for, and patient response. Record temperature and respiratory rate every 4 hours.
At 72 hours post-operative: Oral temperature is below 37.8°C. Cough is productive, with amount of secretions beginning to decrease. Lungs are clear. Respiratory rate is below 30 per minute. Depth of respirations is at pre-operative level.	Supervise patient in deep breathing exercises every 2 to 4 hours. Supervise patient in coughing every 2 hours while awake. Supervise patient in turning, changing positions every 2 hours while in bed. Ambulate patient as frequently as ordered. Perform nasotracheal stimulation as ordered and needed, care for nasogastric tube, administer medication as needed for pain. Assess temperature and respiratory rate every 4 hours as above, advancing to 3 times a day as condition permits.	Record deep breathing, coughing, activity, action taken, medication, temperature and respiratory rate as above. Record when cough nonproductive and respiratory function at preoperative assessment level. Record when respiratory care discontinued.

Table 5-1. *cont.*
Postoperative

Patient Problem	Outcome Criterion
4. Anesthetic interference with autonomic nervous system control of vein walls, contributing to dilatation and peripheral pooling, and leading to potential phlebothrombosis or thrombophlebitis.	Patient's calves are of preoperative size and color and do not elicit feelings of pain or stiffness on palpation or forward dorsiflexion and are not extremely warm to the touch.

Progress Criteria	Nursing Action	Recording Information
At 48 hours postoperative is ambulating 3 to 4 times per day.	Supervise leg exercises every 4 hours until patient is ambulating.	Record every 8 hours exercise undertaken and level of toleration, until patient is actively ambulating.
	Ambulate patient 3 to 4 times per day (as ordered and as condition permits). Increase activity as tolerated.	
	Monitor patient's intake and output, maintaining intake at least 500 cc. more than output (to ensure adequate hydration).	Record intake and output, stating action taken if intake is less than 500 cc. more than output.
	Assess condition of calves every 8 hours until patient is actively ambulating and then assess every 24 hours until discharge.	Record condition of calves every 8 hours until patient is actively ambulating, and then every 24 hours.

	Place patient on bedrest and notify physician if the following occur:
	  1. Redness with or without increase in calf temperature.
	  2. Tenderness of calf with or without palpation or forward dorsiflexion.
	  3. Stiffness or pain in calf with active motion.
	  4. Pain in calf with dorsiflexion.
	  5. Increase in calf temperature.
		Record any adverse symptoms and action taken.

	Apply thigh-high TED stockings as ordered, moving at least once every 24 hours and reapplying before legs are placed in a dependent position.	Record TEDs in place and removed at least once every 24 hours.
	Avoid raising knee gatch and using pillows under calves while patient is in bed.	

Table 5-1. *cont.*
Postoperative

Patient Problem	Outcome Criterion
5. Cardiac depression and maldistribution of blood resulting from general anesthesia and leading to potential shock due to hypovolemia or neurogenic factors.	Patient's pulse, blood pressure, urinary output, and orientation level are equal to or improved from the preoperative assessment.

Progress Criteria	Nursing Action	Recording Information
At 6 hours post-operative: Peripheral pulses are full. Extremities are warm to the touch. Skin color is pink. Capillary filling time is immediate. Pulse rate is stable between 60 to 120 per minute. Blood pressure is stable at or above 100 mm. Hg. systolic, but not more than 20 mm. Hg. above preoperative level. Urinary output is 30 cc. per hour. CVP is within 5–10 mm H_2O.	Assess blood pressure, peripheral pulses, extremity temperature and color, capillary filling time, urinary output, CVP, and orientation every 15 minutes until stable, then every 30 minutes times 4, every hour times 4, then every 4 hours. If pulse rate is above 120 per minute, check for bleeding, pain, PVCs. Report to physician if bleeding, frequent PVCs, or pulse rate remains above 120 per minute. Compare with preoperative level.	Record data after each assessment. If Foley in place, record patency status. Total output every 8 hours. Record assessment and action taken if pulse, blood pressure, urinary output not within acceptable limits.
	If pulse rate is below 60 per minute, report to physician. Compare with preoperative level. If blood pressure is below 100 mm. Hg. systolic or urinary output is below 30 cc. per hour, check for bleeding, fluid intake. Increase fluids 20 to 30 cc. per minute and recheck in 15 minutes. Report to physician the decreased pressure and/or output, and action taken. Compare with preoperative level.	
Patient is oriented to time, place and person and responds appropriately to questions.	If patient appears anxious or confused, monitor pulse and blood pressure more frequently. Check need for pain medication and administer if appropriate. Assess other possible causes—respiratory deficiency, electrolyte imbalance, medication toxicity—and notify physician.	Record patient's orientation level and action taken if patient is anxious or confused.
Visible bleeding is absent.	Monitor incisional drain output every 2 to 4 hours or until drainage ceases. Measure output every 8 hours.	Record amount and characteristics of incisional drainage.
At 36 hours post-operative: Pulse rate and blood pressure are stable within preoperative range.	Assess blood pressure and pulse rate every 4 hours, advancing to every 8 hours as condition permits.	Record blood pressure, pulse rate after each assessment.
Urinary output is greater than 30 cc. per hour.	Assess urinary output every 4 hours. If vital signs and output are not within the stated acceptable limits, take action as above.	Record urinary output every 8 hours. Record assessment as above.
Orientation and response are same as or improved from preoperative assessment.	If patient appears anxious or confused, take action as above. Continue to monitor any drainage output every 4 hours	Record assessment as above. Record assessment as above.
Visible bleeding is absent.		

Table 5-1. *cont.*
Postoperative

Patient Problem	Outcome Criterion
6. Diminished smooth muscle tone and peristalsis of the gastrointestinal tract resulting from anesthesia and leading to potential paralytic ileus with resulting obstruction.	Patient is able to eat solid foods, has a minimum fluid intake of approximately 2000 cc. per day or 500 cc. in excess of output, has not vomited for 24 hours and is having regular, soft, formed bowel movements.

Progress Criteria	*Nursing Action*	*Recording Information*
At 2 to 5 days postoperative (depending on type of surgery), is free from distention, nausea, and vomiting and is expelling flatus.	Maintain patient on nothing-by-mouth while nasogastric tube is in place or bowel sounds are absent. Irrigate nasogastric tube as ordered to ensure patency and measure output every 8 hours.	Record patient maintained NPO, bowel sounds absent, every 8 hours. Record irrigation and characteristics, amount of output.
	Assist patient in turning every 2 hours while on bedrest and ambulate as frequently as tolerated when able to be out of bed.	Record patient turned or ambulated. Record distance, frequency and toleration of ambulation.
	If patient is nauseated, ensure patency of nasogastric tube and administer antiemetic as ordered. If nausea continues check for distention, notify physician.	Record presence of nausea and action taken.
	After nasogastric tube is removed and patient remains NPO, monitor for returning peristalsis every 8 hours (absence of nausea and vomiting, presence of flatus and bowel sounds).	Record every 8 hours if nausea and vomiting present and action taken. Record presence or absence of flatus, bowel sounds.
At 4 to 7 days postoperative (depending upon type of surgery), is tolerating a clear liquid to soft diet, and is having loose formed bowel movements.	Monitor intake and output for at least 48 hours after clear liquids are initiated. If intake is less than 2000 cc. per 24 hours or less than 500 cc. greater than output, notify physician.	Record intake and output every 8 hours. Record action taken if intake is low.
	When intake and output are discontinued, monitor by observing meal tray and recording bowel movements (frequency, consistency).	Record every 24 hours toleration of diet and frequency, characteristics of bowel movements.
	If patient cannot tolerate the advancing of diet and develops nausea and vomiting: 1. Administer antiemetic if ordered. 2. Place on diet previously tolerated. 3. Notify physician if it persists.	Record type of diet tolerated, symptoms experienced and action taken.
	When toleration permits encourage intake of fruits, vegetables, cereals. Encourage adequate fluid intake (two liters per day).	Record every 24 hours type of food consumed.

Table 5-1. *cont.*
Postoperative

Patient Problem	Outcome Criterion
7. Hemodynamic changes and antidiuresis resulting from anesthesia, trauma, and narcotics, leading to potential fluid and electrolyte imbalance.	

Progress Criteria	Nursing Action	Recording Information
At 5 days post-operative intake is 500 to 1500 cc. greater than output, extremities are free from edema, and electrolyte levels are within normal limits.	Maintain accurate record of intake (peripheral intravenous, subclavian intravenous, nasogastric replacement, oral) and output (nasogastric, urine, stool, other drainage) every 8 hours. Compare total intake and output every 24 hours. If intake is less than 500 cc. more than output, report to physician need for fluid adjustments.	Record intake and output every 8 hours. Describe all drainage. Record any action taken.
	Infuse intravenous solutions as prescribed and at safe rate: 1. Maximum rate for hypertonic solutions—200 cc. per hour. 2. Maximum rate for isotonic solutions (without CVP monitoring)—480 cc. per hour. 3. Maximum of 20 meq. potassium per hour. 4. Maximum of 80 meq. potassium per liter.	Record solution, amount, rate administration.
	Monitor patient for edema and accompanying symptoms (weight gain, increased blood pressure, dyspnea). If symptoms noted, decrease infusion rates and notify physician.	Record any symptoms and action taken.
	For patient who is vomiting or has gastric suction, monitor for symptoms of fluid volume, sodium, potassium, magnesium deficits, metabolic alkalosis, ketosis. If symptoms noted, notify physician.	
	For patient with intestinal drainage or suction, monitor for symptoms of sodium, potassium deficits, dehydration, acidosis. If symptoms noted, notify physician.	
	Continue accurate intake and output while patient is receiving intravenous fluids and has gastrointestinal drainage. Maintain record for a minimum of 24 hours after intravenous is discontinued and drainage ceases.	Record intake and output every 8 hours. Describe all drainage. Note times of discontinuations, cessations.

PROGRAM OF CARE FOR PATIENTS UNDERGOING A FEMOROPOPLITEAL BYPASS GRAFT

Just as anesthesia's predictable effects on a patient give rise to a program of nursing care, patient groups can be understood and dealt with in the context of their common diagnosis. Knowledge of normal anatomy and physiology provides a basis for understanding the pathology and treatment of an individual patient's condition. In this particular group of patients the circulatory system provides the starting point.

Distribution of blood to the lower extremities is accomplished via the femoral artery, a continuation of the external iliac artery. The femoral artery originates at the inguinal ligament and terminates at the adductor magnus tendon hiatus. The profunda femoris, one of its seven branches, extends deep and supplies the muscles of the thigh. Extending from the termination of the femoral artery is the popliteal artery, which terminates distal to the knee joint and branches into the anterior and posterior tibial arteries. This network of vessels and their many branches supplies the entire lower extremities.

Muscular arteries, such as the femoral and popliteal, are composed of three layers—the intima, media, and adventitia. The intima, or inner layer, is composed of endothelial cells and a thick layer of loose connective tissue. Fibromuscular tissue bounded by external and internal elastic membranes forms the media, and connective tissue constitutes the adventitia. The adventitia is supplied by the vasa vasorum (small vessels) and contains both motor and sensory fibers[25–27].

Vascular vasomotion is regulated in part by the hypothalamus, the subcortical integrator for sympathetic and parasympathetic action. Stimulation of the sympathetic system induces vasoconstriction, whereas sympathectomy leads to vasodilatation. Vasoconstriction is also produced through the release of such substances as epinephrine, norepinephrine, and angioten-

sin into the blood stream. Other factors affect vessels locally—acetylcholine, vasopressin, histamine, metabolites, bradykinin, and serotonin. Local trauma is a vasoconstrictor and moderate heat a vasodilator. Cold initially constricts vessels and then relaxes them[28].

In chronic obstructive arterial disease, the disturbance of peripheral blood flow can lead to ischemia and tissue damage. If the narrowing is gradual, collateral circulation may develop in response to tissue need. The femoral and popliteal arteries are common sites for atherosclerotic degenerative disease, with the superficial femoral artery being affected in approximately 90 percent of all cases. The occlusion usually occurs at a bifurcation and produces symptoms of oxygen deprivation distal to the lesion[29–32].

With atherosclerosis focal changes appear in the intima and then later in the media. Lipids, carbohydrates, fibrous tissue, calcium, and blood products accumulate in the intima. Lipid-filled cells are thought to degenerate and release irritants, which in turn initiate the production of scar tissue. Smooth muscle cells originating in the media also migrate into the intima. Atheromatous abscesses invade the media and focal necrosis occurs. This altered surface provides a site for thrombus formations. The theoretical explanations concerning the uptake and synthesis of the lipids are still tentative. However, many associated factors have been postulated—high cholesterol diet, diabetes, hypertension, smoking, obesity, hormone activity, and stress[33–35].

This pathological process produces a set of signs and symptoms leading to the diagnosis of chronic occlusive arterial disease: intermittent claudication, rest pain, increased pallor of the feet when elevated, a delay in venous filling time after elevation, dependent rubor, paleness of the skin after exercise, atrophic changes (shiny and dry skin, thickened nails, decreased amount of hair), sensory disturbances, cold extremities, diminished or absent peripheral pulses, cellulitis, arterial ulcers, and gangrene. Segmental occlusion of the superficial femoral artery usually produces claudication in the calf with moderate exercise and no discomfort at rest. Nutrition of the foot appears normal, even though popliteal and pedal pulses are often absent. When the popliteal artery is also involved, trophic changes in the feet occur and the patient often experiences severe claudication or rest pain[36–45].

The bases of the signs and symptoms are related to the inability of the obstructed or sclerosed arteries to supply the tissues with the required amount of oxygenated blood. With exercise the metabolic tissue requirements increase and lactic acid accumulates. Ischemia compounded by the buildup of lactic acid produces painful muscle spasms (claudication). With severe disease ischemic pain may be experienced even at rest. Pale, cold extremities and blanching on elevation occur when arterial flow is reduced to a critical level. When vessels are so damaged that they can no longer constrict, rubor is seen. Prolonged ischemia contributes to tissue malnutrition and trophic changes, which can lead eventually to the development of gangrene[46–48].

Recurrent superficial and deep venous thrombosis is common in those with a history of obliterative arterial disease. It has been estimated that half of all those between the ages of 60 and 70 years will die of some manifestation of this disorder [49,50].

The patient population affected by femoral-popliteal arterial occlusive disease consists primarily of males in their late fifties[51,52]. Indications for femoral-popliteal bypass grafting include claudication that affects quality of life, rest pain, ischemic necrosis, and pregangrenous changes, adequate inflow, and distal runoff. It has been estimated that approximately 80 percent of patients with lower limb occlusive disease are affected in the femoral-popliteal region and most are also afflicted with associated illnesses—prior myocardial infarction, chronic heart fail-

ure, hypertension, angina pectoris, diabetes, and thrombophlebitis[53–58].

Before surgical intervention patients are usually evaluated for a definitive point of obstruction and distal runoff status, via aortography or femoral arteriography. Contrast material is injected into the arterial tree and the lower extremity vessels are visualized on films. The degree of patency of vessels distal to the occlusion determines operability. Patients undergoing these diagnostic evaluations may experience hemorrhage as a complication[59].

When the autogenous saphenous vein is used for the bypass graft, a vertical groin incision is made lateral to the pulse of the common femoral artery. Additional vertical incisions are made on the medial aspect of the thigh to expedite vein removal. The arteries involved in the reverse vein bypass are then visualized and the tunnel that is to accommodate the graft is made. Operative arteriography is often done upon completion of the anastomosis to ensure graft function. The placement of incisions is dictated through individual patient evaluation[60–61].

The reversed saphenous vein is preferred over the use of knitted dacron bypass grafts because it tends to remain patent more often in the presence of poor runoff, to resist kinking when extended beyond the knee joint, to be associated with fewer thrombotic occlusions, and to give the best long-term patency results[62–64]. However, both types of grafting have been associated with several complications—hemorrhage, wound infection and occlusion[65–67]. The postoperative prognosis of these patients is determined by the extent of arterial involvement present and the presence of gangrenous changes and other disease processes. Of those presenting with claudication, more than half will expire from myocardial infarctions[68–70].

Initial graft function, assessed within the first eight postoperative weeks, is evidenced by palpable distal pulses and other signs of improved arterial tissue perfusion—increase in temperature, loss of pallor on elevation, and dependent rubor. The risk of occlusion postoperatively appears to increase when the preoperative blood flow is less than 100 ml./minute[71-72].

Long-term graft patency is greatest with good arteriographic distal runoff, despite the ischemic symptoms experienced. Improved patency is seen with older patients, concomitant sympathectomy, good immediate postoperative outflow, and the use of vein grafting. Poor long-term patency rates have been seen in patients with associated illnesses and where veins with a diameter of less than four to five millimeters were used for grafting. However, functional results can be better than long-term patency rates, because of the development of collateral circulation with initial graft function[73-77].

This patient population has several definable problem areas, each of which has patient care goals and learning need goals to be met. Management goals aim at maintaining tissue viability and integrity, improving blood flow, increasing collateral circulation, decreasing oxygen needs, preventing disease progression, relieving pain, and improving general health. Educational goals focus on the development of physical independence, therapeutic and psychological competence, and a knowledge base concerning the atherosclerotic disease process and its management[78,79]. (See Table 5-2.) This information constitutes a basic body of knowledge. Nursing programs of care exist as a basis for planning specific care for an individual patient. Reference to the appropriate programs helps the nurse develop a specific, individualized plan of nursing care. (See Table 5-3.) They guide the nurse in determining what she needs to know about the patient and what she expects to accomplish in meeting his needs. The effectiveness of the nursing care given can be measured by use of a retrospective audit. (See Table 5-4.)

PATIENT PROFILE

John Smith is a 54-year-old white male who was admitted December 7 for a left femoropopliteal reversed saphenous vein bypass graft with an operative arteriogram. The translumbar aortogram, completed in November, showed an occlusion of the left superficial femoral artery at midfemur level. Mr. Smith had been experiencing claudication in his left calf for two years and recently the pain was beginning to place limitations on his ability to carry out his daily activities—"can't even walk down the block anymore."

Upon admission, Mrs. Smith informed the nurse that her husband "had been told how to take care of himself, but didn't understand why, so he didn't do what was best." During the admission interview and assessment, he had his legs crossed and propped up in bed and he kept tapping his fingers nervously on the bedside stand. Both lower extremities appeared dry and scaly. He mentioned frequently that he has pain in his left leg when he walks too far down the hall.

On the night of admission he complained of a slight burning upon urination. After breakfast on his second hospital day, Mr. Smith told the nurse that he just couldn't eat the terrible food that was served. Surgery was scheduled for 0730 on December 14. (See Table 5-3.)

Table 5-2. Program of Care for Patients Undergoing a Femoropopliteal Bypass Graft

Patient Problem	Outcome Criterion
1. Lack of knowledge and understanding about the change in behavior necessary to enhance peripheral circulation and to prevent mechanical, thermal, or chemical trauma to the lower extremities.	Patient's behavior includes activities that augment circulation to the lower extremities and protect against peripheral trauma.

Progress Criteria	Nursing Action	Recording Information
At the time of discharge is able to demonstrate activities to enhance circulation and prevent trauma and state reason for activities.	On admission: Instruct patient on means of improving circulation to lower extremities by alternating vasodilation and vasoconstriction: 1. Walk to toleration frequently, increasing distance by decreasing length of stride and pace. 2. Flex and relax lower extremity muscles at least once per hour when not ambulating. 3. Change extremity positions frequently (not helpful when trophic changes are present). Instruct patient on means of relaxing arteries to enhance arterial flow: 1. Keep HOB elevated 30 to 45°, with legs horizontal or 3 to 6 inches below heart level. 2. Flex lower extremities and change positions frequently. 3. Take vasodilation and adrenergic blocking agents as prescribed. Instruct patient on increasing tissue perfusion by the use of warmth: 1. Keep extremities loosely covered at all times (encourage use of bed cradle if trophic changes present). 2. Avoid drafts (keep environmental temperature between 75 to 85° F.). Instruct patient on means of preventing thromboembolic phenomenon: 1. Contract and relax extremity muscles frequently. 2. Avoid standing, especially in one position, for long periods. 3. Vary position frequently. 4. Avoid external pressure, trauma, infection (encourage use of sheepskin). 5. Consume at least 2000 cc. of fluid per day. Instruct patient on means of promoting collateral circulation: 1. Practice Buerger Allen exercises for 15 minutes 3 to 4 times per day, observing skin color and pain tolerance.	Record instruction completed on enhancing circulation and preventing trauma.

Table 5–2. *cont.*

Progress Criteria	Nursing Action	Recording Information
	2. Provide for extremity warmth—white cotton socks, warm environment.	

Instruct patient to avoid pressure on popliteal area—avoid sitting, crossing legs, placing pillows under knees, putting foot of bed up (knee gatch).

Inform patient about vasoconstrictive action of tobacco and encourage patient, by diversional or replacement therapy, to quit smoking.

Instruct patient to space daily activities to decrease oxygen consumption.

Inform patient about the vasoconstrictive action of stress and assist patient in identifying stressful situations, so they can be dealt with.

Explain all procedures and activities to patient to lessen the likelihood of an anxiety response, which contributes to vasoconstriction.

Instruct patient to keep skin of lower extremities clean, dry and soft:

1. Clean daily with warm water and mild soap.
2. Gently pat dry with soft towel.
3. Place lamb's wool between toes.
4. Apply lanolin or cocoa butter.

Instruct patient to inspect feet and legs daily for changes in integument. Instruct to report to physician immediately if cuts or abrasions are found.

Instruct patient to prevent mechanical trauma:

1. Wear nonconstrictive clothing, dressings.
2. Avoid tight bed coverings.
3. Wear well-fitting shoes.
4. Place sheepskin under extremities in bed.
5. Avoid scratching.
6. Have physician trim toenails, remove calluses.

Instruct patient to prevent thermal trauma:

1. Avoid use of dry or moist heat (heating pads, hot packs).
2. Take warm baths and soaks (90°F).
3. Avoid environmental extremes of temperature.
4. Wear white cotton socks.

Instruct patient to prevent chemical trauma:

1. Use mild soaps and solutions.
2. Avoid use of local medications.

Table 5-2. *cont.*

Progress Criteria	Nursing Action	Recording Information
	Inform patient concerning benefits of maintaining weight within range for height and adhering to a low cholesterol diet (See Program of Care for Patients on a Low Cholesterol Diet Management Regimen).	
	Inform patient about symptoms of arterial occlusion (decreased or absent peripheral pulses, pallor and blanching, cooling and mottling, pain that is distal initially and increases with movement, loss of sensation beginning distally, increased muscle weakness, decreased capillary filling). Instruct patient to keep head elevated with legs flat or dependent, keep environment warm, protect legs from trauma or pressure, avoid rubbing extremities. Instruct to report to physician immediately.	
	On discharge: Assess patient's understanding of above information and provide reinforcement and additional instruction as required.	Record a time of discharge patient is able to state reason for activities and actions. Record action taken if patient is unable to state reason for activities or does not demonstrate activities.

Patient Problem	Outcome Criterion
2. Potential mechanical, thermal, or chemical trauma to lower extremities.	Patient's lower extremity integument is intact.

Progress Criteria	Nursing Action	Recording Information
	On admission assess extremities for evidence of trauma, injuries. Notify physician concerning any injuries present.	Record condition of integument and action taken.
	Provide skin care as described in Patient Problem 1.	Record action taken.
	Inspect feet every 8 hours for changes in integument. Report to physician cuts, cracks.	Record condition of integument and comparison to initial assessment. Record action taken.
	Prevent mechanical trauma: Implement instructions as described in Patient Problem 1.	Record measures taken to prevent trauma.
	Prevent thermal trauma: Implement instructions as described in Patient Problem 1.	
	Prevent chemical trauma as described in Patient Problem 1.	

Table 5–2. *cont.*
Preoperative Period

Patient Problem	Outcome Criterion
3. Interruption of arterial blood flow to the lower extremities resulting in decreased tissue perfusion.	

Progress Criteria	Nursing Action	Recording Information
	On admission assess patient for: 1. Extremity color. 2. Change in skin color of feet after exercise (pallor?). 3. Change in skin color with elevation and dependency (elevate legs 30 cm. above heart level for 3 minutes and note time of pallor onset; place legs dependent and note time of color return). 4. Venous filling time. 5. Capillary filling time. 6. Presence of swelling or redness after prolonged dependency. 7. Trophic changes of extremities bilaterally—size and symmetry, absence of hair, shiny and thick skin, thick toe nails. 8. Skin temperature (compare bilaterally after exposed and at rest for 10 minutes). 9. Presence of peripheral pulses (femoral, popliteal, posterior tibial, dorsalis pedis)—rate, rhythm, amplitude, symmetry. 10. Leg circumferences. 11. Blood pressure.	Record peripheral vascular circulatory assessment. Record any action taken on assessment data.
At the end of the preoperative period: Intermittent claudication or rest pain remain at a tolerable level. Peripheral pulse status remains stable. Muscle weakness remains stable or improved. No further tissue breakdown has occurred. Skin pallor is stable or decreased. Skin temperature is stable or increased.	Improve circulation to lower extremities by alternating vasodilation and vasoconstriction. 1. Assist patient in walking to toleration several times per day (increase distance by decreasing length of stride and pace). 2. Supervise flexing and relaxing of lower extremity muscles at least once per hour when not ambulating. 3. Assure that patient changes extreme positions frequently. Assist patient in relaxing arteries and enhancing arterial flow: 1. Elevate HOB in low Fowlers position with legs horizontal or 3 to 6 inches below heart level. 2. Supervise in flexing of lower extremities once per hour and changing positions frequently. 3. Administer vasodilation and adrenergic blocking agents as ordered, noting patient response. Assist patient in using warmth to increase tissue perfusion:	Record measures taken to increase arterial perfusion to lower extremities.

Table 5-2. *cont.*
Preoperative

Progress Criteria	Nursing Action	Recording Information
	1. Keep extremities loosely covered at all times (use of bed cradle). 2. Use heat cradle, if available. 3. Keep environmental temperature between 75–85°F (prevent chilling). Prevent thromboembolic phenomenon: 1. Supervise hourly contraction and relaxation of lower extremity muscle groups. 2. Assure frequent position changes. 3. Avoid external pressure, trauma, infection (use sheepskin under extremities). 4. Encourage fluid intake of 2000 cc./day. Promote collateral circulation: 1. Supervise Buerger Allen exercises (15 minutes 3 to 4 times per day). Observe skin color and pain tolerance. 2. Provide for extremity warmth (avoid hot water bottles or heating pads). Avoid placing pressure on popliteal area—discourage sitting, leg crossing, pillows under legs, use of knee gatch when in bed. Discourage smoking (provide diversional activity or therapy). Supervise spacing of daily activities to decrease oxygen consumption and metabolic demands. Assist patient in identifying stressful activities so they can be coped with constructively or avoided (prevents vasoconstriction). Explain all procedures and activities to patient to lessen the likelihood of an anxiety response. Monitor patient for symptoms of arterial occlusion (described under Problem 1). If symptoms occur elevate HOB with legs flat or dependent, keep patient warm, protect legs from trauma or pressure, avoid rubbing extremities, report findings to physician, and start anticoagulants or fibrinolytic agents as ordered. Assess peripheral pulses, extremity color and warmth, amount and type of pain, and muscle strength and tissue integrity every 8 hours, comparing assessment to admission baseline. Report any changes to physician.	 Record symptoms of arterial occlusion and action taken. Record physician notified. Record assessment and comparison every 8 hours. Record action taken.

Table 5-2. *cont.*
Preoperative

Progress Criteria	Nursing Action	Recording Information
On preoperative evening is able to correctly demonstrate leg exercises and state reason for and frequency of regimen.	Demonstrate leg exercises for unaffected leg, relate reason for, supervise and reinforce as outlined in Program of Care for Patients Undergoing General Anesthesia: Problem 2. For affected extremity, demonstrate quadriceps drills (contract muscles that pull patella toward hips). Instruct to repeat 3 times hourly, beginning on the first postoperative day. Relate to patient why drills are necessary—to prevent excessive muscle weakness and aid circulation. Supervise return demonstration and assess understanding. Provide reinforcement when appropriate.	Record as in Program of Care for Patients Undergoing General Anesthesia: Problem 2. Record instruction on quadriceps drills completed. Record patient is able to demonstrate drills and state frequency and reason for. Record action taken if patient is unable to return demonstration or state rationale.

Patient Problem	Outcome Criterion
4. Ischemic pain due to decreased arterial tissue perfusion.	

Progress Criteria	Nursing Action	Recording Information

At the end of the preoperative period intermittent claudication or rest pain remains at a tolerable level.	On admission assess:
	  1. Character and location of pain—intermittent or constant.
	  2. Effect of dependent position and environmental temperature on pain.
	  3. Association of pain with walking a certain distance.
	  4. Effect of present medications on pain.
	  5. Sensitivity of skin.
	  6. How quickly relief comes with rest.
	  7. Provoking and relieving factors.
		Record assessment and any action taken.

	Instruct patient on means of increasing circulation to lower extremities (described under Problem 1), stressing use of warmth, dependent positioning, avoidance of tobacco, and prevention of pressure.	Record instruction completed as previously described.
	Enhance arterial tissue perfusion via activities described under Problem 3.	Record as previously described.
	For patients with intermittent claudication, stress exercising frequently to the point of pain development and then resting until there is relief. Also stress a slower gait, loss of excess weight, and protection from cold (see Problem 1).	Record as previously described.
	For patients with rest pain, keep extremities 20 to 30° below horizontal level and provide environmental warmth (no direct heat).	Record positioning of extremities and patient response.

Table 5–2. *cont.*
Preoperative

Progress Criteria	Nursing Action	Recording Information
	Note patient response (in terms of amount of pain) to above measures. Alter interventions as needed.	Record response to actions to decrease pain. Note alterations made and rationale for. Record follow-up evaluation.
	Assist patient in tailoring activities to pain tolerance.	Record pain tolerance in relation to activity and action taken.
	Assess character and location of pain every 8 hours. If pain characteristic of occlusion occurs (distal initially and increases with movement), take action as described under Problem 3.	Record assessment every 8 hours and action taken.
	Medicate patient for pain if symptoms are not indicative of acute occlusion.	Record medications given and patient response.

Patient Problem	Outcome Criterion
5. Undergoing an arteriographic procedure for purposes of preoperative evaluation.	

Progress Criteria	Nursing Action	Recording Information
	See Program of Care for Patients Undergoing Arteriography.	

Patient Problem	Outcome Criterion
6. Lack of knowledge and understanding concerning the importance of post-operative turning, coughing and deep breathing.	

Progress Criteria	Nursing Action	Recording Information
	See Program of Care for Patients Undergoing General Anesthesia: Problem 1.	

Table 5-2. *cont.*
Postoperative Period

Patient Problem	Outcome Criterion
7. Potential obstruction of arterial blood flow to the lower extremities resulting from occluded graft or thrombophlebitis.	Patient's affected extremity has pulses present in the vessels designated by the physician as patent postoperatively and the nonaffected extremity is of preoperative size and color and is free from pain and excessive warmth.

Progress Criteria	Nursing Action	Recording Information
At 24 to 36 hours postoperative: Extremities are warm and pink. Peripheral pulses (i.e., popliteal, posterior tibial, dorsalis pedis) are present in the vessels designated by the physician as patent postoperatively. Affected extremity is free from numbness and possibly hypersensitive. Affected extremity is of the preoperative size and is just warm (not hot) to the touch.	On return from recovery room assess patient for: 1. Extremity color, circumference. 2. Capillary filling time. 3. Skin temperature. 4. Presence of peripheral pulses bilaterally —rate, rhythm, amplitude, symmetry (check with physician to verify which pulses should be present). 5. Leg circumference. 6. Blood pressure. Compare with preoperative assessment level and report any deficits. Assess vital signs, peripheral pulses and extremity temperature, color and circumference: every 15 minutes until stable every 30 minutes times 2 every 1 hour times 2 every 2 hours times 2, then every 4 hours. Compare with initial postoperative assessment. Report any changes. Monitor for symptoms of arterial occlusion and act as described previously (under Problem 3).	Record peripheral vascular circulatory assessment and comparison. Record any action taken. Record assessments when completed, noting comparisons. Record any action taken. Record symptoms and action taken.
Within 5 days nonaffected extremity is of preoperative size and color and is not painful or stiff upon palpation or forward dorsiflexion and is just warm (not hot) to the touch.	Assess color, warmth, presence of pain on movement of nonaffected extremity every 8 hours. Report symptoms to physician. Ambulate as ordered (usually TID to QID on first postoperative day). Progressively advance and note toleration and distance (do not allow flexion of knee). Administer pain medication prior to activity (may have initial increase in pain postoperatively because of quick blood flow to extremity). Note response. Continue to instruct, assess, and reinforce information presented preoperatively. Note patient response and alter activities as needed.	Record characteristics every 8 hours and any action taken. Record frequency, distance and toleration of ambulation. Record time of and reason for medication. Record response. Record as previously described.

Table 5-2. *cont.*
Postoperative

Progress Criteria	Nursing Action	Recording Information
	Initiate quadriceps exercises for affected extremity and ROM exercises for unaffected extremity. Note toleration. (ROM described in Program of Care for Patients Undergoing General Anesthesia: Problem 4).	Record frequency and toleration of exercise.
	Monitor BP, P, R, CVP, and I & O as described in Program of Care for Patients Undergoing General Anesthesia: Problem 5).	Record when assessed and any action taken.
	Place patient on bedrest and notify physician if symptoms of thrombophlebitis occur (see Program of Care for Patients Undergoing General Anesthesia: Problem 4).	Record presenting symptoms and action taken.

Patient Problem	Outcome Criterion
8. Incisional pain.	Patient's incisional pain is minimal with activity.

Progress Criteria	Nursing Action	Recording Information
At 72 hours post-operative incisional pain is minimal with limited activity.	Assess comfort level every 4 hours and compare to symptoms of ischemia and infection. If pain is incisional, administer medication and evaluate response. If pain is ischemic, caused by an infectious process, or is not relieved via medication or positioning, report findings to physician and take action described for acute occlusion.	Record comfort level every 4 hours for 3 days, and then every 8 hours. Record action taken and response.
	Administer pain medication 30 minutes before activity and before pain becomes severe.	Record administration of medication and toleration of activity in relation to pain level.

Table 5-2. *cont.*
Postoperative

Patient Problem	Outcome Criterion
9. Potential wound infection.	Patient's incisional lines are pink to red in color, free from exudate, approximated, and minimally tender and patient's temperature is below 37.8 °C.

Progress Criteria	Nursing Action	Recording Information
At 48 hours post-operative, oral temperature is below 37.8 °C.	Assess temperature every 4 hours. Notify physician if elevation occurs consistently.	Record temperature and any action taken.
At time of initial dressing change or removal: Minimal serous/ serosanguinous drainage is present.	Assess incisional dressings every 8 hours. Notify physician if bright red blood or purulent drainage is present or if surrounding skin is reddened. If bleeding occurs apply pressure at site and place in shock position. Assess comfort level as previously described.	Record dressing status every 8 hours. Record any action taken. Record as previously described.
Edges of incisions are approximated.	Administer antibiotics as ordered to maintain a constant blood level (usually every 6 hours through postoperative day 6).	Record antibiotics administered.
Skin surrounding incision is free from redness and blistering.		
At 72 hours post-operative: Incisional drainage is absent.	Assess incisions every 8 hours. Notify physician if serosanguinous or purulent drainage is present or if skin surrounding incision is reddened and warm.	Record as previously described. Record assessment every 8 hours and action taken.
	Administer antibiotics as above.	Record antibiotics.
	Cleanse incisional lines every 8 hours with H_2O_2.	Record incisional care completed.

Patient Problem	Outcome Criterion
10. Undergoing general anesthesia.	

Progress Criteria	Nursing Action	Recording Information
	See Program of Care for Patients Undergoing General Anesthesia: Problems 3, 5, 6, 7.	

Table 5-3. Nursing Plan for Patient Care

Name: John Smith
Age: 54 years
Hospital Number: 3514524
Physician: Dr. Marc Jones

Admission Date: 12/7
Admission Complaint: Pain in left calf
Diagnosis: Left superficial femoral artery occlusion
Medical Plan of Care: Left femoropopliteal bypass graft

Outcome Criteria:

1. Behavior includes activities which augment circulation to the lower extremities and protect against peripheral trauma.

2. Lower extremity integument is intact.

3. Dietary intake is balanced and consists of at least 1800 calories per 24 hours.

4. The affected extremity has pulses present in the vessels designated by the physician as patent postoperatively and the nonaffected extremity is of preoperative size and color and is free from pain and excessive warmth.

5. Incisional pain is minimal with activity.

6. Incisional lines are pink to red in color, free from exudate, approximated and minimally tender and patient's temperature is below 37.8°C.

7. Lungs are fully expanded and clear on percussion and auscultation.

8. Pulse, blood pressure, urinary output, and orientation level are equal to or improved from the pre-operative assessment.

9. Able to eat solid foods, has a minimum fluid intake of approximately 2000 cc. per day or 500 cc. in excess of output, has not vomited for 24 hours, and is having regular, soft, formed bowel movements.

Date	Patient Problem	Progress Criteria	Nursing Activity
12/7	Does not know why prescribed activities are necessary to increase circulation and prevent injury.	By 12/9 Mr. Smith is demonstrating prescribed activities and his wife can state what activities are beneficial. By the evening of 12/13 Mr. Smith and his wife can both state the reason for prescribed activities.	On admission begin activities described under Problem 1 in Program of Care for Patients Undergoing a Femoropopliteal Bypass Graft. Stress rationale for the activities prescribed. Stress importance of good skin care once a day—wash with warm water, use mild soap, pat dry, apply lanolin or cocoa butter. Explain material in half-hour sessions, allowing plenty of time for questions, which should be answered honestly. Include wife in sessions so she can reinforce and validate information for Mr. Smith.
12/7	Dry and scaly lower extremity skin, with possible excoriation.	By 12/9 skin of both legs is soft and intact.	On admission begin activities described under Problem 2 in Program of Care for Patients Undergoing a Femoropopliteal Bypass Graft. Apply lanolin to both legs at 0900, 1300, 2000. Use nonallergenic soap for cleansing during morning care.
12/7	Pain in left calf.	By 12/9 Mr. Smith states that pain is at a tolerable level.	On admission begin activities described under Problem 4 in Program of Care for Patients Undergoing a Femoropopliteal Bypass Graft. Stress walking to toleration only.

Table 5–3. *cont.*

Date	Patient Problem	Progress Criteria	Nursing Activity
			Assure legs are 20 to 30° below horizontal level while in bed and up in chair.
			Remind not to cross legs.
			Ask about comfort level every 2 hours and medicate if warranted.
12/7	Poor blood supply to legs.	On 12/14 Mr. Smith states that pain is tolerable and his pulses are stable, skin is soft and skin temperature is stable.	On admission begin activities described under Problem 3 in Program of Care for Patients Undergoing a Femoropopliteal Bypass Graft.
			Explain all procedures slowly and clearly and answer all questions honestly. Repeat at least twice a day—he is very anxious.
12/8	Cystitis.	By 12/13 Mr. Smith states that he can urinate without burning, frequency, or urgency. Urine is clear and straw-colored.	Administer 1 gram Gantanol at 0900 and 2000 (keep blood levels constant).
			Force fluids to at least 3000 cc. per 24 hours (1200 on days, 1200 on evenings, 600 on nights).
			Offer apple and orange juice—he likes them best.
12/9	Refuses to eat because he does not like the food.	By the evening of 12/9 Mr. Smith is beginning to eat portions of the food served.	Continually assess Mr. Smith's likes and dislikes, providing him with nutritious foods he likes that are low in animal fat: squash, spinach, string beans, skim milk, apples, oranges, lean hamburger.
		By 12/10 Mr. Smith is eating at least three-fourths of the total food served and states he likes the items served.	Offer foods Mr. Smith likes at snack time.
			Arrange for dietitian to see him.
			Visit Mr. Smith sometime during meals.
			Assure that his tray is attractively arranged.
			Check with him after each meal to see if food was satisfactory and make alterations if necessary.
12/13	Does not have information about postoperative breathing and leg exercises.	By the evening of 12/13 Mr. Smith is able to demonstrate breathing and leg exercises and state reason for and frequency of process. Mrs. Smith is able to describe activities and state reason for and frequency of.	On afternoon of 12/13 begin activities described under Problems 1 and 2 in Program of Care for Patients Undergoing General Anesthesia and Problem 3 in Program of Care for Patients Undergoing a Femoropopliteal Bypass Graft.
			Explain slowly and answer questions thoroughly—Mr. Smith is very anxious.
			Include Mrs. Smith in teaching so she can support her husband postoperatively.

Table 5-4. Retrospective Audit Plan

Audit Criteria   Topic: The Patient Undergoing a Femoropopliteal Bypass Graft

Criteria	Standard 100% 0%	Exceptions	Instructions for Data Retrieval
Preoperative Progress Criteria			
1. Ischemic pain is controlled at a tolerable level.	X	None	Statement in nurses' detailed notes within 8 hours before surgery that patient states pain is remaining at a tolerable level.
2. Peripheral pulses remain stable.	X	None	Statement in nurses' detailed notes within 8 hours of surgery that all peripheral pulses present on admission are present in immediate preoperative period.
3. Understands preoperative instruction.	X	None	Statement in nurses' detailed notes within 24 hours of surgery that patient can demonstrate leg exercises for affected and unaffected legs and breathing exercises and states reason for and frequency of postoperative regimen.
Postoperative Progress Criteria			
4. Circulatory status in affected extremity within 36 hours postoperatively is the same as or improved from preoperative evaluation.	X	None	Statement in nurses' detailed notes at 36 hours postoperative that affected extremity has an immediate capillary filling time, is pink and warm to touch, and has peripheral pulses present as stated in operative note.
5. Circulatory status in nonaffected extremity is adequate.	X	None	Statement in nurses' detailed notes by fifth postoperative day that unaffected leg is of preoperative size and color and moves freely without pain or local tenderness.
6. Incisional pain is controlled.	X	None	Statement every 4 hours in nurses' detailed notes (for first 72 hours) that patient is free from pain (comfortable) or obtains relief from medication.
7. Remains afebrile.	X	None	Notation on temperature chart by 48 hours postoperative that temperature is 37.8°C or below.
8. Surgical wounds are clean.	X	None	Statement in nurses' detailed notes at time of initial dressing change or removal that minimal serous or serosanguinous drainage is present, edges of incision approximated. Statement by 72 hours postoperative that wound is clean with no drainage present.
9. Lungs are clear.	X	None	Statement in nurses' detailed notes by 48 hours postoperative that cough is productive, secretions loose enough to be expectorated.
10. Ambulating.	X	Patient is amputee or paraplegic.	Statement in nurses' detailed notes that patient is ambulating by postoperative day one.

Table 5-4. *cont.*

Criteria	Standard 100% 0%		Exceptions	Instructions for Data Retrieval
11. Fluid and electrolyte balance is maintained.	X		None	Statement in nurses' detailed notes or temperature chart sheet by fifth postoperative day that intake is at least 2000 cc., with intake within 500 to 1500 cc. greater than output.
12. Tolerating diet.	X		None	Statement in nurses' detailed notes by fourth postoperative day—tolerating clear liquids to soft diet.
13. Bowels are functioning.	X		None	Statement in nurses' detailed notes or temperature chart sheet—having soft stools by fifth day postoperative.
14. Immediate postoperative vital signs are stable.	X		None	Statement in nurses' detailed notes by 6 hours postoperative—BP is at or above 100 mm. Hg. systolic, but not more than 20 mm. Hg. above preoperative level.
Outcome Criteria				
15. Understands rationale for home regimen.	X		None	Statement in nurses' detailed notes (discharge summary)—patient states that reason for activities is to increase circulation and prevent trauma.
16. Demonstrates activities to enhance circulation and prevent trauma.	X		None	Statement in nurses' detailed notes (discharge summary)—patient demonstrated activities/exercises effectively.
17. Lower extremity integument is intact or admitting lesions are improved.	X		None	Statement in nurses' detailed notes (discharge summary)—skin of legs and feet intact or admission lesion or incision is healed or improved.
18. Full circulation in operative leg.	X		None	Statement in nurses' detailed notes written within 16 hours of discharge—pulses present in vessels designated by physician as patent postoperative.
19. Ambulating.	X		Patient is amputee or paraplegic.	Statement in nurses' detailed notes (discharge summary)—ambulating with minimal discomfort.
20. Pain is under control.	X		None	Statement in nurses' detailed notes (discharge summary)—free from pain except for incisional tenderness.
21. Incision is free from infection.	X		None	Statement in nurses' detailed notes—incisional lines pink to red in color, free from exudate, approximated, minimally tender.
22. Afebrile.	X		None	Statement on temperature chart sheet within 24 hours of discharge—temperature below 37.8°C.
Complications				
23. Wound infection.		X		Statement in clinical notes, temperature chart sheet, nurses' detailed notes—purulent incisional drainage, presence of abscesses, red or blistering skin peripheral to incision, temperature above 37.8°C.

Table 5-4. *cont.*

Criteria	Standard 100% 0% Exceptions			Instructions for Data Retrieval
24. Pneumonia.		X		Statement in clinical notes, temperature chart sheet, nurses' detailed notes—respiratory rate above 30 per minute, temperature above 38 °C, chest pain, purulent or bloody sputum.
25. Hemorrhage or shock.		X		Statement in clinical notes, nurses' detailed notes—pale skin, cyanosis of lips or nailbeds, restlessness, increased thirst, pulse rate above 120 per minute, blood pressure below 100 mm. Hg. systolic, urinary output less than 30 cc. per hour.
26. Graft occlusion.		X		Statement in clinical notes or nurses' detailed notes—decreased or absent peripheral pulses, pallor and blanching, mottling, increased pain, loss of sensation, increased muscle weakness, decreased capillary filling.
27. Thrombophlebitis.		X		Statement in clinical notes or nurses' detailed notes—redness with or without increase in calf temperature, tenderness of calf with or without palpation or forward dorsiflexion, stiffness or pain in calf with active motion, pain in calf with dorsiflexion, increase in calf temperature.
28. Injury to extremities.		X		Statement in clinical notes or nurses' detailed notes—mechanical, thermal, or chemical trauma on lower extremities (cuts, bruises, burns).

REFERENCES

1. Cohen, P. J. and Dripps, R. D. "History and Theories of General Anesthesia" in *The Pharmacological Basis of Therapeutics*, L. S. Goodman and A. Gilman, (eds.), New York: Macmillan Co., 1970.
2. Kaufman, R. D. Biophysical mechanisms of anesthetic action: historical perspective and review of current concepts. *Anesthesiology*, 46:1:49–62, 1977.
3. Brunner, E. A. and Eckenhoff, J. E. "Anesthesia" in D.C., Sabistan, Jr., (ed.), *Davis-Christopher Textbook of Surgery* 10th ed., Philadelphia: W. B. Saunders Co., 1972.
4. Cohen and Dripps. "Signs and Stages of Anesthesia" in *The Pharmacological Basis of Therapeutics*, L. S. Goodman and A. Gilman, (eds.), New York: Macmillan, 1970.
5. Dripps, R. D., Eckenhoff, J. E. and Vandam, L. D. *Introduction to Anesthesia: The Principles of Safe Practice* 4th ed. Philadelphia: W. B. Saunders Co., 1972.
6. Brunner, E. A. and Eckenhoff, J. E. 1972.
7. Dripps, R. D., Eckenhoff, J. E. and Vandam, L. D. 1972.
8. Hamilton, W. K. "Anesthesia" in *Synopsis of Surgery*, R. D. Liechty and R. T. Soper, (eds.), St. Louis: C. V. Mosby Co., 1972.
9. Hamilton, W. K. 1972.
10. Home, D. M. "Endocrine and Metabolic Responses to Injury" in *Principles of Surgery*, S. I. Schwartz, (ed.), New York: McGraw-Hill Book Company, 1969.
11. Lee, J. A. and Atkinson, R. S. *A Synopsis of Anaesthesia* 7th ed. Baltimore: Williams and Wilkins Co., 1973.
12. Nunn, J. F. *Applied Respiratory Physiology with Special Reference to Anaesthesia*. New York: Appleton-Century-Crofts, 1969.
13. Brunner, E. A. and Eckenhoff, J. E. 1972.
14. Dripps, R. D., Eckenhoff, J. E. and Vandam, L. D. 1972.
15. Hamilton, W. K. 1972.

16. Home, D. M. 1969.
17. Merin, R. G. Effect of anesthetics on the heart. *Surgical Clinics of North America*, 55:4:759–774, 1975.
18. Dripps, R. D., Eckenhoff, S. E. and Vandam, L. D. 1972.
19. Jones, R. S. "Intestinal Obstruction" in *Davis-Christopher Textbook of Surgery* 10th ed., D.C. Sabiston, Jr., (ed.), Philadelphia: W. B. Saunders Co., 1972.
20. Deutsch, S. Effects of anesthetics on the kidneys. *Surgical Clinics of North America*, 55:4:775–786, 1975.
21. Dripps, R. D., Eckenhoff, S. E. and Vandam, L. D. 1972.
22. Home, D. M. 1969.
23. Robertson, J. D. "Influence of Renal Disease on Anaesthesia" in *General Anaesthesia* Vol. 2, T. C. Gray and J. F. Nunn, (eds.), New York: Appleton-Century-Crofts, 1971.
24. Taylor, W. H. "Fluid, Electrolyte and Metabolic Responses to Injury and Operation" in *General Anaesthesia* Vol. 2, T. C. Gray and J. F. Nunn, (eds.), New York: Appleton-Century-Crofts, 1971.
25. Dawson, L. *Basic Human Anatomy*. New York: Appleton-Century-Crofts, 1966.
26. Fagen-Dubin, L. Atherosclerosis: a major cause of peripheral vascular disease. *Nursing Clinics of North America*, 12:1:101–108, 1977.
27. Luckmann, J. and Sorensen, K. C. (eds.), *Medical-Surgical Nursing: A Psychophysiologic Approach*. Philadelphia: W. B. Saunders Company, 1974.
28. Luckmann, J. and Sorensen, K. C. 1974.
29. Coffman, J. D. "Diseases of the Peripheral Vessels" in *Cecil-Loeb Textbook of Medicine* Vol. 2, P. B. Beeson and W. McDermott, (eds.), Philadelphia: W. B. Saunders Company, 1971.
30. Jackson, B. B. *Surgery of Acquired Vascular Disorders*. Springfield, Illinois: Charles C. Thomas, 1969.
31. Sexton, D. L. The patient with peripheral arterial occlusive disease. *Nursing Clinics of North America*, 12:1:89–99, 1977.
32. Spencer, F. C. "Peripheral Arterial Disease" in *Principles of Surgery*, S. I. Schwartz, (ed.), New York: McGraw-Hill Book Company, 1969.
33. Fagan-Dubin, L. 1977.
34. Jackson, B. S. Chronic peripheral arterial disease. *American Journal of Nursing*, 72:5:928–934, 1972.
35. Luckmann, J. and Sorensen, K. C. 1974.
36. Baker, W. H. "Peripheral Arteries" in *Synopsis of Surgery*, R. D. Liechty and R. T. Soper, (eds.), St. Louis: C. V. Mosby Company, 1976.
37. Cobey, J. C. and Cobey, J. H. Chronic leg ulcers. *American Journal of Nursing*, 72:2:258–259, 1974.
38. Coffman, J. D. 1971.
39. Dedichen, H. Hemodynamics in arterial reconstructions of the lower limb: II. Blood Pressure. *Acta Chirurgica Scandinavia*, 142:3:221–225, 1976.
40. Garrison, G. E. Peripheral arterial insufficiency. *Hospital Medicine*, 11:3:64–79, 1975.
41. Jackson, B. S. 1972.
42. Luckmann, J. and Sorensen, K. C. 1974.
43. Reichle, F. A. and Tyson, R. R. Comparison of long-term results of 364 femoropopliteal or femorotibial bypasses for revascularization of severely ischemic lower extremities. *Annals of Surgery*, 182:4:449–455, 1975.
44. Sexton, D. L. 1977.
45. Spencer, F. C. 1969.
46. Garrison, G. E. 1975.
47. Luckmann, J. and Sorensen, K. C. 1974.
48. Stead, E. A. "Vascular Disease of the Extremities" in *Harrison's Principles of Internal Medicine*, M. M. Wintrobe, et al., (eds.), New York: McGraw-Hill Book Company, 1970.
49. Luckmann, J. and Sorensen, K. C. 1974.
50. Stead, E. A. 1970.
51. Collins, G. J., Rich, N. and Andersen, C. A. Limb salvage procedures for lower extremity ischemia. *American Journal of Surgery*, 132:6:707–709, 1976.
52. Vanttinen, E., Inberg, M. V. and Scheinin, T. M. Femoropopliteal and femorotibial arterial reconstructive surgery. *Acta Chirorgica Scandinavia*, 141:5:341–352, 1975.
53. Baker, W. H. 1976.
54. Collins, G. J., Rich, N. and Andersen, C. A. 1976.
55. Luckmann, J. and Sorensen, K. C. 1974.
56. Reichle, F. A. and Tyson, R. R. 1975.
57. Thomas, G. I., et al. Prosthetic grafts in the femoropopliteal system: an acceptable violation in some cases. *American Surgeon*, 42:7:527–534, 1976.
58. Vanttinen, E., Inberg, N. V. and Scheinin, T. M. 1975.
59. Fenn, J. E. Reconstructive arterial surgery and for ischemic lower extremities. *Nursing Clinics of North America*, 12:1:129–142, 1977.
60. Collins, G. J., Rich, N. and Andersen, C. A. 1976.
61. Fenn, J. E. 1977.
62. Friedmann, P., DeLaurentis, D. A. and Rhee, S. W. The sequential femoropopliteal bypass graft: a five year experience. *American Journal of Surgery*, 131:4:452–456, 1976.
63. Luckmann, J. and Sorensen, K. C. 1974.
64. Spencer, F. C. 1969.
65. Cannon, J. A. Discusses care of infection in wound that contains vascular prosthesis. *Hospital Topics*, 50:2:68–69, 1972.
66. Roberts, B. The acutely ischemic limb. *Heart and Lung*, 5:2:273–276, 1976.
67. Vanttinen, E., Inberg, M. V. and Scheinin, T. M. 1975.
68. Coffman, J. D. 1971.
69. Lawson, L. J. Reconstructive surgery for lower limb ischaemia. *Nursing Times*, 70:8:261–265, 1974.
70. Luckmann, J. and Sorensen, K. C. 1974.
71. Dedichen, H. Hemodynamics in arterial reconstructions of the lower limb: I. Blood Flow. *Acta Chirurgica Scandinavia*, 142:3:213–220, 1976.
72. Reichle, F. A. and Tyson, R. R. 1975.

73. Buda, J. A., et al. Factors influencing patency of femoropopliteal artery bypass grafts. *American Journal of Surgery*, 132:1:8–12, 1976.
74. Cutler, B. S. et al. Autologous saphenous vein femoropopliteal bypass: analysis of 298 cases. *Surgery*, 79:3:325–331, 1976.
75. Freidmann, P., DeLaurentis, D. A. and Rhee, S. W. 1976.
76. Thomas, G. I., et al. 1976.
77. Vanttinen, E., Inberg, M. V. and Scheinin, T. M. 1975.
78. Eddy, M. E. Teaching patients with peripheral vascular disease. *Nursing Clinics of North America*, 12:1:151–159, 1977.
79. Jackson, B. S. 1972.

BIBLIOGRAPHY

Barker, W. R., et al. The current status of femoropopliteal bypass for arteriosclerotic occlusive disease: a panel discussion. *Surgery*, 79:1:30–36, 1976.

Bergersen, B. S. and Krug, E. E. *Pharmacology in Nursing* 11th ed. St. Louis: C. V. Mosby Co., 1969.

Clark, S. C. and MacCannell, K. L. Vascular responses to anesthetic agents. *Canadian Anaesthetists' Society Journal*, 22:1:20–33, 1975.

Cross, L. Surgery in arterial occlusion. *Nursing Mirror and Midwives Journal*, 141:18:51–53, 1975.

DeBakey, M. E. and Noon, G. "Surgical Treatment of Chronic Occlusive Disease of the Aorta and Major Arteries" in *Cardiovascular Surgery*, G. K. Danielson, (ed.), New York: Harper and Row, 1975.

Eisenberg, R. L. and Mani, R. L. Pressure dressings and postangiographic care of the femoral puncture site. *Radiology*, 122:3:677–678, 1977.

Hallin, R. W. Femoropopliteal verses femorotibial bypass grafting for lower extremity revascularization. *American Surgeon*, 42:7:522–526, 1976.

Johnson, M. and Keen, P. "Program of Care for Patients Undergoing Abdominal Surgery and Requiring a General Anesthetic." Unpublished paper, University of Iowa Hospitals and Clinics, Department of Nursing, 1975.

Kernicki, J., Bullock, B. L. and Matthews, J. *Cardiovascular Nursing: Rationale for Therapy and Nursing Intervention*. New York: G. P. Putnam's Sons, 1970.

Kessro, B. Peripheral arterial insufficiency: postoperative nursing care. *Nursing Clinics of North America*, 12:1:143–149, 1977.

Pierce, P. F. Gains and losses of vascular surgery patients. *Nursing Clinics of North America*, 12:1:119–127, 1977.

Price, H. L. and Dripps, R. D. "General Anesthetics" in *The Pharmacological Basis of Therapeutics*, L. S. Goodman and A. Gilman, (eds.), New York: Macmillan, 1970.

Rose, M. A. Home care after peripheral vascular surgery. *American Journal of Nursing*, 74:2:260–262, 1974.

Ryzewski, J. Factors in the rehabilitation of patients with peripheral vascular disease. *Nursing Clinics of North America*, 12:1:161–168, 1977.

Taggert, E. Physical assessment of the patient with arterial disease. *Nursing Clinics of North America*, 12:1:109–117, 1977.

Vanttinen, E. Postoperative changes in bypass vein grafts and collateral arteries after femoropopliteal arterial reconstructive surgery. *Acta Chirorgica Scandinavia*, 141:8:731–738, 1975.

Vanttinen, E. and Inberg, M. V. Aorto-ilicofemoral arterial reconstructive surgery. *Acta Chirorgica Scandinavia*, 141:7:600–608, 1975.

Welch, E. L. and Geary, J. E. Femoro-popliteal bypass with bovine heterografts. *Journal of Cardiovascular Surgery*, 17:1:62–68, 1976.

PART III

Standards of Process

CHAPTER 6

Performance Standards: Derivation and Maintenance

Nurses are not alone in recognizing the need for performance standards. At present, the desire to improve the quality of the product by improving the quality of the worker producing the product appears to be widespread. Individuals developing performance standards in their various fields may have different reasons for establishing such standards or methods for their use, but the task is the same for all—to determine valid criteria that will explicitly indicate acceptable levels of job performance. If such criteria are to measure successful performance in a particular ongoing activity, it should be possible to relate them to other measures of success relevant to that work[1].

In nursing, four such components can be stipulated: (1) ongoing nursing activity (such as teaching patient to manage diabetic condition) designed to help the patient with his or her current health problems; (2) performance standards applicable to the nurse's activity (such as criteria for appropriate procedures for teaching diabetic patient); (3) short-term, patient-oriented criteria (patient's ability to demonstrate knowledge and skills required); and (4) longer-term, patient-oriented criteria that determine whether major goals (patient's maintaining complication-free life) have been achieved. However, sometimes such long-term criteria are not available or they are poorly defined.

In some cases, fortunately, the usefulness of selected performance standards can be judged by examining the end product. When the quality of that product can be assessed in explicit terms and the activities that relate to desirable outcomes identified, it should be easy to develop performance standards that are predictive of successful functioning. However, performance criteria have been successfully used to predict long-term outcomes primarily in activities with easily recognizable skills (for example, typing or machine operations). In contrast, in positions that involve more complex skills or difficult judgment components, the likelihood of predicting success on the job from performance criteria diminishes considerably[2].

DEVELOPMENT OF STANDARDS

In nursing, the usual practice when performance standards or evaluation scales are being developed is to identify desirable behaviors without referring to criteria that define the purpose of those behaviors. The most prevalent approach to validating performance standards has been the use of experts who are asked either to identify the behavioral characteristics that are descriptive of the most effective nurses[3,4,5] or to evaluate anecdotes regarding nurse behavior by use of the Flanagan Critical Incident Technique[6-9]. Although such panels might include doctors and patients as well as nurses, none of the cases just cited indicate that patient-welfare indices were used to validate the effectiveness of the nursing action. The developers of standards seem concerned with establishing standards that focus on *what the nurse does*, rather than on *what is accomplished for the patient.*

The Joint Commission for Accreditation of Hospitals has been trying to help nurses focus on patient outcomes, but day-by-day observation of nurses functioning indicates that nurses rarely think of patient-outcome results as the appropriate basis for developing nursing performance standards. Indeed, many individuals are still deriving standards of patient care from standards of nursing practice, rather than the other way around. A prime example can be found in the Quality Patient Care Scale developed by Wandelt and Ager, who state that the scale "originates from the Slater Nursing Performance Rating Scale"[10].

If hospital staff nurses were asked where they would look for the performance standards that govern the nursing practices in their hospitals, some might identify the various job descriptions, and others might designate the performance evaluation criteria. But it is unlikely that many would recognize a relationship between either of these documents and the programs of care being provided patients in those hospitals. My impression is that most hospital nurses would be surprised at the suggestion that patient-outcome criteria should be developed before it would be meaningful to develop performance standards. They have simply not seen this approach taken.

The use of patient-outcome criteria to establish general, all-purpose performance standards does present some problems. Which criteria should become the ultimate indices of patient welfare? Values as well as factual issues enter into consideration. Prevention of or relief from pain might well be regarded as one such criterion, but what others might be adopted? Medical research provides some bases for making

such selections, but research in the field of nursing adds little relevant information.

Lists of performance standards have been developed and their reliability established by competent nursing researchers. Such standards are in the literature, one notable example being the *Slater Nursing Performance Rating Scale*[11]. Some individuals may find that performance standards developed via painstaking standardization procedures, as in the Slater scale, dovetail well with their concepts of effective nursing care. However, service agencies have an immediate need for standards by which to evaluate the functioning of staff members to assure that acceptable care is provided patients on a day-by-day basis. In such situations, standardized performance scales may be too time-consuming to administer, because they are designed for use outside the framework of nurses' daily activities. Furthermore, available instruments must be judged on the extent to which they are directly associated with identifiable patient benefits. Because most of the available standards have been selected on the basis of consensus of opinion (albeit expert opinion), with no subsequent examination of the extent to which their use leads to desired patient results, the chances seem great that factors irrelevant to desirable patient outcomes exist. Available evidence suggests that we can accurately anticipate what people will designate as important aspects of a particular job, but not what will turn out to be good predictors of success in that job[12].

Service agencies that have an immediate need for standards might find it more useful and less time-consuming in the long run if the staff members developed their own performance standards. Such standards could then reflect their own philosophies of nursing and patient-care objectives. Performance standards developed by the American Nurses' Association or other such organizations might be useful as guidelines[13]. However, they are not specific enough to be applied directly to the typical practice setting.

If both the information on which the programs of care were developed and the information gleaned from audit procedures are used, performance standards involving a minimum of extraneous considerations can be established.

The programs of nursing care prescribe the nursing activity requirements for a given group of patients. The performance standards can provide the means by which those nursing activities are incorporated into practice on the unit or division. In addition, they can establish the level of functioning needed to assure that the activity will be effective.

CATEGORIES OF STANDARDS

Those performance standards which derive directly from the activities identified in the programs of care will be appropriate for the typical staff nurse position. The staff nurse might well be designated the implementer of the program of care. She is responsible for providing the nursing care that is most likely to benefit the patient. The measure of her effectiveness would be the extent to which she is able to perform the activities prescribed in the program of care. Thus, the performance standards derived from the programs of care can be translated directly into evaluation criteria to assess the performance of the staff nurse.

Those below or above the level of staff nurse have different responsibilities; they must either supplement the work of the staff nurse or organize such work to achieve better functioning in the unit or department. Different sets of standards should be used to evaluate various types of staff members.

The performance standards for the licensed practical nurse, the nursing assistant, the unit clerk, the unit manager, and the unit secretary pertain to different responsibilities, but the work of all such individuals ought to ultimately help the staff nurse perform those activities which implement programs of care effectively.

Each job designation should play a different role to achieve this goal and the performance of any individual staff member should be assessed only by criteria that examine how much that individual's work assists the staff nurse in effective performance. Some individuals—particularly practical nurses—may actually perform some of the nursing actions required. Most important, however, is that the performance standards for subordinate personnel be determined by carefully specifying the activities such individuals can be expected to perform, either on the basis of already acquired knowledge or knowledge they can realistically be expected to acquire through an inservice training program.

An effective nursing care delivery system requires that all staff members devote their energies to activities that they are capable of handling and that those who are more subordinate cannot handle. Each level should have its own set of performance standards developed according to the knowledge and skills required to perform given activities effectively.

Positions in the hierarchy above the staff nurse level (such as head nurse, supervisor, and clinical specialist) have different responsibilities from the staff nurse and from each other. Staff nurse performance standards are not appropriate for any other staff level. However, the performance standards for these job designations can be derived by studying the activity requirements incorporated in the programs of care.

But administrative positions and positions that call for special expertise require knowledge beyond that required by the staff nurse for ordinary bedside activities. Although individuals in these higher-level positions are indeed responsible for the direct care provided the patient, they should *not* be placed in the position of relieving the staff nurse to allow her to engage in other activities. Lower-level staff—such as the licensed practical nurses or the nursing assistants—should be able to supply such relief. If the head nurse cleans up a unit to make it possible for a staff nurse to move on to a patient in need of attention, then it must be assumed that the activities the head nurse should perform are being neglected. Although such activity may solve an immediate and pressing problem, no long-term solution will result because the very individual who should be doing the planning that would eliminate the problem is otherwise occupied.

If the performance standards for one category of worker are the same as those for another category, then one of these categories is obviously superfluous. If a presumably more experienced and knowledgeable head nurse is being paid a higher salary than a staff nurse but both are doing the same kinds of work, then the pay differential must be considered inappropriate. A clinical nursing specialist who provides bedside nursing care to only a limited number of patients (even though that care may reflect her advanced knowledge and skill) is doing little more than what could be done by a very good staff nurse; the specialist's activities should result in improved care for *all* patients.

Either nursing care criteria, as they apply to the individual patient, are met or they are not. Every patient is entitled to have them met, regardless of who gives the care. If the same level of care is provided by a staff nurse and by a nurse with master's degree training, there is no advantage to the patient in having the care given by the latter. For the total nursing care delivery system to be effective, the system must be analyzed to identify its requirements and the skills needed to meet those requirements. Job descriptions should be hierarchically developed so that a position at each succeeding level calls for skills and knowledge not possessed by individuals at the lower levels.

RELATION TO JOB DESCRIPTIONS

Although developing job descriptions for different positions is important, the term *job description* is not synonymous with the term *performance standard* or *performance evaluation criterion*. Job descriptions are merely statements of what the individual is generally expected to do. Performance standards and evaluative criteria may be regarded as synonymous because both are concerned with judgments about the quality of actions. A job description might state that a staff nurse will "Develop and implement nursing plans that enhance the effectiveness of the general therapeutic plan for each patient"[14]. But, one could develop a poor nursing care plan and implement it well, or one could develop a good nursing plan and implement it poorly. There is no inherent judgment that the action taken "enhances effectiveness."

Although many individuals would doubtless start by using job descriptions to develop performance standards, I feel that just the reverse should be done. One should begin by determining the nursing care requirements of patients and the skills and knowledge needed by nurses to meet those requirements; then, one can make sensible decisions about the activities to be assigned the personnel on the various levels of the nursing staff.

ADAPTATION OF STANDARDS

Performance standards for a given unit are geared to the specific activities it requires. As one moves farther away from the individual patient and patient group, the standards become broader. Thus, the standards for the whole nursing department should include all patient groups and the activities required in all clinical units. Such general department standards can serve as a basis for developing standards at the unit level. This process has both circular and progressive features. Specifics associated with the various patient groups are used to develop generalizations applicable to all patients, while general standards of performance can be guidelines for delineating specifics applicable to individual units and patients.

In all conceivable programs of care a categorization system can be developed that deals with the problems most apt to occur in a given setting. For example, a system for an acute-care hospital setting might take the following form:

1. Problems associated with the need for immediate emergency treatment.
2. Complication problems occurring because of the course the disease may take, the treatments that must be administered, or the environmental restrictions placed on the hospitalized individual.
3. Problems associated with the fear and anxiety brought on by the disease, the treatments, and the deprivation of normal social contacts.
4. Problems associated with the patient's pain and discomfort.
5. Problems associated with the nursing staff's effectiveness in carrying out prescribed treatment procedures.
6. Problems associated with the patient's adaptation to the changes involved in being discharged or transferred.

Assuming that all individual patient problems can be placed in one of these categories, a statement of patient care objectives stated in patient-outcome terms and applicable to all patients can be formulated. Thus, a department might have the following nursing care objectives:

1. Emergency conditions are kept to the lowest possible level of threat to the patient by timely and effective intervention.
2. The patient is free of preventable complications.
3. Fear and anxiety related to illness and hospitalization are reduced.
4. Pain and discomfort are minimized.
5. The maximum benefits of the diagnostic and therapeutic procedures ordered by the physician and performed by the nursing staff are realized by the patient.
6. The patient is prepared for or arrangements are made for continuation of the necessary regimen of care or readjustment of life pattern posthospitalization[15].

Patient care outcomes are easily translated into general statements of performance standards to be met by the individuals designated to implement the program. For example, the performance standard pertaining to the first outcome statement might be worded, "Recognizes emergency situations immediately and institutes the appropriate nursing intervention procedures without delay." Such a statement obviously contains too many undefined terms to be anything more than a guideline for further development. The statement must be translated into specifics that identify what behaviors are acceptable in various emergency situations.

In an emergency cardiac arrest situation, the specific performance standards might include the requirements for certification listed by the American Heart Association, with any needed additions to accommodate unique aspects of the hospital or department involved[16]. All patient care standards can be converted into performance standards in the same way. One then needs to identify the facilitating activities that, in association with the direct care provided the patient, might be required by particular staff members (such as the staff nurses) who are to implement the program of care. When this has been accomplished, the performance standards for one level in the hierarchy have been completed. The specific patient care standards for the staff nurse with supervisory responsibilities, however, might be supplemented with standards for directing auxiliary personnel and organizing assignments.

Performance standards for other staff members should derive from their roles in facilitating the provision of direct care to patients. The unit secretary would doubtless play a key role in maintaining records and in handling communications, both of which are important in facilitating patient care. Performance standards for a unit manager might include such criteria as, "Maintains and checks all emergency treatment materials and equipment so that they are always immediately available and functioning properly." Such a standard would require further delineation of specific activities, such as adequate testing schedules for electrical and mechanical equipment, establishing recordkeeping and storage systems, and devising a dating system for consumables.

The head nurse and other supervisory personnel have programming responsibilities. The head nurse, for example, may be required to establish a system for administering emergency care. A relevant general standard might state "Establishes a system for preparation and review that verifies the competency of staff to function effectively in the administration of emergency treatments at all times." Again, this general standard would guide the drawing up of specific requirements to assure the readiness of staff members to achieve the desired outcome.

Rather than concentrating on each patient outcome separately, one might prefer to establish standards for the head nurse encompassing all her activities necessary to ensure adequate staff functioning. Removing the phrase "in the administration of emergency treatments" would generalize the previous standard. In any event, provisions should be made for ensuring that staff competencies are acquired and maintained to maximize the possibility of meeting every patient care objective for every patient in the unit.

PROCESS VERSUS GOAL ORIENTATION

As one moves farther away from the patient's bedside, the development of standards may involve an increasing tendency to substitute a *process* for a *goal* orientation. It is particularly difficult to relate the performances of administrative and supportive staff to patient benefits. As a consequence, standards taken from other disciplines are frequently adopted. Thus, performance standards developed for supervisors, staff development instructors, clinical nursing specialists, researchers, or directors may make sense from the standpoint of processes that play an integral role in certain other disciplines, but there may be no proof that the same relevance exists for nursing. Standards for the staff development coordinator might require that she use the principles of adult education in developing her program even though the goals of adult education are different from those of inservice education. Head nurses might be required to apply techniques from the field of counseling in working with personnel with the consequence that focus is placed on attempting to develop a therapeutic relationship with the employee rather than on the job. The values, goals, and knowledge that led to such process-oriented criteria in those other disciplines may not be at all compatible with the values, goals, and knowledge of nursing. Other fields *can* be examined for relevant processes if the role of each job is defined in terms of what the employee must *accomplish* to meet specified goals rather than in terms of what she must *do*.

If the role of each job is defined in terms of what the employee must *accomplish* in the way of specified patient care goals (rather than in terms of what she must *do* without reference to such goals), then other fields can be examined for processes or activities relevant to the facilitation of nursing care delivery.

It is important to differentiate between standards of performance for nurses who actually deliver bedside care and standards for personnel who do not. In any case, one should be able to show that whatever standards are adopted contribute to the achievement of departmental goals. If an individual has been appointed to a position because she possesses specialized knowledge, it would be a mistake to set standards that might restrict her ability to use her knowledge, to be creative, and to go beyond the bounds of conventional practice. But one could still formulate requirements that call for fulfilling specified responsibilities. For example, a standard for an inservice educator might require that her classroom offerings focus on activities that pertain to patient care, in contrast to the more usual practice of simply requiring that objectives be developed for each class offering. A nurse supervisor is expected to delegate authority; relevant standards might focus on her ability to judge which skills are crucial in an assignment and to choose the most qualified individual.

Although performance standards pertain to *processes* they can be stated in terms of what should be *accomplished*. Regardless of the job designation and its distance from the actual bedside nursing care, it should be possible to relate the activity to patient outcomes. If such roles are not considered according to how they facilitate the provision of high quality care, a danger exists that what Etzioni calls "goal replacement" will occur, and the primary mission of an institution or unit is interfered with or sidetracked[17].

In sum, patient outcomes and progress criteria constitute the standards by which the effectiveness of the total system is evaluated. Performance criteria are the standards by which individual staff members are evaluated. Performance standards are derived from an identification and analysis of the activities required, both at the bedside and elsewhere, so to achieve optimal patient outcomes. Having determined what types of personnel are most appropriate for the particular activities, one assigns available personnel accordingly. Having ascertained what constitutes desirable performance, one formulates performance standards accordingly. Those standards provide the bases for preparation of relevant job descriptions.

THE USE OF PERFORMANCE STANDARDS IN NURSING PRACTICE

Performance standards in any kind of endeavor have three major purposes: (1) to establish the level of functioning expected of the worker and to help prepare the worker to perform an assigned job effectively; (2) to establish a basis for evaluating staff effectiveness in maintaining high-quality service and correcting existing deficiencies in that service; and (3) to provide a basis for selecting individuals with the most potential for meeting the requirements of the position.

Performance standards for any job designation can be used to evaluate the individual's effectiveness in achieving the job's goals. Performance standards that are not specifically related to the goals of the organization will not provide the information needed to make wise decisions about staff assignments and evaluations.

Information gathered from performance standards is relevant for three major kinds of decisions: (1) decisions regarding the employee's educational needs to make effective job performance possible; (2) decisions regarding the awarding of salary increases and tenure, the writing of references, and so on; and (3) decisions pertaining to appointments and promotions.

The information required for each decision is likely to differ in amount or kind and will depend on the degree of precision needed to make valid predictions.

Performance standards obviously constitute the most appropriate basis for making personnel evaluations, but formulating the standards constitutes only a beginning step in developing an evaluation system.

In preparing the performance standards for a given position, one starts with the general performance standards established by the department. These are statements of the level of performance that must be achieved by the individuals in a particular job category to assure the provision of high quality care. If one uses a rating scale for assessing performance, the standard would define the highest point on the scale. Thus, in a 6-point rating scale, the standard would delineate the behaviors that merit a rating of 6. Such a rating should be within the reach of most of the employees concerned, rather than by only the most exceptional performers. The standards should reflect the desired patient care goals.

Performance standards for the staff nurse are derived from the patient care objectives. The nursing department's standard directed to prevention of complications, for example, might read, "Potential complications are identified and appropriate measures are taken to prevent those that are preventable and avoid exacerbation of those that are not." As this statement stands, it can serve as a standard for all staff nurses who provide bedside nursing care. However, the statement is too general to be practicable. For application, it would have to be stated in more explicit terms and, perhaps, differently for different clinical nursing services. Personnel in each clinical area would have to restate the terms to be directly applicable to the patients within that service. The clinical experts would apply their knowledge of the nursing needs of their patients to formulate the specific performance requirements. Thus, the obstetrical unit, the coronary care unit, or the pediatric unit would each function with a different definition of the behaviors that would merit a top rating regarding the problem of complications. But, in each case, the expected complications and the actions to combat them would be delineated specifically and completely.

Ideally, each staff member can and should achieve the top rating, thus maximizing the probability that patients will receive high-quality care. Given their explicit formulations and their applicability as bases for evaluation, the standards can also serve as objectives toward which staff nurses can work. At the same time, the head nurse can use them to determine any additional training or remediation steps her staff members might need.

Use of the evaluation criteria and process begins as soon as the individual joins the staff within a clinical service. For example, the head nurse immediately acquaints new staff nurses with the evaluation criteria; thus, they are aware at the outset of what they must do to meet the unit's performance standards. The head nurse should evaluate a new employee as soon as an assignment has been accepted so that any deficiencies can be remedied as quickly as possible.

In addition to criteria specifying the level of performance required of the staff nurse, the head nurse should set up a system to collect information needed to monitor the staff nurse's progress. Various sources of information may be used, but in each case the data should be based either on direct observations of performance or on performance outcomes relevant to the unit's per-

formance standards, whether the head nurse makes the observations herself or delegates this task to an associate.

Much of the staff evaluation can be done in conjunction with assessing the quality of care received by patients. A head nurse, to be knowledgeable about the quality of care given her patients, must evaluate that care. When the patient's current status is assessed, the individual doing the checking should ascertain whether all the care needed by that patient has been provided. If this is not the case, the staff member whose performance fell short should be helped to make up for the deficiencies. Remedial measures might involve new educational content or performance of the necessary activities under direct supervision. However, it is crucial that the head nurse ascertain that the appropriate behaviors have been incorporated into the staff member's subsequent activities.

Generally, the application of evaluation criteria will indicate how the individual is performing in the actual nursing setting. Because of the infrequent occurrence of extreme emergency situations, the opportunity to observe certain crucial behaviors performed by the staff member may not be readily available. In such cases, the evaluation criteria may be stipulated in terms of the staff member's ability to perform adequately in mock situations or her ability to demonstrate the requisite knowledge in a test.

Thus, the evaluation process begins as soon as the staff member enters the unit and continues daily by continually monitoring the quality of care provided the patients. Careful, detailed information gathering is required if appropriate decisions are to be made about the individual staff member's need for help and the kind of assistance that will satisfy that need.

THE SUMMARY EVALUATION

Generally, the references used in staff evaluations are the periodic summaries frequently associated with salary adjustments and tenure decisions. The summary evaluation, a necessary task in most institutions, is an extension of the frequent and continuing evaluation. It measures an individual's general performance level against the department standards. However, the decisions for which the summary evaluation is performed do not require information as specific as that needed to detect inadequate ongoing performance. Basically, what is needed is some indication of the individual's present and future level of performance.

The information gathered to improve and maintain the individual's performance can be used to compose the summary evaluation, but only some of those characterizations are required to make a decision involving a limited number of options. For example, one may need only to decide whether the individual is to receive a raise, to be put on probation, or to be given a termination notice. The summary evaluation is not the time to diagnose that staff member's educational problems.

Frequently, the evaluator does not make the final decision about a salary adjustment. The supervisor or a director on nursing who does make the final decisions may not be able to judge the significance of certain detailed information about a staff member's performance. She may require an interpretation of the specifics to help her put that information into perspective with what she knows about all the staff members. Thus, the immediate supervisor of the employee must process all the information obtained about the individual, interpret that information in terms of its predictive significance, and put it into a meaningful form for those who will make decisions about the employee's job and salary status.

For example, the criterion pertaining to preventing complications can illustrate how such standards might be used in a summary evaluation.

The head nurse will have made observations about the extent to which the staff nurse prevents complications or minimizes their effects. Obtaining such information would be deliberate and not a matter left to chance. The head nurse should be as certain as possible that the employee will not neglect any activity that will prevent or minimize the effects of complications. In the process, she should be using standards defined in terms of *observable behaviors*. Such observations will help assure that a complete appraisal of each staff member is being made for every standard relevant to patient complications. It is by no means necessary that the head nurse collect all the pertinent data regarding all employees at the same time. But to assure herself that adequate patient care is continuously being provided, she ought to have either checked the employee as functioning effectively or arranged appropriate remedial steps to correct existing deficiencies in the employee's performance. Information about her staff's functioning should be collected continuously, because *evaluation of the adequacy of staff performance is a major part of the head nurse's supervisory responsibilities concerned with the maintenance of high-quality care for her patients.*

The Author's Approach

Particular performance standards preventing complications are adopted because of demonstrated relationships between certain nursing activities and certain patient outcomes (that is, absence of complications). Once these standards have been adopted, the functioning of individual nurses can be rated. In a traditional approach, the employee would be rated by level of performance on each activity involved and then, perhaps, given an overall, average rating.

The approach I recommend is different. The employee is checked off as either performing or not performing each activity adequately. An overall rating is then assigned, based on the *number* of activities performed in acceptable fashion. This approach stresses the notion that *each* component activity must be performed adequately. Half-way measures and good intentions are given no credit. In recommending such an approach, I recognize that there are varying degrees of success in preventing of complications and that some preventive measures may require more skill and knowledge than others. But the crucial question is: Did the employee recognize the possibility of a complication in a given case and proceed in the preventive activities called for by the unit's performance standards? The staff nurse who performs acceptably with all her patients would receive a top rating. To the extent that she fails to do so, her rating would fall short. In determining how far short it ought to be, one might take into account the knowledge manifested by the employee in her successful activities and the degree of difficulty associated with such activities. Most important, each staff member would be evaluated on the same basis and the judgment about the acceptability of *a given activity* would be certain—either the individual performed that activity adequately or she did not.

The rating will reflect the level at which the individual is functioning at the time of the evaluation. For objectivity, the rating and any accompanying descriptions should not reflect the speed with which the employee acquired the skills or estimates about her prospects for the future. Also, performance, not the person, is being evaluated. If the evaluator incorporates her personal feelings about the employee and the employee's future in her rating, the meaning of such ratings will vary by staff member. Once such subjectivity enters the process, the value of a staff evaluation standard—a standard that provides the best information for making decisions, and treating each staff member fairly and objectively—is lost.

Other Considerations

Although the same rating reflecting comparable performances may be given to two different staff members, it does not necessarily mean these individuals ought to be treated identically. If two staff nurses each receive a rating of 3 on a 5-point scale, it does not follow that both are performing at "average" levels. A nurse who has been on the staff for two years is probably performing less than adequately if she earns no more than a 3 rating. In contrast, a recent graduate who has been on the staff only six months who re-

ceives a rating of 3 may be performing quite admirably, given the limited time she has had to learn about the types of complications likely to occur in her unit.

This kind of scale is based on a direct translation of observations into scale scores. Interpretation is left until the ratings have been examined and considered together with other factors that enter in the decision-making process. Attaching particular salary increases to particular scale scores would not be appropriate. Although such a score is an objective index of the quality of a staff member's performance, the *interpretation* that follows must be based on other information as well and will inevitably be somewhat subjective. For example, a staff nurse might have an average rating of less than 4 after three years of service. If her evaluations were based on an objective assessment of her ability to satisfy her unit's performance criteria, one could conclude that her performance has not been sufficient to guarantee that the essentials of high-quality care are provided her patients, at least without some form of supervising her activities. And given her failure to improve beyond her present rating after three years, it might seem highly unlikely that such improvement would occur during the next three years. Even though one presumably has enough information here to accurately predict her future performance, the decision in this case may include other factors—such as the hospital's policies regarding salary increases and retention or dismissal of employees; certain standards or policies held outside the nurse's unit, even outside the nursing department, frequently enter in the decision process. But even if the head nurse could make recommendations she considered appropriate and such recommendations would be followed, the decision should not be automatic based simply on how the worker measures up to the performance standards in her unit. One must weigh the value of retaining the services of an employee whose limitations are known and who has mastered at least some of the activities carried on in the unit against the prospects of replacing her with an unknown and possibly inexperienced individual who might be even less effective.

At the same time, one ought to attempt to determine if the current employee's strengths are sufficient to outweigh her inadequacies. If her lowest ratings occur in functions with serious consequences for the wellbeing of patients, then relatively high ratings on desirable but less crucial traits (such as kindness and consideration for patients) should not tip the balance in her favor. The evaluation process can only provide information on which to base a decision. The most objective measure one can contrive will not substitute for wisdom. Nor, as already suggested, will the performance evaluation necessarily comprise the totality of what must be considered in reaching a final decision.

The principles applicable to the evaluation of staff nurses will apply to other categories of workers as well. Information gathered about any employee ought to provide a basis for making effective decisions. For workers who assist the staff nurse in providing patient care the situation is very similar, although the standards will, of course, be different. In drawing up evaluative standards for auxiliary personnel, it might be necessary to routinely include certain traits that, in the case of registered nurses, would only be considered when infractions are apparent. For example, personal or clothing cleanliness and professional conduct should be taken for granted in drawing up standards for the performance of registered nurses. Including such criteria would only draw attention away from characteristics that are crucial in the provision of high-quality patient care.

EVALUATION OF ADMINISTRATIVE PERSONNEL

Evaluating staff in administrative or supervisory roles is more difficult. The results they are supposed to achieve are not as well defined. Standards that appear to facilitate the delivery of nursing care may have readily been adopted for administrators, but gathering the information to evaluate such standards is likely to pose serious difficulties. What would one look at to determine whether a supervisor was providing adequate supervision of her head nurses? The nursing department's director (and assistant directors) have very likely delegated responsibilities to supervisors because of the impossibility of keeping abreast of all the personnel and all the work required to meet the department's goals. But the director of nursing is nevertheless still responsible for the effective functioning of the total department. The director is undoubtedly concerned about the quality of work performed by staff members to whom she has delegated major responsibilities. But it would be unreasonable to expect her to observe their performances directly. She can, however, observe the functioning of the systems they have established. If she wishes to know whether her supervisors are providing appropriate support for their head nurses, she can examine components of the system that are likely to reflect such support.

Evaluating this aspect of the supervisor's work is more difficult because we know a good deal less about this realm than, for example, what constitutes adequate or superior bedside nursing. In both cases, we are interested in results—well-prepared head nurses in one case, high-quality patient care in the other. Obviously, the methods for achieving these desired outcomes differ markedly.

If the focus is on well-prepared head nurses, one must identify the activities and conditions that produce this outcome and then use those events to formulate performance standards for the administrator. If one finds that the head nurses are not well prepared, then obviously whatever activities the supervisor is pursuing are not effective. But the supervisor must be prepared to engage in, and be evaluated on, whatever activities are considered at the time most likely to produce the desired results.

For example, the skills of the supervisor in helping head nurses achieve professional growth might be assessed by the following standards:

1. A profile for each staff nurse is prepared after six months experience to determine her potential for development as a head nurse.
2. A system for providing staff members with the continuing education experiences needed to assume leadership roles in the department has been established; staff members are attending such sessions and are evaluated for their acquisition of content.
3. Turnovers in head nurses are projected in sufficient time to ensure that replacements can be found without disruptions in the system.
4. A supervisory system provides for the identification of problems presented by head nurses and the undertaking of necessary remedial steps.

All these standards are rather general and would require further explication depending on the knowledge and values of those responsible for selecting the outcomes. But, even these general standards would at least give the supervisor an idea of the goals she is expected to achieve and the evaluator a basis for determining if the supervisor has been performing effectively.

The supervisor could be asked to submit a plan for identifying potential candidates for head nurse positions, together with evidence of its success, as one indication of her ability to meet the standard. Plans for leadership development, methods of evaluating the success of plans, and her use of information obtained from supervisors regarding the functioning of head nurses constitute additional possibilities. A system for assigning values to these items would help the evaluator establish a rating. Because of the subjective nature of the judgments called for, these evaluations will probably be more difficult than will evaluations of staff nurses.

Invariably, an element of subjectivity enters a judgment about quality of performance or outcomes. To the extent that standards are defined carefully, one can reduce the amount of bias. The qualitative nature of the standard can even be eliminated when judgments are restricted to characteristics that can be reliably rated even by individuals lacking substantial knowledge.

However, Ebel has indicated that it is possible to reduce the validity of a test while at the same time raising its reliability by selecting items for their ease of measurement rather than for their relevance to the behavior to be assessed[18]. In much the same fashion, using a performance-appraisal tool can be made easy and reliable by limiting the behavior to be judged to what can be understood and handled by the least knowledgeable of the judges. The gain in reliability associated with such an approach would be far outweighed by the resulting loss in significance.

Successful recognition of high quality performance in any complex endeavor depends largely on the knowledge and judgment of the evaluator. An evaluator cannot do a decent job if he or she is not knowledgeable about what is being evaluated. A tool that does not require some degree of knowledge about the delivery of high-quality nursing care will probably not guarantee the provision of such care. An inadequate director of nursing or head nurse will interpret existing standards using her own values and whatever knowledge she possesses.

When the knowledge base is sound and reasonably complete, the activities and effects to be observed can be explicitly described. Designating the steps involved in preparing and applying a dressing, for example, is the kind of standard that can be formulated explicitly enough to permit reliable evaluations by a large number of individuals with minimal backgrounds. In contrast, the bases for criteria for such areas as teaching, planning, or delegating responsibility are not as well established, and such criteria are likely to be vaguely defined. Nevertheless, these abilities may be much more important in determining the quality of a nursing program than some of the more easily defined procedural abilities. As we gain additional knowledge in the more complex areas, we will become better able to explicate the nature of the skills required to meet specified goals. In the meantime, sacrificing a degree of objectivity makes it possible to gather certain types of significant information.

I feel that relatively imprecise assessments of traits or activities that play an important role in high priority nursing care are of more significance than reliable measures made of traits or activities that are unrelated to the achievement of departmental goals. More emphasis should be placed on identifying and achieving the goals of the department than on the mechanics of the measuring process.

EVALUATION COUNSELING

The evaluation conference is assumed to be an integral part of the evaluation system[19]. In this process, the supervisor meets with the staff member to review her evaluation; in theory, the staff member presents her views and the supervisor provides additional information to help the employee understand the evaluation. The meeting might terminate with the employee signing a form to indicate she has been apprised of the evaluation. In certain cases consideration may be given to what the employee must do to improve her performance, as well as to shortcomings the employee believes exist in the system and that might be remedied through the supervisor's efforts.

However, in many instances, neither the employee nor the supervisor has a clear idea of the purpose of the evaluation conference, but both nonetheless consider it a necessary part of the evaluation system. Even if an employee regularly received feedback as a part of the daily routine, it seems quite possible that she would still not regard herself as having been evaluated without a formal conference with her supervisor. In my view, such conferences do not contribute much to improved employee performance or evaluation and could in many cases be abandoned, particularly if provisions are made to counsel the employee for any specific prob-

lems. Those who believe strongly in the need for a formal discussion with the staff member every six or twelve months, should carefully consider what can and cannot be achieved in such sessions.

Without question, an employee who is not going to receive an expected salary increase or promotion is entitled to know why. She is also entitled to know what modifications in her behavior would guarantee favorable outcomes. But if the six month or one year period has elapsed without the employee having already been made aware of her deficiencies, the supervisor has been extremely negligent in handling the case.

Some supervisors believe the evaluation conference provides an opportunity to relate to their staff members and to engage in a mutually satisfying exchange about the problems they are working together to solve. Regularly scheduled, formally organized conferences might indeed have beneficial effects, including favorable effects on unit morale. But it should be clear that there are limitations to what such conferences can achieve and the likelihood of their being successful hinges on ensuring that the sessions are explicitly designed to serve their stated purposes. For example, if the conference is mainly a tool for improving employee-supervisor relations, then it should be designed with that express purpose in mind.

The evaluation constitutes a form of either reward or punishment, depending on its consequences. The evaluation conference is likely to involve whatever affect or feelings the evaluation itself elicits. The individual is rewarded or punished, not her specific behaviors. As a result, neither the evaluation nor the evaluation conference provides an effective means of motivating the individual to perform more effectively. The individual who feels she has been rewarded is not likely to discriminate among the behaviors that were rewarded and behaviors that may need modification. The individual who experiences what she perceives as punishment is not likely to conclude that she needs to improve her performance to obtain the desired reward. In most cases, neither delayed reward nor delayed punishment has the desired effect of encouraging desirable behaviors[20].

Identifying undesirable behaviors— whether in an evaluation or for any other purpose—is not likely to produce desired behaviors. Some behaviors may cease, but these may not be the ones that were criticized. The behaviors most closely associated in the individual's mind with the punitive situation are the likeliest to be suppressed [21]. A list of deficiencies may be useful documentation for a decision to terminate an employee or to withhold a salary raise, but it will not facilitate improved behavior. Undesirable behaviors are most effectively discouraged at the time they occur; furthermore, unless the individual is at the same time also taught the desired behaviors, such discouragement can only be counted on, at best, to suppress the undesirable behaviors[22].

Using the evaluation process and conference as a vehicle to promote interactions between staff and supervisor entails other possible risks—for example, the danger associated with either participant perceiving the evaluation as a disciplinary measure. At times, undue consideration is given to behaviors that annoy the supervisor but that do not affect the employee's functioning. This is most likely to occur when the performance standards are not explicitly stated, are not pertinent to the provision of high-quality care, or the supervisor has personal biases that interfere with her ability to apply the standards effectively.

Another problem exists when the supervisor overlooks inadequate performance because of a staff member's affability, industry, or conscientiousness. The worker who is disruptive or who needlessly challenges the supervisor's authority may be a frequent cause of administrative problems, but the individual whose inadequate performance has been overlooked because of her attractive traits can pose a threat to patients. Both situations can be avoided if evaluations are based on valid performance criteria and if the supervisory system uses

performance evaluations to maintain high-quality patient care and not simply as a retrospective correction mechanism.

For those who believe that the formal conferences associated with the summary evaluation are useful or who are required by departmental standards to hold them, I would not recommend their discontinuation. But, the purposes of holding the conferences should be explicitly stipulated, the features that will maximize accomplishing those purposes identified, and the conferences conducted with these considerations continually in mind. Additionally, the formal summary evaluation and the evaluation conference do not by themselves comprise sufficient evaluative activity. At best, they are procedures that supplement the day-by-day positive and negative feedback provided the employee on the job.

EVALUATION FOR APPOINTMENT, REAPPOINTMENT, OR PROMOTION

In addition to decisions about job retention and salary raises, new appointments, reappointments and promotions must also be considered. Each instance requires information that will help predict the individual's potential for success. In the case of an appointment to a position similar to one an applicant has held elsewhere or a reappointment to a position the applicant held earlier, the same information that would be useful in deciding about job retention or granting a salary raise would be applicable.

In many cases, individuals in one hospital are asked to write recommendations that will be used for making decisions in another hospital. The appropriate information to be included would be in the summary evaluation. Although the hospital requesting the evaluation may not share identical values and beliefs about the data, virtually any information that pertains to the individual's ability to meet the goals of patient care is nevertheless useful. If the request for the references includes questions about social habits or other characteristics that may not be of concern to the responding unit, such information may simply not be obtainable. Personnel in the referring hospital surely should not feel obligated to forward information they consider irrelevant.

On occasion, references are used to discharge an undesirable staff member. In such cases, they may conceal serious problems, out of fear of reprisal from the employee if critical information were provided the inquiring institution. The safety and welfare of patients are at stake in such instances. Misrepresenting an employee's significant shortcomings or refraining from commenting on them, to the extent that those shortcomings bear on patients' wellbeing, is a serious breach of ethics. Any concern about possible violations of employees' rights in such instances seems totally inappropriate. If an employee has been fairly and honestly evaluated on the basis of quality care standards, communicating unfavorable information seems eminently defensible, since employee defects could result in inadequate or harmful care to patients.

Uses of the evaluation process for promotion decisions entails evaluation of an individual's performance in one job with a view toward promoting her to another one. However, one fallacy in this particular use of the evaluation process is illustrated by the Peter Principle: the qualities that make a worker successful in one position may be the very qualities that make him unsuitable for another position[23].

A candidate should be considered for promotion because a job opening exists that needs to be filled by a capable person. Promotions should not be manufactured simply as a way of rewarding individuals for their efforts. Unfortunately, both the supervisors and the staff members in some institutions look upon promotions as a means of rewarding favored employees. When this attitude prevails, it is frequently accompanied by an emphasis on employee relations that overshadows any concerns about the quality of care provided patients. Furthermore, any problems in such settings are not apt to be viewed as resulting from

the competencies of the leaders involved. A sound promotion decision frequently requires information that will predict potential success in an entirely new type of job. The evaluation of her work in her present job may simply not be relevant to the job she is seeking. For example, the excellent staff nurse will be a poor head nurse if she is unable to remove herself from the bedside care situation or is unable to convey her knowledge about patient care to other personnel. The evaluation criteria associated with the job to which the individual aspires may provide a better basis for assessing her qualifications than do the criteria pertaining to her present position.

As pointed out earlier, the criteria for evaluation of supervisory staff tend to be ambiguous; and difficult to define. Certain personality attributes may be relevant to an individual's leadership potential, but attempts to pin down and measure such traits as a basis for reaching decisions about promotions are likely to meet serious obstacles. Despite the fact that an individual's personality characteristics undoubtedly play a role in determining leadership potential, the use of personality tests to predict one's job performance has met with little success[24].

In some situations, a trial period may allow the candidate to demonstrate explicitly whether she has the potential to fill the position. This approach is not particularly useful, however, because the practicalities of the typical situation make it impossible to employ the procedure on a widespread basis. Even when it is practicable—as, for example, when an employee fills in for a vacationing supervisor—the duties and responsibilities assumed temporarily are not likely to closely duplicate those required of the permanent leader.

In my view, the most efficient approach to this problem is to identify some activity relevant to significant aspects of the supervisory job and then have the individual prepare a project that demonstrates her competence in that activity. For example, in the nursing department at the University of Iowa Hospitals and Clinics, an initial promotion step was made available to the general staff nurse. The position emphasized clinical leadership rather than administrative activities and had no line responsibilities. It was designed to assist the head nurse in her efforts to provide continuing high-quality patient care and also aid staff members in improving their clinical performances. The position required expertise in bedside care and the ability to program for quality of care given patients, and for teaching staff members. The criteria for promotion to the position were set accordingly. A 4.5 average on a 5-point scale on the staff-nurse evaluation form was set as the *minimum to be considered* for appointment.

Two projects demonstrating the individual's ability to develop and implement programs were required of candidates. The first project, developing a program of patient care, reflected the candidate's ability to organize clinical content and to program for improved patient care. The second project, an educational offering for staff members, actually required the candidate to follow through with the educational effort, teaching the material involved to a group of staff members and then evaluating the effectiveness of that teaching. The assumption was made that such projects provide sample activities actually called for in more advanced positions and that should be valid predictors of ultimate performance. By requiring a candidate to present relevant evidence that can be judged objectively, one is in a good position to select effective leaders and provide a fair opportunity for candidates to compete on the basis of their competencies.

Obviously, instituting such a procedure can generate problems if either the candidates or the evaluators do not understand the purpose of the program and logic underlying its development. If the skills required on the job are not represented in the project, then the procedure will be useless at best and, at worst, will fill responsible positions with incompetent leaders and

draw legitimate charges about discriminatory employment practices that emphasize characteristics irrelevant to the job.

Such projects also entail numerous other problems. The most difficult idea to convey to individuals unfamiliar with such an approach is the conceptualization of the project as a way of sampling behaviors that play an important role in the job situation. Frequently, both candidates and evaluators tend to look on the projects as "papers" like those prepared in school or college. In these cases, the size of the bibliography and the amount of information transferred from book to paper tend to be emphasized, rather than the relevance of the project's content to the improvement of nursing care delivery. The project may not predict job performance at all, but may satisfy the individual needs of the evaluators and/or the candidates for promotion.

A serious misunderstanding is to identify the development of programs of care with the promotion process—that is, the mistaken assumption that the only way to generate a program of care is by having someone in the setting who wants to be promoted. Another allied misunderstanding is that a nurse clinician position is assured once a project has been done, that a promotion is due regardless of the quality of the finished product, and that the project obviates the need for any similar future projects. If the projects are not viewed as a basis for predicting future performance, an individual might be selected for promotion first and then pushed to complete the projects as a way of legitimatizing the decision.

Standards for carrying out and evaluating such projects must be developed and maintained. The specific project chosen is not as important as its relevance as a predictor of future performance (see chapter 7).

Identifying relevant work samples is a major challenge for filling leadership jobs, and one that becomes exaggerated if the leadership jobs are viewed in diverse ways by different persons with significant roles.

Some view leadership positions as simply adding a certain amount of breadth to whatever is done in the job one step below in the departmental hierarchy; others see them as calling for the coordination of a number of independent systems, with the relevant knowledge base existing elsewhere (such as in management and business administration); and still others view them as involving programming for patient care delivery, with the relevant knowledge base located in the sciences. Reconciling such diverse views in one department is exceedingly difficult but necessary. Without a prevailing philosophy, the mechanics of the chosen system may be put in motion, but the criteria used from unit to unit and from situation to situation will vary and so will the benefits enjoyed by patients.

PEER REVIEW, SELF-EVALUATION, AND EVALUATION BY SUBORDINATES

Periodically, staff members may request adoption of performance appraisal methods that will give them some degree of control over their own evaluations. Peer review for evaluation of registered nurses is in current favor[25]. Self-evaluation as an addition to evaluation by peers and even appraisal of supervisors by subordinates have their advocates[26, 27]. The adoption of any of these approaches would depend on the extent to which they contribute to the department goals and their users' objectives. The advantages of the approaches should be weighed against their disadvantages.

A nursing administrator might consider three questions as she assesses the strengths and weaknesses of the three procedures: (1) What purpose will the information obtained in this fashion serve? (2) In whose hands would the system place the power to reward and discipline? and (3) Who would control the establishment of the performance standards that would actually be adopted under the evaluation system chosen?

In all three approaches, the assumption seems to be that individuals *other than those who are directly accountable for the quality of care afforded patients* could determine what system would be used to reward staff performance. I have grave reservations about such an approach. Among its unfortunate and probable consequences, it deprives the individual responsible for the quality of care of a major means of exerting constructive control over her employees. Furthermore, it may commit the administrator to the use of information that has a rather high likelihood of being erroneous or irrelevant.

Perhaps self-evaluations along with other evaluative procedures can be used as an educational tool and to assist the individual to internalize department standards. But the time and effort they require, together with the potential problems that could arise from discrepancies in judgments, should be carefully weighed against their potential benefits. More direct ways of accomplishing the purpose are available that would not commit the administrator to the use of forthcoming information. Taking advantage of existing staff development and performance maintenance systems are good possibilities.

The purpose served by subordinates' evaluations of their superiors remains obscure. It seems highly implausible that a responsible nursing administrator would use evaluations made by a subordinate of a supervisor to obtain information about the supervisor's effectiveness. The administrator who would resort to this kind of information gathering has very likely not sufficiently defined the supervisor's responsibilities to judge the effectiveness of her functioning.

But why would an administrator at any level ask to be evaluated by her subordinates? What information could the subordinate have about how the supervisor is meeting the objectives that have been set up for her? The subordinate sees only a limited segment of the activities that go on in a unit; at best, she can only judge how she "feels" about her superior. Some may believe that an employee should be able to anonymously evaluate *her* subordinates. But what would a supervisor do with information obtained this way? One could hardly be expected to modify her behavior in accordance with every critical comment made because such criticisms may not even be pertinent to her job performance. The administrator who asks for evaluations for any purpose other than that of assessing job performances must be acting out of her own personal needs. The administrator can obtain the information she needs by examining the operation of the system itself.

Peer review involves an aspect of professionalism that calls for special consideration. As I understand peer review, it is the assessment of one individual by another of equal status or rank. For example, peer review in medicine involves physicians assessing their fellow physicians. Those with specialized knowledge or skills are obviously more qualified to evaluate the caliber of the work done by their professional colleagues than those who lack such background.

But the definition of "peer" deserves crucial consideration. One does not ordinarily regard the resident physician as being the peer of the staff physician simply because they both have the basic MD degree. Nor does the staff physician relinquish the responsibility of judging a resident's work to other residents. Presumably, the senior members of a law firm evaluate the performances of junior members, even though they all possess law degrees. In academic settings, an individual at a given rank is not typically evaluated by colleagues possessing that same rank; rather, individuals at the rank to which the candidate aspires (or higher) ordinarily fulfill this obligation.

Nurses tend to describe the evaluation of staff nurses by head nurses as the "bureaucratic model" of evaluation which suggests that head nurses and supervisors are not in their positions because of their knowledge of nursing practice, but because of their grasp of the content in some other discipline or their knowledge of practices in business or industry[28]. The typical hospital is indeed a bureaucratic organization within which pro-

fessional divisions exist and whose leaders were presumably assigned to their administrative posts because of, among other considerations, their knowledge of their own disciplines.

If, for example, the supervisory staff know less about patient care than do the head nurses or even the staff nurses, then the possibility of high-quality care is minimal and the administrative structure rather than the evaluation system is at fault. The head nurse's assumption of responsibility for evaluating the work of the staff nurse, licensed practical nurse, or nursing assistant is in keeping with the practice by which the senior members of a law firm assess the work of the firm's junior members, or by which the staff physicians in a hospital evaluate the performances of interns and residents.

If the quality of care given patients does depend on knowledge and achievement of the objectives of care and if the evaluation system used by the department has a role in ensuring that those objectives are met, then it seems sensible to insist that the individuals doing the assessments possess the requisite knowledge. If several members of the department are equally competent in this regard, then of course the responsibility for evaluative activity can be shared.

THE ROLE OF SUPERVISION IN THE MAINTENANCE OF PERFORMANCE STANDARDS

The systems established to maintain standards will be effective if they are seen as leading to, and forming part of, the whole supervisory system. A supervisor who uses certain standards to evaluate individuals on a retrospective basis but fails to ensure that those standards are met on a daily basis is working against the goal. Performance standards are not maintained by periodic performance evaluations, but by daily encouragement of desired behaviors and discouragement of undesirable behaviors. If the standards that are adopted mandate what must be done to assure high-quality patient care, their violation is never excusable. Vigilant application of those standards should be the responsibility of any individual who supervises the performance of others.

The hallmark of an effective supervisor is not skilled handling of frequently occurring performance problems but is the ability to establish a system that *prevents problems from occurring.* She not only can identify staff members' failures to meet standards, but can also pinpoint the features of her own behavior and of the conditions she has established that facilitate or inhibit meeting those standards.

One of the biggest problems faced by a supervisor is relinquishing favored supervisory approaches that are not producing desired results. To change someone else's behavior, one must often—however reluctantly—change one's own behavior. Many supervisors like to try to control the behavior of others by using exhortations to change in counseling sessions or staff meetings. As Mager has pointed out, such approaches seldom prove effective[29]. Even teaching is ineffective if the problem does not arise from a lack of knowledge of the appropriate behaviors in the situation. Frequently, a supervisor may be exhorting her staff to perform in a given way, while at the same time reinforcing or encouraging the very behaviors she wants to eliminate. One operating room head nurse complained because her staff continually asked her about room set-ups, instead of using the file cards containing the necessary information. It never occurred to her that, by consistently giving them the information, rather than directing them to the card file, she was fostering the very behavior about which she was complaining. Another head nurse could not understand that vigorous efforts to reduce the number of staff members coming to work while carrying infections were rendered ineffectual by her obvious concern about the amount of sick leave being taken in her unit[30].

It is well to remind oneself periodically that standards are not simply directives set by one group to be adhered to by another.

One cannot reasonably expect standards to be met simply because they have been formulated and adopted. The supervisor should be committed to establishing conditions that make meeting the standards possible and give fair, consistent treatment to staff members in their adherence to those standards.

The supervisor's own commitment to standards will be manifested by the actions—rather than the words—that make it possible for her staff members to meet those standards without undue hardship. Just patting a nurse on the back for a job well done is often not enough. For example, a conscientious supervisor will reinforce a head nurse for challenging physicians on important policy or patient safety matters. But providing truly adequate support requires that the supervisor make certain the head nurse will not have to endure unfair criticism and abuse as a consequence of her actions and will be forced to battle alone for the principle involved. Furthermore, a constructive approach would require that the supervisor not view the problem as an adversary situation in which more concern is directed toward defending nursing than toward determining whose behaviors need to be altered.

Personnel at each supervisory level have an obligation to help those working under them to understand and successfully meet the standards that have been set up to ensure high-quality nursing care. The happiness and contentment of staff members, although an important element in the total picture, is not a major reason for a hospital's existence. Obviously, good patient care will not be forthcoming if strained and disruptive interpersonal relations exist among the hospital's personnel. But when patient care goals are *replaced* by such goals as administrator-employee relations, one has lost sight of what matters most in the total situation. It seems likely that the farther one departs from bedside nursing the greater the possibility that employee relations standards will replace patient care–performance standards as the focus of her attention. Thus, a clinical supervisor, when dealing with a dispute between a head nurse and a staff nurse, might show great concern over the dispute itself, while virtually ignoring its implications for the quality of patient care.

Being required to meet certain specified standards is not a source of pleasure for some. At any level in the hierarchy of a nursing department, some individuals consider it an infringement of their rights if they are required to do anything they would rather not do. Certain employees will be unable to meet the standards that have been adopted for the positions they would like to fill. They may on occasion expect the standards to be modified to suit their knowledge and skills. The superior who cannot tolerate the discomfort of dealing with employees who are not meeting standards, or who values her relationships with her subordinates more than meeting standards, will probably not be able to maintain rigorous standards consistently. Regrettably, occasions arise when, for example, a supervisor will actually prevent her head nurse meeting

certain standards, because of fears about her inability to sort out the human relations problems that might be entailed.

Vigilance in maintaining performance standards developed from a firm knowledge base and with a clear understanding of what constitutes superior nursing care is vital, if such care is to be provided. Standards of performance applied to the functioning of supervisory personnel, holding these individuals to certain expectations in determining the quality of their subordinates' work, are of considerable significance. To serve their purpose successfully, such standards must be built on a firm knowledge base that includes an understanding of sound personnel practices and an understanding of the nature of human behavior in general. Institutions differ considerably in the extent to which employee appeals are permitted on such matters as leave policies and working hours. Appeals should never be allowed when the issue pertains to performance standards that have been explicitly designed to assure the provision of high-quality patient care.

NOTES AND REFERENCES

1. Nagle, B. R. "Criterion Development" in *Perspective on the Measurement of Human Performance*, W. W. Ronan, E. P. Prien, (eds.), New York: Appleton-Century-Crofts, Education Division, Meredith Corporation, 1971, p. 580.
2. Wallane, S. R. "Criteria for What?" in *Perspective on the Measurement of Human Performance*, W. W. Ronan, E. P. Prien, (eds.), New York: Appleton-Century-Crofts, Education Division, Meredith Corporation, 1971, p. 48.
3. Dyer, E. D. *Nurse Performance Description: Criteria Predictors, and Correlates.* Salt Lake City, Utah: University of Utah Press, 1967.
4. Tate, B. L. Evaluation of clinical performance of the staff nurse. *Nursing Research,* 11:7–9, Winter 1962.
5. Wandelt, M. A. and Slater, D. S. *Slater Nursing Competencies Rating Scale.* New York: Appleton-Century-Crofts, 1975.
6. Flanagan, J. C. The critical incident technique. *Psychological Bulletin,* 51:327–358, July 1954.
7. Gorham, W. A. Methods for measuring staff nursing performance. *Nursing Research,* 12:1:4–11, Winter 1963.
8. Jensen, A. C. Determining the critical requirement for nurses. *Nursing Research,* 9:8–11, Winter 1960.
9. Bailey, J. T. The critical incident technique in identifying behavioral criteria of professional nursing effectiveness. *Nursing Research,* 4:52–63, October 1956.
10. Wandelt, M. A. and Ager, J. W. *Quality Patient Care Scale.* New York: Appleton-Century-Crofts, 1974, p. v.
11. Wandelt, M. A. and Slater, D. S. 1975.
12. Wallane, S. R. 1971, p. 48.
13. American Nurses Association. "Standards of Nursing Practice" *The American Nurse,* July 1974, pp. 11–22.
14. Job Description, "Staff Nurse III." *Administrative Nursing Policy and Procedure Manual.* Department of Nursing, University of Iowa Hospitals and Clinics, 1974, pp. II:36–37.
15. Adapted from the "Department of Nursing Objectives." *Administrative Nursing Policy and Procedure Manual,* Department of Nursing, University of Iowa Hospitals and Clinics, 1974, p. I-4.
16. Committee on Cardiopulmonary Resuscitation and Emergency Cardiac Care Task Force on CPR-ECC Learning. *A Manual for Instructing—Trainees and Instructors of Basic Cardiac Life Support.* New York: American Heart Association, 1974.

17. Etzioni, A. *Modern Organizations.* Englewood Cliffs, New Jersey: Prentice-Hall, Inc., 1964.
18. Ebel, R. L. *Measuring Educational Achievement.* Englewood Cliffs, New Jersey: Prentice-Hall, Inc., 1965, p. 389.
19. O'Brien, M. J. Evaluation: a positive, constructive approach to the development of potential. *Supervisor Nurse,* 2:4:24-39, 971.
20. Lawson, R. *Learning and Behavior.* New York: Macmillan, 1960, p. 281.
21. Lawson, R. 1960, pp. 246-287.
22. Lawson, R., 1960, pp. 246-287.
23. Peter, L. J. and Hull, R. *The Peter Principle.* New York: William Morrow and Company, Inc., 1969.
24. Cronback, L. J. *Essentials of Psychological Testing.* New York: Harper and Row, 1960, p. 485.
25. Maas, M., Specht, J. and Jacox, A. Nursing autonomy: reality not rhetoric. *American Journal of Nursing,* 75:2201-2208, December 1975.
26. O'Brien, M. J.
27. Moore, T. F. and Simendinger, E. Evaluation as a two-way street. *Supervisor Nurse,* 7:6:58, June 1976.
28. Hinshaw, A. S. and Field, M. A. An investigation of variables that underlie collegical evaluation: peer review. *Nursing Research,* 23:292-300, July-August 1974.
29. Mager, R. and Pipe, P. *Analyzing Performance Problems.* Belmont, California: Fearon Publishers, Lear Siegler, Inc., Education Division, 1970, pp. 1-2.
30. Mager and Pipe present a useful, more complete discussion of this topic.

BIBLIOGRAPHY

Bechtold, H. P. "Problems in Establishing Criterion Measures" in *Personnel Research and Test Development,* D. B. Stuit, (ed.), U.S. Bureau of Naval Personnel, Princeton, N.J.: Princeton University Press, 1947, pp. 357-379.

CHAPTER 7 | # Performance Standards: Staff Preparation

Assuring the provision of high-quality nursing care depends greatly on successful use of personnel performance standards. Such success, in turn, requires an effective staff development program. The major function of the department's educational program is to assure that nursing personnel acquire the knowledge and skills needed to provide prescribed care to patients. Two basic tasks constitute the major challenges in structuring a staff development program: (1) identifying staff members' *general* learning needs; and (2) pinpointing *individual* needs. The first task can be further subdivided: (1) planning the total curriculum for the department, service, or unit; and (2) developing the specific content of the curriculum's classes or workshops.

Inexperienced inservice educators often plan their programs to meet what new employees perceive as their needs, without reference to the actual demands of their particular jobs. Because a newcomer does not yet know what these demands are, it makes little sense to ask what they regard as their inservice education needs. They can, of course, indicate activities in which they would like to have more experience or specify areas in which they feel insecure, but they have no way of knowing whether such remediation would in fact improve their functioning within the department.

New staff members frequently cannot even effectively evaluate their orientation program. Anyone who tries to assess the usefulness of a given educational offering must do so within the limits of her own knowledge, likes and dislikes, and past experience. A particular topic may seem relevant to a newcomer for her own purposes, but could in fact have no significance for the job she is about to assume.

Inservice educators who use new staff members' evaluations of their programs are likely to modify their approaches for flimsy and superficial reasons. The one major way in which newcomers could be useful in evaluating educational offerings would be to indicate, *after some time on the job*, how much time they spend in various clinical settings and how frequently they are called on to engage in various nursing procedures. Using this information, the instructor may decide to alter her inservice program if it does not match well with what the staff member has subsequently been called on to do and her competence in such procedures. Any other useful information about the new employee's educational needs could, in my view, be obtained only from a formalized, specific testing program. The new graduate's *own* appraisal of her educational needs, strengths, and weaknesses is not likely to be of much value.

The conscientious inservice educator might look to the older, experienced staff members for advice about the structure and content of the staff development program. It seems reasonable to assume that the skilled practitioners could best determine the learning needs of the new graduate and the form an ongoing staff development program should take. However, experienced staff members are often only slightly better prepared to make such judgments than are newcomers. Nurses can discuss past experiences in working with new graduates with the inservice educator. They can identify their own pet irritations stemming from what they perceive as deficiencies in the functioning of new and recent additions to the staff. But few have the background needed to analyze their work situation to identify what should be taught and what priorities to establish.

Many individuals believe that virtually *everything* pertaining to hospital policies, procedures, and routines should be covered in the educational program. Special emphasis is frequently given to the newcomer's mastery of established procedures and routines. However, it may entail the rote memorization of a great deal of material, with little attention paid to the time allotted for such learning or to the relevance of such material to her work. Because experienced staff members will frequently not have evaluated the effectiveness of long-standing practices on achieving desirable patient care results, they may be perpetuating poor nursing practices by teaching what *is* done, rather than first determining what *ought* to be done.

These individuals may show even less discrimination when they meet in committee to plan the continuing staff education program. There is no magic in consensus. Although everyone in the group may agree that a particular topic or activity is essential, their collective judgment may be as mistaken as a single individual's. A group of individuals who possess little knowledge about a subject will not be likely to reach valid conclusions simply because all the members of the group made the decision. Few practicing nurses, whether staff members or supervisors, have learned to relate nursing practice to content that is essential to that practice. For many, simply presenting some material to the

trainee suffices, and the newcomer is left to relate such information to practice. The inservice coordinator who depends on the unstudied opinions of staff members to decide what constitutes adequate staff preparation is likely to perpetuate the very deficiencies that the program is supposed to remedy.

The inservice educator who looks to other disciplines for help in developing a useful educational program may receive less assistance than from her nursing colleagues. There is no dearth of people ready to advise the nursing department about its educational needs. Many will even volunteer to provide the content themselves. Dietitians, social workers, physicians, and hospital administrators all feel confident that they are qualified to offer classes containing essential information for the development of nursing personnel. Many nurses, in turn, believe that content provided by specialists in other fields can somehow be translated into effective nursing practice.

But inexperienced individuals by themselves cannot, generally speaking, select from such content those aspects they must retain and apply to their own practices. Nor can a person from outside nursing be expected to make these achievements possible for the nurse. The teacher herself may lack confidence in her own abilities or knowledge in certain areas. If she is herself unable to determine what content is relevant to nursing practice, let alone show how such content can be applied to patient care activities, then it is highly unlikely that such inservice training will produce its intended benefits.

The inservice educator who teaches certain content because it is currently in vogue or is being discussed by well-known authorities in nursing may fare no better than those who rely on specialists from outside the field. Although a feeling of security may arise from adopting programs advocated by recognized authorities or by following patterns already established by others, there is no guarantee that such programs will meet the educational needs of the staff. This is not to say that all educational programs conceived and developed by nursing authorities or other fields are unsound. What *is* unsound is the practice of adopting programs without first ascertaining that their content will serve the purpose at hand. The wise inservice educator *first determines what goals are to be achieved* and *then* selects those programs which should meet those goals.

Obviously, education is not the main business of a service agency but a necessary component if the system is to provide optimal care to its patient population. But education is not the major function of the unit, nor does it produce the unit's main product. Rather, inservice education should be planned with economy and efficiency, as well as effectiveness. Each individual engaged in educational endeavors is spending time away from direct bedside care. In some form or other, the patient pays for the time devoted to preparing the nurse to take better care of him. If the educational program is ineffective, uneconomical, or inefficient, the patient pays more for service that is no better than what would otherwise have been provided.

The individual coordinating the educational program must possess certain basic information to plan a total program. Her first, most crucial, and probably most difficult task involves developing a basis for deciding what educational content is needed and how the educational program that evolves will be evaluated. The learning needs of employees cannot be identified if the expected results of the learning experience are not clearly specified. If the performance standards have already been developed from a study of the activities necessary to bring about particular patient care results, then the task is already partly—but only partly—completed. One must still specify the content needed, how that content should be presented to maximize its retention, and how to evaluate the effectiveness of the teaching activity.

It is helpful to discuss the development of a single educational offering before considering the formulation of a total educational program for a department of nursing. In this discussion, the topic of determining learning needs is included because it is an integral part of educational planning.

DEVELOPMENT OF A SINGLE EDUCATIONAL OFFERING

Just as the program of nursing care provides a basis for developing a system to achieve optimal patient care, the individual educational offering becomes a basis for defining individual learning needs and programming the entire departmental educational curriculum. The kind of planning needed to formulate an educational offering is the same as that needed to develop the program of care. If a given educational offering emphasizes a particular aspect of a program of care, the first part of the planning has already been accomplished. Any educational offering provided within a service agency, whether concerned with a nursing procedure or an administrative activity, should ensure that the patient is being given the care he needs. Hence, the first step is specifying patient benefits. The second step is identifying required nursing procedures. This sequence is the same one recommended for developing a program of care.

Many people find it difficult to think of educational programs in terms of patient results. They feel more comfortable starting with content they consider pertinent to a topic and teaching it without first determining where and how such knowledge will be used. Unless the content is geared to patient results, essential content may be eliminated or extraneous content included. If the teacher always *validates* what she teaches by *relating the knowledge to the use to which it will be put*, she can assure the appropriateness of the content.

Verifying Criteria as Short-Term Objectives

The activities required to achieve specified patient results can be considered the long-range objectives of the educational offering. The task then remains of developing the short-term or immediate objectives of the program—the learner's behaviors that predict whether she will be able to meet the ultimate objectives. They provide verification for the teacher that the learner can now be allowed to assume the responsibilities entailed in performing the activities. Thus, these behaviors are both criteria, indicating the learner has successfully assimilated the content, and predictors of the learner's future performance.

These predictors, or criteria, are critical to the achievement of the teacher's goal of developing educational offerings that form part of the quality assurance program. They help her assure herself that her teaching is contributing to the quality of patient care. By developing these criteria the educator demonstrates her willingness to assume her share of the responsibility for the functioning of staff members.

Decisions are constantly being made about assignments of tasks or responsibilities to staff members. The more information the supervisor possesses that validly indexes the individual's potential for competent performance, the more secure she can feel in making such assignments. When she delegates to the inservice educator the responsibility for evaluating a new employee's readiness for an assignment, she should be able to expect that the educator has obtained the information needed to arrive at sound recommendations.

Criteria developed for this purpose can range in applicability from simple nursing procedures to extremely complex assignments. The most important consideration for the educator, in any case, is to develop verifying criteria by assembling as much information as possible with the least possible expenditure of time and effort, with the outcome of making decisions that safeguard the patient's welfare.

"Passing" an individual who in fact needs remedial teaching would subvert this outcome. The educator cannot, of course, check out the individual on every activity required in a job, which means that the *critical* activities associated with the position must be identified. The educator must use these activities to set up a *test* situation to identify

responses that must be made in specified forms and under specified conditions.

The extent to which the individual can simply give back information acquired in class should not be a major interest. The more closely the test situation simulates the actual job situation, the more significantly will the resulting information predict job performance. Sometimes the testing can take place in the actual practice setting, in which case the duplication is exact. For example, one might observe the learner performing a catheterization procedure. However, it would still be necessary to select those steps in the procedure that are crucial indicators of the individual's readiness to proceed without further supervision or additional instruction.

The written procedure may involve steps that are included for efficiency or because of requirements that are peculiar to the department or hospital. Under these circumstances, time and effort can be saved by limiting the screening just to those steps which are of crucial significance to patient welfare. Variations in the order of performing prescribed steps and even poor organization on the nurse's part can be discounted if such lapses have no deleterious effect on patient welfare. If the *crucial* aspects of the learner's performance are satisfactory, assistance in remedying the noncrucial defects can be given by the educator during the test or subsequently by the head nurse in the actual job situation. The crucial aspects of the procedure in some tasks may be limited to only a few features (such as maintaining sterile conditions) that would be considered in assessing the learner's competence.

Whenever the learner is required to repeat a test until certain criteria have been met, it is particularly crucial that the test be restricted to *essential* content. Otherwise, a new staff member might take repeated tests that would needlessly delay her assumption of responsibilities.

As the teacher develops her verifying criteria, she can test their usefulness by specifying the behaviors she expects from the individual who passes the test. If a test item requires the individual to diagram the urinary system, label the parts, and describe the function of each part, the teacher could verify that the individual who successfully responded to the item would in the future be able to perform those three tasks again. However, one could *not* predict that the individual would make appropriate use of such information in her daily practice with patients suffering from urinary problems.

Considerably more evidence indicating how well the individual would use the content would result if the educator's criteria required applying the information in a realistic situation. The criteria should be developed on the basis of the activity requirements for competent practice. An analysis of this type would make it possible to determine if it is even necessary to teach the entire anatomy and physiology of the urinary system for the purpose at hand.

Development of effective verifying criteria can also reveal to the teacher what content ought to be included in the educational program. The teacher is in fact going to teach to the test. Although such an idea may shock those accustomed to thinking about teaching and testing in traditional terms, teaching content that will prepare the individual to meet and demonstrate mastery of the criteria is precisely what the instructor should do, assuming she is confident that meeting the criteria is clear evidence of ability to perform competently in the nursing practice situation.

When particular criteria are used as a basis for a given educational offering, the instructor may have difficulty restricting her teaching to content directly relevant to those criteria, especially when much information and numerous resources cover the topical area. Most nursing instructors are accustomed to starting with content when planning an educational offering. Thus, even though they may have learned along the way to develop objectives they rarely *use* objectives in selecting educational content.

Moreover, if objectives *are* developed and used, they frequently have little relevance to the activities for which the learner is supposedly being prepared. Rather, their selection is often suggested by *content choices that have already been made* by the instructor. A more efficient and meaningful approach would entail the instructor's first ascertaining what knowledge the learner needs to make appropriate decisions, what skills the learner must possess to carry out the required activities, which of these have already been mastered, and which remain to be acquired.

It is also helpful to determine what set, or predisposition to act, must be present to ensure that appropriate behavior will be performed when needed. On occasion, inadequate performance by the staff member may not involve a lack of knowledge. The individual may in fact know what must be done, but lacks a set that maximizes the performance of necessary behaviors. This elusive quality in a nurse cannot be taught in any direct sense. Presumably, complex environmental factors difficult to identify, isolate, or simulate, are involved. But a teaching program can include content that helps to establish a set to perform appropriate behaviors in a given situation. For example, repeated laboratory practice of certain emergency procedures may not only help to assure retention of those procedures, but may also facilitate the establishment of a set that maximizes the individual's appropriate and immediate response in an emergency.

Making certain that the learner will always discard a contaminated catheter and begin every catheterization with sterile equipment can be conceptualized as involving the establishment of an appropriate set. It may be accomplished by: providing information about urinary infections; documenting the relationship between failure to follow strict aseptic procedures and incidence of infection; requiring drills in the manipulation of materials used in surgical asepsis situations; presenting relevant content as a basic part of a specific procedure, with an expectation that reinforcement of the set would occur in daily practice.

In the final analysis, the educator must be concerned with the quality of the daily activities in the practice setting. If that quality is high, then the educator is in an ideal position, because her job is to prepare staff members to perform activities that will subsequently be reinforced in the clinical area. In contrast, if performance standards in the practice setting are low, the educator's efforts in training staff members are likely to be in vain. In this case, the problem is administrative rather than one that can be solved by altering the educational program.

By analyzing the various skills, the knowledge, and the sets required for adequate or superior performance, one can determine what must be taught. Some content will be new. In many cases, however, the learner will already have certain background information. Knowledge of surgical asepsis is a crucial component in many procedures, particularly in catheterization. Most registered and licensed practical nurses who might be learning or relearning the skill already know the basic principles of surgical asepsis. Thus, although the content is clearly relevant to the procedure, it is probably not necessary to include that *basic information* in a class devoted to catheterization procedures. The *skill* of maintaining sterility while inserting the catheter, however, would necessarily form part of the procedure taught to the staff member.

When the subject matter is a procedure such as a catheterization, in which the specific behaviors are well defined, it is not difficult to select relevant content. But when the topic concerns psychological or sociological patient problems or more amorphous professional matters (such as leadership development in nursing), it may prove difficult to relate teaching content to the specific behaviors expected. In these cases educators are frequently tempted simply to present content that someone else has deemed relevant and hope that the information thus acquired by the staff member will eventually have some beneficial effect on patients.

Educators are likely to defend such a practice by arguing that the behaviors in question are not measurable, but that the information is nonetheless necessary. However, even the teacher herself often does not know how the information could be used in actual practice. When nursing activities are ill-defined and their relation to patient outcomes are left unspecified, the learner must acquire certain content although she is unable to use it—an undesirable situation. I suspect that, in many such instances, the learner considers the content *useful* because she found it *interesting* or *entertaining*. Teachers receive a good deal of reinforcement on these grounds—reinforcement that perpetuates this kind of teaching activity.

The responsible educator, aware of the value of time, knows it is inefficient to pack one's teaching content with information that cannot be translated into practice. She resists the tendency to include material that has nothing to recommend it aside from its interest value or the fact that it has been advocated by others with authority or prestige.

The efficient and effective teacher knows why she has selected every bit of content included in her course offerings. Justifiable rationale, in my view, includes the following arguments: (1) the content involves knowledge that is essential for making effective decisions and judgments; (2) it pertains to skills required in activities that benefit the patient; or (3) it promotes the acquisition of sets that help determine whether the individual will make appropriate use of her skills or knowledge.

Of course, sometimes the content will not be reflected in the direct care given patients but rather in the programs and systems that facilitate the provision of such care. These facilitative effects can be identified and made part of the basis for choosing educational content.

Sometimes nurses are so strongly oriented toward content that they find it difficult to eliminate content that even *seems* relevant. Such reluctance can be rationalized by arguing that at least some learners can process information in new ways to arrive at creative solutions to problems. This being the case, one might argue, the educator should not exclude content that holds *any* promise of stimulating such creativity. But it is important to differentiate between staff development offerings designed to improve staff functioning directly related to patient care and continuing education offerings intended for the advanced and self-directed nurse-scholar. Obviously, because scholarly content would not be directly useful to most staff members, the cost of its large-scale distribution is not justifiable.

When the content offered to staff members has been analyzed for its relevance to specific goals defined in clear nursing practice terms, its tangible benefits will be maximized. An effective educational offering can be developed according to a useful principle: educational objectives (verifying criteria) should determine the choice of content and not vice-versa. An analogy between this principle and that used in developing a program of care (chapter 3) is clear: patient outcome criteria should determine the choice of activities to be carried out on the patient's behalf and not vice-versa.

The Method of Instruction

When the content has been selected, the teacher is then ready to choose the method of instruction. The choice of teaching method depends on the content, and also on the nature of the actual nursing setting. Regardless of choice of content and method, one principle is broadly applicable: whatever skills the individual is acquiring, their practice in the appropriate setting is a highly effective means of ensuring their good use.

The amount of practice to be provided in the educational setting depends on several factors, for example:

1. The more complex a skill, the more practice it requires[1]. Learning to read a thermometer, for example, requires less practice time than does learning to take an accurate blood pressure reading.
2. Skills that will be used immediately and frequently in the clinical setting need less practice and formal review than do those that are rarely used. Skills that are routinely employed are,

in effect, practiced on a continuing basis and hence should not be lost or diminish in strength. In contrast, skills that are used only occasionally can be forgotten and should be practiced (in a contrived situation, if necessary) periodically[2].

3. The circumstance under which the activity will be performed helps determine the amount of practice needed. In general, the higher the stress level characterizing a performance situation, the greater the need for reinforced practice[3]. Those situations in which error or functioning inadequately has serious consequences for the patient will require greater practice, particularly when decisions must be made and actions taken without time for reflection or review.
4. The individual's background can contribute in a negative or positive way in determining the amount of practice needed. If the staff member has had previous experience with certain aspects of an activity and if her already acquired knowledge and skills are highly similar to what the learning situation demands, then only a minimum amount of practice is needed. However, if the individual had learned to perform a task in ways that *conflict* with what is presently expected, she is apt to require a good deal of practice—perhaps even more than that needed by someone lacking any experience at all[4].

Obviously, no matter how much practice is provided, the activity will not be helpful unless it simulates the actual task to be performed in the job setting. It is easy to recognize the need for practice on specific skills involving physical manipulation of the patient (such as venipuncture, colostomy care, or cardiopulmonary resuscitation). But when the skill involves making judgments about conditions and decisions regarding courses of action, it is more difficult to provide practice.

However, just as individuals need practice in performing a nursing procedure, so do they require practice in assessing situations that present decision choices, the correctness of which depends on observations made by the staff member. The kind and amount of practice needed here depends on the number of variables to be considered, the subtlety of the distinctions to be made, and the degree of precision called for in choosing among alternatives. The nurse who is asked to read a monitor simply to differentiate normal from abnormal needs far less practice than does the nurse who must detect subtle changes in a reading and choose a subsequent course of action. Skill in assessing patients to determine whether they should be maintained on an existing nursing program or be shifted to another regimen will often require considerable experience, especially if the signs to be observed are difficult to perceive.

Determining whether a patient who has had a transurethal resection of the prostate is manifesting the expected amount of bleeding calls for inspection of the patient's urinary drainage. Individual staff members might require several opportunities to make relevant observations and estimations to master this skill. Similarly, extensive practice might be needed before one can accurately judge whether a patient's skin color is normal under his particular circumstances, or whether another patient's dyspnea is still within safe limits. Assessing the extent of a patient's pain and choosing the appropriate action to take necessitates considerable experience in making such judgments. The teacher should not assume that information she has presented will necessarily be translated into appropriate actions by the learner. Guided practice in applying newly acquired information is frequently necessary.

Such practice need not necessarily occur within a clinical setting. Sometimes the skills the instructor is trying to develop are best acquired in the classroom. Other skills, however, require practicing on real patients. Thus, skills in reading monitors and in making differential judgments and decisions based on such readings can be developed by using a variety of monitor readouts and by asking the trainee to practice readings and decide appropriate actions within a classroom setting. In contrast, teaching a nurse to make appropriate neurological assessments on neurologically impaired patients would probably require using actual patients who exhibit relevant signs. In this case, one may not have to provide many practice sessions, since each relevant sign would appear in only a limited number of variations.

An important aspect of such practice—one to consider seriously when practice sessions involve patients—is adequate exposure to the variety of conditions and decisions that are apt to be encountered by the staff member during the course of her actual job. A new staff member might easily pass a test requiring assessment of a patient with a given illness whose condition is obvious, but fail that test in actual practice when a patient with the same illness presents less obvious signs and symptoms. An important feature of practice in the classroom or the clinical setting is the extent to which it faithfully duplicates the conditions of the daily job situation.

Other decisions about teaching methods should be governed by *what constitutes the most effective and efficient means of assuring skill and knowledge acquisition*, considering the individuals who do the learning and the content to be acquired. Whether one lectures to the group, sets up discussion groups, or uses audiovisual materials, that question should be foremost in one's mind. When considering a variety of possibilities, it is wise to weigh the potential benefits of each against its costs in time, effort, and money. It is also beneficial to remind oneself that the utility of a method should not be determined by assessing its entertainment value or its value as a promoter of a department's or hospital's image. The most humble teaching method may frequently be the most effective and efficient when evaluated against the objectives.

When the skills and knowledge acquired by the learner are evaluated, the educator is likely to interpret a disappointing outcome as evidence of the learner's lack of ability or motivation. But other possibilities exist, especially when one encounters high rates of failure in successive groups of trainees. For example, the teaching method used may be at fault. A particular method may have proven effective in other contexts, but its utility in the situation at hand may not be high. Another possibility is that inappropriate content that interferes with learning has been included.

The evaluation procedure does not provide information limited just to the progress made by the individual learner. Implications about the quality of the teaching present themselves for examination as well.

Evaluating Effectiveness of Instruction

Making certain that inservice education programs are effective, efficient, and economical should be an important part of the educational efforts of the nursing department. Otherwise, one is in danger of perpetuating educational programs that not only do not contribute to the quality of care provided patients, but in fact lower the quality by inhibiting the development of other, more effective programs. Verifying criteria used as objectives in the development of an educational offering also provide a sound basis for evaluating both the learner and the educational program.

The structure within which the learner will be tested is important. It is imperative that the educator focus on the predictive relationship between test results and on-the-job performance. Determining how much information the learner has acquired will not do; nor should one be concerned with individual differences in test scores. When on-the-job performance is at stake, only *mastery* is acceptable. The criteria used to verify the individual's competence should have been selected because they pertain to essential components of effective nursing practice. The skill has either been acquired or it has not. It would not make sense to think in terms of 95 percent correct functioning in a

cardiopulmonary resuscitation procedure; the individual receiving that score needs additional help in whichever aspect of the procedure she has failed to master.

Every test item should be handled correctly by the learner before she is allowed responsibility for the activity in an actual nursing setting. If a written test is administered, the responses to all of its items should be considered individually as a means of obtaining information to assess the learner's preparation for on-the-job responsibilities. Test performance reveals the individual learner's grasp of the essentials that constitute safe and effective nursing practice. Whenever a teacher preparing staff members for certain nursing activities sets a passing score of less than 100 percent, she is indicating that some test items do not tap knowledge that is really essential to safe and effective nursing practice. If the teacher specifies a passing level of 85 percent without indicating which items can safely be included among the incorrect 15 percent, she is indicating that she considers no part of the test content essential to on-the-job practice. If the teacher could think of the test as a *diagnostic tool* rather than as a final step in her teaching activities, she would develop a useful educational evaluation system.

A pretest can be a useful diagnostic tool. However, I have found that many teachers use pretests and posttests simply to demonstrate that their students know more after classes than before. In such cases, the pretest is not used to determine what content the learner needs; its use simply documents the acquisition of whatever content the teacher presents. That a new employee moved from 60 percent on a pretest to 95 percent on a posttest is of little interest if such improvement tells nothing about the individual's readiness to function in the nursing practice situation.

If the teacher is uncertain about the amount of content to be mastered before the staff member can assume certain responsibilities, a pretest could provide useful information. Much time can be saved if only those parts of an educational program clearly needed by the individual are included in her orientation sessions. If the teacher knows that the staff member lacks certain content or skills, the administration of a pretest is a waste of time. For example, a service teacher would know that new graduates do not have certain content because basic educational programs do not include it or provide minimum exposure to it. In a large medical center, care of patients with complex medical problems might be unique content not available in other settings. In a smaller community hospital, nurses might be required to assume responsibilities that are customarily assumed by physicians in other settings. She may have found that new graduates no longer know how to perform procedures such as catheterization.

In effect, I am arguing that comparisons between pretest and posttest scores are meaningless when the educational offering is presented to prepare the learner to assume certain specific responsibilities in an applied nursing setting. Pretest-posttest comparisons are of course valuable for some purposes— for example, in comparing the effectiveness of different teaching methods. But this is a research-oriented problem rather than one concerned with the preparation of an employee to assume nursing care responsibilities.

Testing that takes place immediately after a class or practice session may not accurately predict the amount of long-term retention. For this reason, particularly in the case of manipulative procedures, it is useful to allow a period of time to elapse between the final learning session and the test administration. To make certain an employee is prepared to perform the cardiopulmonary procedure, for example, one might require the individual to come for testing on successive days until she has successfully administered the procedure on the dummy on the first attempt. Passing the test for the basic resuscitation procedure might require the behaviors in the following list:

All patient care staff, after a lapse of at least one day following the last practice session, can:

A. On a written test:
   1. State how they would recognize and check for cardiac arrest.
   2. State where the crash cart can be found on the area.
   3. Give phone number for Code Blue.
B. On the first trial with the manikin
   1. Raise chest with ventilation
      a. Alternating.
      b. Simultaneous.
   2. Massage effectively
      a. Hands in position.
      b. Adequate pressure.
      c. Rhythm 1 per second.

Another way to help ensure retention is to require a given number of perfect performances in succession. For example, in teaching a group of nursing assistants to measure blood pressure, one might require that the learner report the same reading as that obtained by the instructor on three different patients assessed successively. A registered nurse might be required to establish an intravenous site by venipuncture successfully on five successive patients before being considered competent to perform that task without supervision. In the event of an error, the count would start again. The number of successful performances (as well as the amount of practice) required would depend on the following considerations: (1) the number of variations in the actual situation; (2) the degree of skill required by the task; and (3) the risk involved when inadequate performance occurs.

The first consideration is perhaps the most important determinant of the number of times an individual should be required to demonstrate her skill. Two ways of dealing with situational variations suggest themselves; the test could either include the whole range of possible features one might expect, or it could emphasize those features which would cause the most difficult problems for the practitioner.

Consider, for example, a respondent who can effectively plan for the discharge of a patient with limited resources faced by multiple problems requiring drastic modifications in his life patterns. A nurse with this ability could be depended on to perform effectively in related but less complex situations. Thus, one such complex problem could serve as the basis for constructing a test item to assess the learner's capabilities.

Situations such as the discharge planning example might best be presented as standardized *hypothetical* cases for all individuals in the educational program. However, although the teacher's task would become more complicated, it is possible to set up a standard testing situation calling for nonstandardized responses. In this case, the test would involve whichever *actual patients* are present on the clinical service at the time. Under this arrangement, the specific responses expected of the learner would differ from patient to patient.

A psychiatric nurse used this approach to ascertain whether the nurses in her class had acquired competency in assessing patients with regard to discharge planning. The test conditions required that the respondent evaluate the patients currently on the unit to determine if any were ready for discharge and to decide what preparations to make for those who were. The instructor in such a situation obviously has to study each patient to decide the correct response at a given time.

The disadvantage of this approach is its relative inefficiency, because of the additional effort required on the tester's part and the necessity of restricting those who evaluate the test responses to individuals highly qualified to make such assessments. It has the advantage of providing immediate and highly significant information about the individual's knowledge of the patients and of the principles governing the decisions to be made. It also avoids the problem common in hypothetical case studies of making the significant cues so obvious that test performance does not meaningfully predict how

well the individual will function in a more ambiguous real-life situation.

Whether one uses patients in the clinical setting or provides hypothetical cases for testing, the overriding consideration ought to be how one can make the best possible predictions based on the information supplied by the test while keeping the expenditure of time and effort to a reasonable minimum. One does not have to find everything the future practitioner knows about a subject, but just those aspects indicating whether the individual has the capability of (or the potential for) performing effectively in the job situation. The best way for teachers to increase the power of their tests is by comparing the testing results with the performances of staff members when they have subsequently been confronted by actual on-the-job situations. The performance evaluation results will supply the latter information. Acceptable test performance should predict acceptable on-the-job performance, if the evaluation criteria were used as a basis for setting the short-term objectives of the educational program.

The plot of the development of an educational offering might take the form below.

THE DEVELOPMENT OF THE INSERVICE CURRICULUM

Some may object that the term "curriculum" is more commonly associated with educational institutions than inservice educational programming. But a departmental or service educational program must be considered in terms of an overall curriculum; otherwise that program is a series of unconnected educational offerings providing a piecemeal and unreliable preparation for the attainment of patient care goals. In certain respects, the nursing service educational setting requires curricular planning as stringent as that in educational institutions.

Form for Development of the Educational Offering

Patient results	Nursing activity	Verifying criteria	Knowledge skills, sets	Method	Evaluation

See chapter 8 for example of the use of this form.

Paradoxically, the need for educational programs to accommodate newcomers in a service agency is likely to become most pressing at the time when the staff has the lowest number of prepared personnel on hand. In university-associated hospitals, for example, periods of major exodus occur when school terms end, the result being a need for many new staff members. Even the nursing services that can afford special teaching positions cannot always ensure that a full-time instructor will be available for every new staff member and for all the kinds of learning experiences that should be provided. Many hospitals must depend on staff members with major service commitments to provide teaching.

Needless to say, an enormous amount of content is relevant to, and necessary for, the provision of safe and effective patient care. The consequences of incorrect decisions about staff preparation can have a serious, undesirable impact on patient welfare. The least harmful outcome resulting from erroneous judgments is increased financial costs to the patient; the most harmful is unnecessary patient suffering and even death.

The inservice coordinator makes some critical decisions when she develops staff education policies and procedures for the department or service, including: (1) choice of the content to be presented to new employees; (2) selection of the content to be presented only to certain individuals (and the method by which those individuals are chosen); (3) choice of the order of presentation (which content can be delayed and which cannot); and (4) designation of the criteria used to determine whether the employee has satisfactorily met the inservice education requirements. Perhaps the most crucial decision involves the choice of the content to be taught. Inservice coordinators are usually responsible for making the new staff member functional as soon as possible so that the staff member's contribution in work quickly becomes commensurate with her salary.

Because their goals differ, service agency educators cannot adhere to the basic premises of educational institutions. In *educational* (academic) settings, the *learner* is given the major focus and the preparation is directed toward an unspecified future position. In *hospital* settings, the *patient* is (or at least ought to be) given the focal status, with educational preparation directed toward specific activities undertaken by staff members appointed to clearly designated positions.

It is possible that many seemingly well-developed educational programs designed for new hospital staff members are never completely tested, because the conditions for realizing the full potential of those programs never materialize. For example, frequently the services of new staff members are too badly needed to allow them to go through all the step-by-step learning experiences required by the staff orientation program. Often the educational content designed for certain new staff members is presented to them only after they have been engaged in the activity for a considerable time—a counterproductive situation. Inadequate staff performance also is often rationalized by the argument that the institutional turnover rate precludes the possibility of complete staff preparation. The inservice educator who resorts to such explanations ought to review the whole basis for the organization and functioning of the inservice education program. For years nurses have used staff shortage to jusify inadequate employee performance when, in fact, the problem is often one of inadequate programming.

Too frequently, the educational program is designed for the ideal situation. A more realistic and appropriate approach determines the most *difficult* circumstances possible for inservice education activities and plans an educational program that will prepare staff members to function safely and effectively in their daily practice even under suboptimal conditions. Thus, contingency plans should assure necessary orientation experiences for new staff members if, for example, an influx of newcomers occurs just when the inservice instructor is ill or on vacation or when few experienced staff members are available to help in the teaching process. One might argue that no serious, long-term harm results from staff members on occasion assuming responsibility for nursing activities for which they are unprepared. But I regard this as an assumption of dubious validity. Inadequate preparation results in patient care of less than optimal quality.

The quality of staff member's educational preparation is affected by the extent to which the inservice educator has identified what *must be taught*, what can be acquired more efficiently by *other means*, and what *cannot be taught*. The latter concern arises because those available to teach lack sufficient expertise, because learners lack sufficient ability, motivation, or background, or because of insufficient time for adequate teaching.

To identify the content requirements, an inservice coordinator must analyze the overall activity requirements of the department, service, or unit for which she is responsible. This entails extending the procedure that is used to analyze an individual offering.

She first identifies the content essential to the conduct of adequate nursing practice within the particular hospital setting. For purposes of analysis, the component activities can be divided into four categories[5]: (1) the staff member's use of information pertaining to standardized practices and routines; (2) the staff member's use of the skills entailed in competent manipulation of equipment and in application of the various therapeutic procedures called for; (3) the staff member's use of factual information to appropriately assess the patient's condition and to take the action most beneficial to the patient; and (4) the staff member's use of her own ability to process information from various sources, to make relevant and valid generalizations, and to plan effective courses of action. This categorization is based on the premise that all these activities are essential to acceptable practice in the given hospital. Although all the activities in these categories are required for successful nursing practice, not all necessarily must be emphasized in the educational program. This categorization system facilitates further examination of

content requirements when deciding what must be taught and what can be provided for in other ways.

Routines

Certain conditions within the nursing environment either contribute to or hinder appropriate behaviors from staff members. Obviously, if necessary equipment is not available or if some administrative practices preclude a particular activity, certain desired outcomes are not achievable. But these concerns are administrative, not educational. In addition, certain policies and routines may have been established to standardize and facilitate activities within the service area. Such policies and routines may have either positive or negative effects on delivery of nursing care. However, because they involve systems established by the hospital, they should not be considered part of the *content of nursing as a discipline*. But in analyzing nursing activities to delineate educational content, one must consider these routines as aspects of the performance of *nursing activities*. For example three general categories of these "policy-routine" activities are:

1. Governmental and legal regulatory practices that are not concerned with the provision of direct care to patients. The procedures for monitoring administration of controlled substances and the methods for reporting errors or accidents are clear examples.
2. Administrative or clerical activities that facilitate interactions between departments and provide certain services from one unit to another. Examples include procedures to schedule patients for x-ray or physical therapy and the system set up to record medications for billing purposes.
3. The particular routines established to systematize and standardize nursing procedures or patterns of nursing activity. The nursing department procedure book has been developed for the express purpose of providing standards of performance for each nursing

activity. The standard procedures, although concerned with activities that definitely relate to the nursing discipline, are also likely to contain routines that reflect the department's particular methods of handling problems. These routines, of themselves, do not involve nursing principles and their existence may or may not facilitate the achievement of nursing goals. Consider, for example, a departmental procedure for administration of medications at certain specified times of the day or night. Such a routine may in fact conflict with sound nursing principles, by its failure to consider the time of maximum effectiveness of the drug or individual patient needs.

In all three categories, the activities form part of the system used by a given hospital. The first two categories are routines that do not contribute to direct nursing care to patients. Rather, such routines consist of additional activities that are necessary for adequate functioning of the total hospital system or for the legal protection of patients and staff members.

New graduates will not know about them, unless they happened to have been students in that hospital. It is not necessary to teach this content in formal classes, however, because most of the information can be made available by circulating easily comprehended policy and procedure statements. An error or inadequate performance in such routines would have less serious consequences than mistakes committed while directly caring for patients. Hence, the priorities attached to learning these procedures is not high.

The third category includes both elements of nursing knowledge and skill and departmental routines that may be unfamiliar to new staff members, but if they already have the necessary nursing knowledge and skills, they can readily use written procedures to adapt their practice to the demands of such routines.

Although such routines and procedures are relevant to successful hospital practice,

teaching the content to the new staff member would be a waste of time and effort. All the information pertaining to hospital and nursing department policies and procedures can be made accessible to the staff member with appropriate resource folders or books. The staff member might have to be taught the use of such resource materials and how they can be obtained.

To engage in competent practice, nurses must clearly be able to handle their hospital's systems that contribute to the services and care provided the patients. Such systems will often not pertain directly to nursing principles or practices as such. They should not be considered a major part of what is to be covered in a staff preparation program. If the staff member concentrates on memorizing hospital routines and in the process neglects information about identifying patient conditions and the nursing care required, errors can result in irreversible damage. Competition between content that is and is not essential for safe and effective patient care must be kept to a minimum.

The amount of information needed in the practice of nursing in a hospital is simply too great for any individual to master in a short period of time. The staff member will doubtless require access to some kind of reference, regardless of whether the routines have been formally taught, when she is about to make out a condition sheet, prepare a requisition for a particular laboratory test, obtain a social service referral, find the EKG laboratory, fill out an application for short-term educational leave, or engage in other nonnursing or quasi-nursing activities. If the policies and procedures are carefully written out and if the reference materials include hospital maps, examples of requisitions, and other illustrative materials that fully explain procedures, then a substantial portion of the job preparation task can be accomplished by teaching the new employee how to use the references.

Nursing Procedures

The individual's ability to capably perform scientifically based procedures contributes to her potential for providing safe and effective nursing care. Expectations held for new employees vary, of course, in relation to their preparation prior to their employment. Unfortunately, knowledge of the individual's general preparation usually provides only a basis for making gross differentiations pertaining to the various job levels. A nursing assistant lacking any prior job experience will need preparation for virtually any procedure required of her. Similarly, one can expect that the licensed practical nurse will be unprepared to administer procedures ordinarily considered the prerogative of the registered nurse (although newly employed practical nurses may have substantial abilities). Completion of a particular type of program (associate degree, diploma, or baccalaureate) or attendance at a particular institution granting one of these degrees does not alone indicate the new employee's experiences in school or the level of her current competencies.

Educators across and even within programs frequently disagree about the choice of procedures to be included in the student's practicum experiences and about the level of competency required for any given procedure. Even knowing the amount of practice a new graduate has had in a particular procedure does not prove that the individual understands its principles or will invariably perform the procedure safely and effectively. Decisions about which procedures should be routinely taught to new employees can better be made by analyzing the procedure's significance to the patient's welfare and the consequences of inadequate functioning to the patient.

Factual Information

The practitioner must obtain certain factual information to make the appropriate assessment of a patient's condition and take the most beneficial course of action. This category can be analyzed by subdividing it into three levels in which information is needed: (1) situations in which an inadequate assessment and/or incorrect action would have immediate, detrimental consequences for the

patient (such as inadequate assessment of signs of hemorrhage); (2) situations in which inadequate assessment and/or incorrect action would have serious and detrimental cumulative effects on patient welfare (such as failure to follow through on a program of motion exercises to prevent contractures); and (3) situations in which inadequate assessment and/or incorrect action may or may not affect the patient's welfare appreciably or in which the detrimental effects are only short term.

Such short-term effects may be intensely felt at the time by some patients, but in all cases the long-term effects are either unperceived or absent. Much of the psychological content involved in the care provided in nonpsychiatric situations is of this nature; the generally used comfort measures may be involved, as well. The content in this category is in general poorly defined and disagreement exists among authorities as to how to conceptualize it. The soundest information relevant to the category is more complex than inservice educators realize.

Ability to Process Information

Processing information requires knowledge of the factors (and their interactions) necessary for appropriate planning or programming. It involves the ability to accurately predict the probable consequences of various approaches to problems. Situations range from simple problems involving only a few factors to complex ones involving a large number of variables. Planning for the discharge of patients from the hospital includes situations ranging from the very simple—such as planning for a patient who has no modifications to make in his life circumstances—to the very complex—such as planning for the patient who must drastically modify his life-style. Solutions in complex cases may involve alternatives with varying degrees of acceptability for the patient. Successfully attending to all of the factors in such situations is no small accomplishment.

Other activities requiring information-processing skills include programming for quality of care and for teaching and directing staff, and investigating nursing problems. The complexity of the situation determines the level of skill required for solutions. Different degrees of ability among nursing staff members are to be expected, given differing amounts of experience and levels of education. Usually, such skills are restricted to the registered nurse level; and, within this group, the staff nurse would generally not be capable of coping with the more complex problem-solving situations. The question of what preparation renders one able to handle complex nursing problems successfully is difficult. A superficial analysis of such requirements will very likely lead to the establishment of educational programs that waste time and that, more significantly, are dangerous: they lead in simplistic fashion to the formulation of rigid rules of behavior for situations that in fact demand varying responses under varying circumstances.

All the previously listed activity areas are relevant to the implementation of an effective nursing care program. They differ in the degree of importance which demands inclusion in an educational program, just as they differ in the likelihood that their emphasis will bring results (depending as they do on the particular teachers and learners who happen to be involved in such a program).

Selection of Curricular Content

After the educator has analyzed the activities required for adequate functioning within her nursing setting (taking into account the range of decisions that must be made in that setting, the knowledge of routines called for, and the ability needed to process information and plan), she has a solid basis for determining what shall be taught, when, and to whom.

In my view, an effectively organized and conducted educational program has several constant characteristics. All of the content to be covered has some significance to patients, thus assuring from the beginning that the program's relevance to practice is continuously being maintained. Some of the content will be chosen to be taught immediately and

in formal, structured, classroom situations. Other content will deliberately be left for the learner to acquire on her own, fairly early in the program, but only after she has been taught how to find it and, by relevant examples, to apply it. Still other content will be presented formally, but not until prerequisite material has been mastered. And, finally, additional content will be left for the learner to acquire on her own late in the program. With respect to *all* of the content being taught, the teacher will have clearly stipulated what will show that the objectives have been met, thus making it possible to determine whether additional exposure is needed.

Several factors should be considered in selecting and placing the content in the educational program:

1. The situation into which the individual will be placed, the amount of responsibility she will assume, the amount and kind of supervision that will be available, and the number of individuals who will perform nursing activities that the individual is not yet prepared to handle should be taken into account. If a long orientation period is available before the individual will be depended upon to provide services, then no problem exists. But in some situations, the new employee is filling a gap and must assume responsibility for certain activities very soon after employment.

If it is uncertain whether the individual will have the benefit of a full orientation period, the program should be planned under the assumption that the staff member will have to move into unsupervised practice, taking on responsibility for some activities while still attending orientation classes. In such a situation, the educator should first schedule content that deals with those activities that carry the most serious implications for patient welfare. If there is any possibility the learner will be in a position to recognize an emergency situation and act on it, then she should be prepared for that possibility first.

Although it might be considered reasonable to start with the least serious situations and work up to more stressful activities, the staff member must be prepared for the latter if she will be exposed to them. Priority should thus be assigned to content concerned with situations in which the learner may have to make decisions and perform on her own, with serious consequences for the patient if the staff member performs inadequately.

2. The amount of time available to the staff member to process the information required to perform satisfactorily must be considered. One could hardly look up and review the procedure for cardiopulmonary resuscitation when a patient is in cardiac arrest. Knowledge of the signs and the procedure must be immediately available to the individual who is the shortest distance from the patient at the time of the arrest.

In contrast, the staff member charged with caring for a patient admitted for a breast biopsy and facing the likelihood of a mastectomy would have ample time to review the program of care. In the first case, a life-saving procedure must be mastered, which requires repeated drill and practice. However, in the second case, a leisurely reading of the program of care will suffice.

3. Another factor involves the learner's recognition that she needs to obtain information. A patient presenting symptoms of a yet undiagnosed problem constitutes an ambiguous situation that might be lost to the inexperienced nurse. The nurse must recognize the unusual symptoms, before she feels the need to obtain more information to help determine her action. One must have some knowledge to recognize that one needs more. The content that provides for this recognition must be taught before she can assume the major responsibility for evaluating patient conditions.

4. The relationship between the time available for teaching and that needed to achieve a necessary level of competence in the learner must be considered. If the situation in which the nursing action is to occur is well structured and alternative actions are clearly delineated, the teacher could probably transmit the content easily. Within limits, one might be able to teach most

nursing skills to most potential learners, given certain minimum capabilities in the learners. But time is usually the crucial factor. Even if one could teach certain skills to nursing assistants or licensed practical nurses, given enough time, the cost of teaching them might outweigh the benefits of having them carry out the activities they have learned. Some things might be taught only to registered nurses—not because other kinds of staff members could not acquire the skills involved, but because the registered nurse can be taught less expensively and more efficiently.

The time needed to teach all of the content required to make a learner efficient is a crucial question. Decisions about what to include in an educational program (whether for the purpose of orientation or continuing education) should hinge, at least in part, on the answers to that question. One must have some certainty that the educational achievement is worth the time entailed. One of the greatest mistakes in developing our continuing education programs is to underestimate the time and teaching that must be invested before the learners achieve a level of competence that improves nursing practice.

An hour's class or even a series of classes that provides a superficial coverage of a complex subject, without follow-up opportunities to practice the skills or apply the principles, is worse than a mere waste of time. It creates a false impression that steps to improve nursing care have been taken and that no further efforts are necessary. If certain content *is* crucial to superior patient care, and if an inadequate amount of time or number of instructors is available to teach that content, then it is incumbent on the in-service coordinator to investigate ways of solving the problem.

To summarize the factors relevant to developing a staff development curriculum, several guidelines are suggested:

1. Include only the content that cannot be presented in any other way. Put everything in written form that can be stated clearly and make certain the informa-

tion is organized to facilitate easy use by individuals who are functioning on the job. Teach the staff to use the written resources.

2. Establish verifying criteria to be used in making decisions about whether to assign an individual to specific nursing activities.

3. Set priorities for scheduling content in the orientation programs according to the seriousness of the consequences to patients if an activity were neglected or inadequately performed.

4. Test for application of content, not for mere retention of information.

5. Develop the test as a diagnostic tool, select for it only those items that have the potential for identifying the learner's remediation needs, treat each item individually, and demand 100 percent success before excusing the individual from further teaching or practice.

6. In designing continuing education programs that cover leadership development, new procedures or new treatment programs, use the same general methods recommended for the development of orientation programs— that is, delineate the behaviors, both short- and long-term, that are expected as a result of the educational experience.

7. Consider the time available and the teaching methods used as relevant to the success of any educational offering. Make certain that the amounts of time and practice needed to achieve *mastery* are provided.

8. Make certain the testing instruments include elements that predict the individual's performance in daily nursing practice, lest erroneous information enter into decisions about the individual's fitness.

Clearly an effective staff development program, considered in all its aspects, cannot be generated unless the coordinator is knowledgeable about the remaining systems within the nursing setting. Many decisions must be based on information and practices that fall outside of the field of education itself. Just as the supervisory and administrative staff need to be informed about the factors affecting the success of a departmental staff education program, a staff development coordinator is expected to function with knowledge of the other department systems. Interactions among the different departmental administrative units are imperative if the various programs are to contribute constructively to departmental functioning. The inservice education coordinator must have realistic staffing predictions to organize the content of educational programs effectively. The staffing coordinator must know what educational achievements are necessary before she can develop a staffing program that best serves the interests of patients.

Most importantly, the individuals providing the educational experiences and those programming and administering the programs of care must work together to ensure that staff members are prepared to accomplish departmental goals. No educational program will succeed if it is not supported within the practice setting. The director of nursing who applauds the staff development program, but at the same time establishes an administrative climate that precludes the application of the education provided, is sabotaging her own department's educational program. She can also have a direct adverse effect on the program if she is unduly influenced by goals unrelated to the quality of patient care or if she permits the staff development coordinator or instructors to pursue other educational goals than such care. Certain premises must be accepted by all staff members if a useful staff development program is to exist.

It seems appropriate to conclude that all members of the department have the best interests of patients in mind if their attitudes toward the educational program conform to the following guidelines:

1. All nursing staff members accept without question the requirement that they demonstrate their ability to perform an activity before they are considered qualified to be assigned the activity, and they understand that attendance at staff development sessions will lead to but will not guarantee the desired qualification status;
2. The nursing supervisors accept the staff development program as the necessary preparation for adequate staff functioning and make it possible for their subordinates to participate in the program at appropriate times and places appropriate to their levels of functioning;
3. The nursing administrators hold staff members to performance standards taught within the staff development program;
4. The inservice educator shares with the administrative staff any culpability for ineffective nursing practices occurring within the department;
5. The inservice educator informs herself about the educational factors associated with the efficient achievement of nursing practice goals and provides the director of nursing with sound advice regarding the feasibility and utility of various programs and methods;
6. The director of nursing acts on the advice of only those with relevant and necessary information pertaining to the issues she faces;
7. The policies, procedures, and goals of other department programs are consistent with those of the staff development program, all of the programs involved bearing mutually complementary relations, and;
8. Educational programs provided solely because of staff members' expressed interest or for the members' (as opposed to the patients') benefit are recognized as components of the department's *employee relations system* and *not* as an integral part of the *staff preparation program* or as a substitute for the content that must be presented if high-quality nursing care is to be provided patients.

NOTES AND REFERENCES

1. Cronback, L. J. *Educational Psychology.* 2nd ed. New York: Harcourt, Brace and World, Inc., 1963, p. 284.
2. Cronback, L. J. 1963, pp. 304–308.
3. Cronback, L. J. 1963, pp. 281–285.
4. Cronback, L. J. 1963, pp. 318–319.
5. The content from this point through to *Selection of Curricular Content* was first developed as part of a research project, "Learning Needs of the New Graduate Entering into Hospital Nursing," in progress at this writing.

BIBLIOGRAPHY

Birch, D. and Veroff, D. *Motivation: a Study of Action.* Belmont, California: Brooks/Cole Publishing Company, 1966.

Lawson, R. *Learning and Behavior.* New York: Macmillan, 1960.

Levitt, E. E. *The Psychology of Anxiety.* New York: Bobbs-Merrill Company, Inc., 1967, pp. 108–138.

Mager, R. *Preparing Instructional Objectives.* Belmont, California: Fearon Publishers, Lear Siegler Inc., 1962.

Mager, R. *Goal Analysis.* Belmont, California: Fearon Publishers, Lear Siegler Inc., 1972.

Mager, R. *Measuring Instructional Intent.* Belmont, California: Fearon Publishers, Lear Siegler Inc., 1973.

Mager, R. and Pipe, P. *Analyzing Performance Problems.* Belmont, California: Fearon Publishers, Lear Siegler Inc., 1973.

Miller, P. "A Comparison of Two Methods of Improving the Decision-Making Abilities of Nurses." Unpublished dissertation, University of Iowa, Iowa City, 1974.

Thorndike, R. L. and Hagen, E. *Measurement and Evaluation in Psychology and Education,* 3d. ed. New York: John Wiley and Sons, Inc.

CHAPTER 8

Performance Standards in Developing a Teaching Program: Examples

Susan W. Kurth and Deborah D. McDougall

One concern of the staff development program is to ensure that the individuals responsible for patient care are indeed competent practitioners. In many instances the orientation period is limited and the RN must assume responsibilities on the unit within a short time. An orientation program must set priorities so that the RN first receives the content immediately necessary to begin work in the practice setting. The following shows the process that was used in designing an orientation program for RNs.

IDENTIFYING EDUCATION CONTENT

The educational program was planned with safe and effective patient care as its outcome. Therefore, it was designed to ensure that the patient care objectives established by the department of nursing would be met. The nursing department's objectives used were:

1. Emergency conditions are kept to the lowest possible level of threat to the patient by timely and effective intervention.
2. The patient is free of preventable complications.
3. Fear and anxiety related to illness and hospitalization are reduced.
4. Pain and discomfort are minimized.
5. The maximum benefits of the diagnostic and therapeutic procedures ordered by the physician and performed by the

nursing staff are realized by the patient.
6. The patient is prepared for or arrangements are made for continuation of the necessary regimen of care or readjustment of life pattern posthospitalization[1].

These objectives were the starting point in developing the orientation program because they indicated the general work requirements that demonstrated what education was needed. The information or content needed by the new RN would be provided partly in a general orientation and partly by service orientation at the unit level. The nursing department's general orientation would cover content applicable across all services, while the service orientation would provide content specific to the patient populations on the individual units.

SETTING PRIORITIES FOR TEACHING

Once the general work requirements were identified, the next step involved setting teaching priorities. The work requirements were analyzed for those which were required for immediate induction and those which could be delayed. The following criteria were applied to the objectives of the department of nursing to determine priorities for including the content in the orientation program:

1. A situation in which failure to perform an activity correctly or neglecting to perform an activity would have serious consequences for the patient.
2. A situation in which the nurse must immediately process information to make a decision or perform an activity for the welfare of the patient.
3. A situation which could have serious consequences for the patient if the nurse failed to recognize the need to obtain more information.
4. A situation in which recurrent inadequate assessment or incorrect action would have cumulative serious and detrimental effects on the patient's welfare.
5. A situation in which inadequate assessment and/or incorrect action may or may not affect the patient's welfare appreciably or the detrimental effects on the patient are of a short-term nature[2].

The first three criteria deal with situations that have immediate serious consequences for the patient. Therefore, such content was placed high in the priority for presentation during orientation. Content related to less serious situations was considered necessary, but involved teaching the new RN where to get the information more than providing the specific content. If the time period in which the nurse was required to act was not critical to the patient's welfare, then it seemed more appropriate to provide information on resources where she could obtain the content when needed.

All emergencies require that the nurse recognize the situation immediately and institute the appropriate nursing activities without delay. In such situations, the consequences would be serious to the patient if the nurse failed to act appropriately. Content relevant to emergency care was included during the orientation period to ensure that the nurse would have the skills and knowledge to meet the needs of the patient in an emergency. The nurse must be able to per-

form the required activities in an emergency situation before she can be given responsibility for patient care.

The next patient care objective states that the patient is free from preventable complications. To meet this objective the RN must institute nursing measures to prevent complications. In these situations recurring inadequate assessment or incorrect action would have cumulative detrimental effects on the patient—for example, failure to turn a patient to prevent formation of a decubitus ulcer.

If a complication should occur which constitutes an emergency, such as a pulmonary embolus, then the patient would require immediate action by the nurse. Content related to prevention of complications was considered second priority during the orientation period. It was decided that the RN should be provided information on available resources dealing with prevention of complications.

The third patient care objective is that the patient's pain and discomfort are minimized. In this area, an inadequate assessment or incorrect action may or may not affect the patient's welfare appreciably, or the detrimental effects are short-term or unrealized. The major exception is sudden acute pain, which may indicate an emergency such as a myocardial infarction. In cases where the patient's pain is unusually severe or unexpected the nurse may need to obtain more information and take appropriate action. In this situation the symptom of pain represents an emergency; relevant content was developed so that this type of situation would not be lost to the inexperienced nurse. Because content regarding comfort is not well-defined, this area is difficult to teach. Because the long-term effects are unperceived or absent and consequences to the patient are not so severe, this content was given third priority during the orientation period.

The objective of reducing the patient's fear and anxiety similarly involves content that is not well-defined. The psychological effect on the patient in a nonpsychiatric situation is not perceived as having long-term effects. There may not be agreement as to the content involved or the content may be very complex. This content was not considered first priority and was not developed for use during the orientation program.

To ensure that the patient receives maximum benefit from procedures performed by the nursing staff, the RN must prepare patients for procedures and execute those procedures safely and effectively. Any procedures ordered by the physician and performed by the nurse for the patient are classified under this objective, including medication, administering intravenous fluids, dressing changes, and nasogastric feedings. Improper administration of medications can have serious consequences on the patient's welfare. Therefore, content pertaining to the administration of medications was considered a first priority for teaching, since this is one of the RNs major activities. Other procedures are required to different extents on the units and the nurse could be checked out on the procedures required in the area.

The final patient care objective concerns discharge planning for the patient. The content varies with each patient population, as well as the individual patient. The consequences to the patient may be serious if there is improper teaching or inadequate planning at discharge. However, the fact that the nurse does not need to make an immediate decision and has time to gather and assimilate the information necessary to teach the patient makes it possible to teach the use of resources and eliminate hours of teaching content. Such resources as the program of care are invaluable, and the discharge planning should be ongoing with continuous evaluation.

Once the work requirements had been identified and priorities for teaching were categorized, the next step was to identify whether the content should be part of the general orientation or the service orientation. This decision was based on the types of activities involved and the number of RNs to which the content was applicable.

PLACING CONTENT IN THE PROGRAM

Because emergency content had first priority, it was necessary to identify the types of emergencies that occur in our hospital. Some of the emergency situations may occur in a large majority of patient populations; therefore, the content is needed by all nurses regardless of where they work. This content was relevant for the majority of the RNs and could be taught more efficiently in the general orientation program. The emergency content specific to special patient populations was included in the clinical service educational program.

The following list of emergencies can occur in our hospital setting. Each emergency listed was evaluated according to its occurrence on the clinical services to determine where relevant content would be placed.

1. *Cardiac arrest* occurs throughout the hospital and the CPR procedure is standardized content presented to all RNs.
2. *Anaphylactic shock* is common throughout all clinical services.
3. *Hemorrhagic shock* may occur on almost any service; it is seen in medical, surgical, OB, and urological patients.
4. *Hypoglycemic shock* is common to all services because diabetics are admitted on many services. Diabetes may not be the primary reason for admission.
5. *Septic shock* is seen on all clinical services.
6. *Myocardial infarction* may occur on all services. Incidence is increased in patients with a history of ischemic heart disease.
7. *Fire* may occur anywhere in the hospital.
8. *Wound dehiscence or evisceration* is usually restricted to areas where patients have abdominal surgery.

9. *Seizures* are most likely to occur in neurological patients, adults or children.
10. *Increased intracranial pressure* occurs in neurological patients, medical or surgical.
11. *Pneumothorax* closed or open is likely on medical areas, or areas of trauma or thoracic surgery.
12. *Pulmonary embolus* is more common on medical, surgical, and orthopedic units.

Content on cardiac arrest, anaphylactic shock, hemorrhagic shock, hypoglycemic shock, septic shock, myocardial infarction, and fire was included in the general orientation. For some of these emergencies, it is necessary to include more specific content in the clinical service orientation. For example, the CPR procedure would be taught in general orientation, but the location of the crash cart and the operation of the defibrillators would be taught at the clinical unit level.

Some general nursing activities pertaining to all emergency care were identified. Then, for each emergency situation, the specific nursing activities were defined and analyzed. From this information, decisions were made concerning the actual content for presentation.

The RN must perform the following general emergency behaviors:

1. Monitors patients for the most significant clues to an emergency condition and at time commensurate with the patient's condition.
2. Has potentially necessary equipment and supplies within easy access and can use them effectively.
3. Recognizes the earliest signs of an emergency condition and makes appropriate judgment for action based on the stage of the emergency.
4. Institutes the most effective procedure for the patient's condition.
5. Checks the patient's response in terms of specific evaluative criteria and determines the next nursing action.
6. Records information in the record that

shows surveillance carried out, appropriate timely care, and patient's response[3].

EXAMPLES OF EMERGENCY CONTENT

Two tables illustrate the development of emergency content. The fire program contains general information as well as specific information provided at a service level. See Table 8-1 on pages 140-141. The program on wound dehiscence is specific for the surgical service orientation. See Table 8-2 on pages 142-143. Decisions about the kind of content to be presented were made on the basis of the analysis shown. First, the patient results were identified and the activity requirements for achieving them defined. The activities were then classified by categories to determine what component elements were involved in bringing about the behavior. The classification of the activities, according to knowledge, set, or skill, helped to define the content necessary for the RN to perform adequately. The evaluative criteria are the means by which the educator can both predict the RN's future performance and test for the critical information with the least time and effort. The method of teaching the defined content and a method for evaluation were determined as the final steps in developing the educational program.

EXAMPLE OF MEDICATION CONTENT

One area of concern early in the orientation program was the administration of medications. It is important to predict the RN's future performance before she is given the responsibility for passing medications. Some content is provided in the general orientation but presentation of other specific content and testing needs to take place at the unit level because of differences among patients and variations in the stocking of medications.

The following general nursing activities

were identified for the RN:

1. Understands effects of drug to be administered and why patient is receiving the drug.
2. Times administration of drugs so that patient will receive maximum effect.
3. Assesses effect of drug on patient.
4. Knows side effects of drug and monitors patient for side effects.
5. Administers right drug to right patient in right amount, and by correct route.

The content related to administration of medications was developed using the same steps as shown for emergency care. The starting point was the patient results. It was impossible to identify specific drugs because there are so many, and many of the drugs are not used widely throughout the hospital. Therefore, the nursing activities are not specific to drugs and much of the content is related to the proper use of resources to obtain needed information. See Table 8–3 on pages 144–145.

CONTENT DEVELOPMENT IN CONTINUING EDUCATION

The same system of content development used in constructing an orientation program can be employed in the department's continuing education unit. When a service area completes an audit, unmet patient results are identified and the nursing interventions necessary to meet them are operationalized. The activities are then classified according to component elements, as done previously. Verifying criteria, method of incorporation, and evaluation are also predetermined, using the nurse's behaviors as the measure of predicting success, based on the desired patient outcomes.

When an audit was completed on the patients who had experienced a femoropopliteal bypass graft, deficiencies were noted in their knowledge of their regimen of care. The audit implied that patients did not understand why they needed to carry out certain activities and therefore, did not follow them through. Deficiencies concerning patient education had been noted previously on this service area. Obviously the method used to correct the deficiencies (referring the nurses to the respective programs of care) was not effective; the staff appeared to lack knowledge of how to use programs of care. Table 8–4, on pages 146–147, is an example of a continuing education program developed to correct the noted audit deficiencies.

NOTES AND REFERENCES

1. See chapter 6.
2. Cantor, M. M. "Learning News of the New Graduate Entering Into Hospital Nursing." Study in progress, University of Iowa Hospitals and Clinics, Iowa City, 1977.
3. Cantor, M. M. 1977.
4. *Fire Reporting and Control Procedure Manual.* Unpublished manual, University of Iowa Hospitals and Clinics, Iowa City.
5. Hahn, B. Film: *Hospital Fire—Dial 195.* Iowa City: University of Iowa Motion Picture Unit, 1977.
6. Hahn, B. Film: *Hospital Fire—Protect the Patient.* Iowa City: University of Iowa Motion Picture Unit, 1976.

BIBLIOGRAPHY

Beelner, C. *Emergency Care Educational Program.* Unpublished manual, University of Iowa Hospitals and Clinics, Department of Surgical Nursing, Iowa City, 1977.

Cantor, M., McDougall, D. and Kurth, S. "Learning Needs of New Graduate Entering the Hospital Setting." Study in progress, University of Iowa Hospitals and Clinics, Iowa City, 1977.

Emergency Situations—Urology Procedure Manual. Unpublished manual, University of Iowa Hospitals and Clinics, Department of Urological Nursing, Iowa City, 1977.

Fuerst, E. and Wolff, L. *Fundamentals of Nursing.* Philadelphia: J. B. Lippincott Co., 1969.

Luckmann, J. and Sorensen, K. *Medical-Surgical Nursing: A Psychophysiologic Approach.* Philadelphia: W. B. Saunders Co., 1974.

Schedule II Narcotic and Non-narcotic Controlled Substances. *Administrative Nursing Policy and Procedure Manual.* Unpublished. University of Iowa Hospitals and Clinics, Iowa City, 1977.

Schwartz, S. *Principles of Surgery.* New York: McGraw-Hill Book Company, 1969.

Table 8-1. Fire

Patient or Structure Results	Nursing Activity	Skill, Knowledge, Set
Patient is away from danger of fire.	1. Quickly remove patient in immediate vicinity of fire to a safer area.	*Knowledge* required concerning location of fire doors and exits. *Knowledge* to make judgments concerning which patients need to be moved. *Knowledge and skill:* knowing patient condition and method that should be used to move patient; ability to move patient using proper body mechanics and correct method of carrying. *Knowledge* to determine what equipment is necessary for patient and *skill* in transporting or disconnecting equipment.
Fire is contained.	2. Close doors and windows in rooms and turn off O_2.	*Knowledge* of need to cut off air supply, and that doors serve as fire break.
	3. Pull fire alarm and call 195 to notify operator. Tell operator who you are, what you are reporting and exactly where fire is located.	*Knowledge* of where fire alarm is located and steps for notifying hospital personnel.
	4. Extinguish fire if possible.	*Knowledge* of location and types of extinguishers, what type of fire they are used for; *skill* in operating extinguisher.
	5. Evacuate patients to safer area of hospital as necessary.[a]	*Knowledge* of which patients should be moved first (order of evacuation), assignment of personnel to ambulatory and nonambulatory patients. *Set:* developing immediate and automatic response.

[a] *Fire Reporting and Control Procedure Manual.* Unpublished manual, University of Iowa Hospitals and Clinics, Iowa City.

Table 8-1. *cont.*

Verifying Criteria	Method	Conditions or Structure for Evaluation
In a written test RN can: 1. State first five steps to take once fire is discovered. Steps must be in order. 2. State the fire number (195) and the information to be given to the operator (name, exact location, and what observed). 3. Determine what equipment should be taken along and what should be left a. if a nonambulatory patient has the following: peripheral IV (discontinue) O_2 (discontinue) NG tube to intermittent suction (clamp NG and disconnect from suction) b. if an ambulatory patient has the following: CVN line (have patient carry IV bottle if able) Foley (have patient carry Foley bag if able) 4. State the types of fire extinguishers and the type of fire they are used for. Can demonstrate the following transportation techniques: 1. knee drop 2. 2-man carry 3. 3-man carry Can locate on the unit: 1. fire extinguishers 2. fire alarm 3. nearest fire doors	Film titled "Hospital Fire—Dial 195" shown in hospital orientation gives five steps to take when fire is discovered.[b] Hospital fire reporting and control procedure manual is given to all personnel and one is posted on every nursing unit. Film entitled "Hospital Fire—Protect the Patient" is shown in nursing orientation and demonstrates methods of moving patients, e.g., knee drop, 2-man carry, and 3-man carry.[c] Explain different fire extinguishers and demonstrate their use. At unit level: Go over equipment commonly used by patient population and how to disconnect it or transport it. Tour unit locating fire exists, fire doors, fire alarm, and fire extinguishers. Establish set using multiple exposure to proper procedure and periodic review.	After one week on unit test RN on verifying criteria by setting up a mock situation and have RN describe action she would take in reporting the fire and moving the patient. Have RN demonstrate 3 methods of moving the patient. (Must have all information correct and properly demonstrated to pass.) Conduct a similar test at 6-month intervals using different patient situations.

[b]Bill Hahn, *Hospital Fire—Dial 195* (Iowa City: University of Iowa Motion Picture Unit, 1977).
[c]Bill Hahn, *Hospital Fire—Protect the Patient* (Iowa City: University of Iowa Motion Picture Unit, 1976).

Table 8-2. Wound Dehiscence or Evisceration

Patient or Structure Results	Nursing Activity	Skill, Knowledge, Set
Patient's internal organs will be protected and the chance of infection will be minimized.	1. Monitors susceptible patient populations for wound healing and provides adequate abdominal support.	*Knowledge* of patient populations prone to dehiscence or evisceration. *Knowledge* of normal wound appearance and healing. *Set:* routine check of abdominal incision.
	2. Nurse recognizes presenting symptoms: a. sudden escape of serosanguinous drainage usually around POD #5 b. rush of peritoneal fluid onto dressing followed by protrusion of bowel or omentum. Notifies MD	*Knowledge* of symptoms of dehiscence or evisceration. *Set:* automatic response once symptoms are recognized.
	3. Place patient in supine position with minimal movement.	
	4. Cover wound with sterile saline dressing.	*Knowledge* of physiologic loss of fluids and susceptibility to infection. *Skill* in aseptic technique.
	5. Prepare patient for surgery if ordered by MD	*Knowledge and skill* in preparation of patient for surgery.

Table 8-2. *cont.*

Verifying Criteria	Method	Conditions or Structure for Evaluation
The RN can identify the patient populations on the clinical unit who are most likely to experience wound dehiscence or evisceration. Given a patient situation the nurse can state the first three actions she would take once she has identified the patient's problem.	On the clinical service present content in lecture covering emergency care.	Test the RN for nursing actions prior to assignment of patient care on unit. (The first three required nursing actions must be identified correctly to pass.) Sample question:[a] Mr. F. is a 60-year-old male who had surgery five days ago for cancer of the colon. Before his surgery, he received radiation therapy to decrease the size of the tumor. He has been coughing when he calls you in and complains of pain and the feeling that something gave away. His gown is saturated with serosanguinous drainage. 1. Notify MD 2. Have Mr. F. lie down in a supine position and restrict his movement. 3. Cover the wound with sterile saline dressings. Check nursing notes and care plans for monitoring of incisional healing after RN is assigned to patient care.

[a]Item on a test on emergencies.

Table 8-3. Medication Administration

Patient or Structure Results	Nursing Activity	Skill, Knowledge, Set	Verifying Criteria	Method	Conditions or Structure for Evaluation
Patient receives only correct drug and dosage.	1. Nurse checks medication Kardex by patient and patient problem and looks up any drug that he or she cannot justify by patient problem or by usual dosage.	1. *Knowledge* of resources available for obtaining information about drugs. *Knowledge* of patient problem and action of drug in relation to patient problem. *Knowledge* of usual dosage. *Set:* familiarizing self with patient and looking up unfamiliar drugs. *Knowledge* of possible harm to patient if incorrect drug or dosage is administered.	Confronted with a medication Kardex and patient profile, the RN will be able to (1) pick out a drug with greater dosage than appropriate for the patient or identifies source of reference if unsure of usual dosage; (2) identify a drug that seems inappropriate for patient's problem; (3) accurately figure dosage when order is not in dosage available; (4) pick out drugs that should not be given together; (5) correctly calculate IV infusion rates; (6) can identify drugs that should not be delayed longer than 1 hour past the ordered time; (7) identifies drugs that should be given in special relation to food or fluids.	Because it would be impossible for an RN to remember every drug, the content is general and geared toward use of resources. Review method of calculating IV rates and work some sample problems. Review calculation of dosage using examples. In lecture form: a. review method of administration for Imferon and heparin b. review locations and techniques of s.c. and IM injections. c. review how to check that IV is in place.	Prior to passing medications on unit, give a written test to the RN, using common medications. Questions should be answerable using patient profiles and sample medication Kardexes. Observe RN and document the other criteria x3 before allowing the RN to pass meds to a group of patients without supervision.
	2. Nurse questions physician's order if drug is inconsistent with patient problem or dosage is unusual.	2. *Set:* questioning drugs before administering a drug or dosage that seems inappropriate.			
	3. Nurse checks for and questions drugs that may have an additive effect or may be antagonistic.	3. *Knowledge* of which drugs are synergistic or antagonistic. *Set:* questioning orders of two drugs may affect one another.			
	4. Determines patient identification before administering drugs.	4. *Set:* routine check of patient ID band.			
	5. Charts all medications given in medication Kardex.	5. *Set:* routine charting to ensure patient receives med and only as ordered.			
	6. If given p.r.n. medications, checks to see when last given.	6. *Knowledge* of length of effect of drug and assessment of patient's need. *Set:* routine check of time interval to avoid possible overdose.			
	7. Correctly calculates IV infusion rates.	7. *Knowledge* of method to calculate IV rate.			
	8. Correctly calculates dosage if order is not in dosage available.	8. *Knowledge* of basic math and method of arriving at correct dosage in needed units.			
Patient experiences optimal effects that drug can provide.	1. Plans medication passing for routine medication administration so that meds required at special times are received by patient; if delays must occur the delayed drugs are those in which time is not a factor.	1. *Knowledge* of length of effect of drugs, peak actions.	RN can describe method of administration for Imferon, insulin, subcutaneous heparin, and IM morphine.	Orient to pharmacy's guidelines concerning administration of antibiotics located on each unit.	
	2. Gives drugs so that maximum effects are received by patient. a. anticipates when pain is most likely to occur and gives med before pain becomes severe. b. schedules medications so maximum effect is reached when need is greatest (such as compazine, pain med before procedures).	*Knowledge* of length of action and peak action of pain meds. *Set:* routine checks and anticipation of need by patient. *Knowledge* of time of greatest need of drug by patient and length of action drug. *Set:* anticipation of patient need.	In a demonstration medication procedure: Checks patient ID before giving med.	Review kinds of information patients will need if discharged on medications.	

	Actions	Knowledge	Strategies

	c. schedules medications accordingly when other factors affect ability to make use of meds (such as food, fluids).
	d. gives medication and arranges environment so that maximum effect of drug is received (such as sleeping pills, tranquilizers).
	3. Monitors effects of drugs after administration.
	4. Gives drugs by prescribed route.
	  a. follow procedure for special drugs (heparin, Imferon).
	  b. selects proper sites for IM injections.
	  c. when giving IV piggyback meds, checks for placement of catheter in vein.
	  d. when giving IV piggyback meds, mixes drug with proper type and amount of diluent and infuses over recommended time period.
		Knowledge of drugs that have effectiveness or absorption affected by food or fluids.
		Knowledge of effect of drug. *Set:* completing procedures and interruptions before patient receives drug.
		Knowledge of expected effect of drug. *Set:* routine follow-up to ensure patient receives desired effect.
		Knowledge of method of administration of drug for effectiveness and minimal side effects.
		Knowledge of sites for intramuscular injection.
		Skill in giving injection.
		Knowledge of indicators that catheter is in place.
		Knowledge of what diluent and how much to use with an IV medication and the length of infusion time.
			Charts medications given to each patient.
			Checks when last p.r.n. med was given and assesses patient need. Documents in nurse's notes.
			Locates information on unit concerning IV diluents for meds and infusion times.
			Checks for IV placement by lowering bottle before administering IV meds.

Patient experiences minimal side effects or has side effects relieved or drug removed.	1. Monitors patient for side effects possibly related to medication and notifies MD. 2. Obtains information from patients necessary for safe and effective use of drug by patient. Charts allergies on drug Kardex and front of chart.	*Knowledge* of side effects of prescribed drug. *Knowledge* of potential shock reaction if patient is allergic to drugs. *Set:* routine check for drug allergies on admission.	
Patient is knowledgeable about drugs and can participate in decisions.	1. Provides patient with information about drugs which will help the patient get maximum effects. 2. Prepares patients who are going home on medication by explaining need for medication, time to administer it, and possible reactions to watch for. 3. Sees that patient has medications on discharge and can get meds once at home.	*Knowledge* of drug action and what factors might affect its utilization or effectiveness. *Knowledge* of drug action and patient need along with knowledge regarding patient compliance. *Set:* routine check to ensure patient will have meds at home; automatic check in discharge planning.	
Drugs are safeguarded to prevent misuse.	1. Locks medication cart when not in use. 2. Documents use of narcotics under narcotic control system. 3. Counts narcotics at beginning and end of shift.	*Set:* automatic response when not using cart. *Knowledge* of controlled substances and policy and procedure established to account for their use.	Go over policy and procedure for narcotic and controlled substances. Use examples to explain how to sign out narcotics. Locate policy on unit.

Table 8-4. Using Programs of Care

Patient or Structure Results	Nursing Activity	Skill, Knowledge, Set
Outcome criteria of programs of care achieved.	Refer to programs of care relevant to patient and his defined problem area.	*Knowledge* of programs of care, the meaning of the component parts and the interrelationship between those parts:
	Using the appropriate programs of care, develop an individualized nursing care plan for the patient, including:	a. patient problem b. outcome criterion c. progress criterion d. nursing action e. recording information
	a. a statement of all outcome and progress criteria the patient is expected to meet. b. a concise, personalized statement concerning each identified problem. c. progress criteria, which can be met during the hospitalization, for each problem statement (if applicable). d. nursing activities designed especially to assist the patient in meeting criteria.	*Set:* employing programs of care to develop individualized nursing care plans.
	Implement care plan and continuously assess patients' progress toward meeting the criteria and make activity revision as necessary.	
	Record evaluative statements about patient's progress in medical record.	

Table 8-4. *cont.*

Verifying Criteria	Method	Conditions or Structure for Evaluation

Given a specific patient, RN can:
a. identify applicable programs of care.
b. develop a nursing care plan from the appropriate programs.
	On a general level present the theoretical base for and construction of programs of care through quality assurance classes, offered on a regular basis by the department of nursing.
	
	On the service level conduct a series of small group sessions on developing care plans through the use of programs of care:
	   a. using a patient on the unit as an example.
	   b. discussing evaluation of criteria attainment and necessary care adjustments.
		Immediately following teaching, present with patient profile (patient on unit), requesting construction of a care plan from available programs of care to be used for the length of hospitalization.
		
		For example, given the following profile:
		
		"J.S. is a 54-year-old white male admitted for a femoropopliteal bypass. A previous Translumber Arteriogram showed a left superficial arterial occlusion at midfemor level. He described the pain in his left calf as being so severe that he could not walk down the block. Mrs. S. informed the nurse that her husband does not follow medical advice because he has trouble understanding why. The nurses have observed J.S. crossing and elevating his legs and tapping nervously on the bedside stand. Both lower extremities are dry and scaly. On the night of admission he complained of burning on urination and on the second hospital day he refused to eat the 'terrible' food."
		
		List:
		   a. patient problems.
		   b. outcome criteria.
		   c. progress criteria.
		   d. nursing activities.
		(See sample nursing care plan in chapter 5.)

PART IV

Standards of Structure

CHAPTER 9 | # *The Model Applied to Elements of Structure*

The primary focus of nursing is the interaction between nurse and patient for the patient's benefit. Although nurses emphasize the *process* as opposed to the *outcome* features of their discipline, they can learn to stipulate desired outcomes and to assess their effectiveness. However, when they practice nursing in institutions, nurses must be concerned with more than the immediate and direct interaction between nurse and patient; they must be concerned with the structural components of the nursing care delivery system—the programs, systems, and environmental conditions established to facilitate the delivery of care. As Donabedian states, the structural components involve the "instrumentalities of care and their organization"[1].

Difficulties Inherent in Applying the Model

Nurses who find it difficult to conceptualize the provision of nursing care in terms of a projection from problem to outcome and choosing nursing activities based on that projection will find the goal-directed model even more difficult to understand when it is applied to the structural elements of nursing care delivery for several reasons:

1. Because of the complexity of the health delivery system, many of the facilitating functions are far removed from the patient's bedside. It is difficult to determine how a policy pertaining to sick leave or to other personnel matters relates to achieving

a particular patient outcome. The purpose of a particular structural element may be to facilitate the functioning of another element, which in turn might critically influence the functioning of still another component. Considering the inevitable complexities of such a system, individuals working within the system can lose sight of its main mission—providing high-quality patient care.

2. People other than nurses may have a great deal to say about the administrative operations of a nursing department. A nursing department is just one unit among several within a hospital. Administrators' goals are not identical to those of nurses. Both groups may claim high-quality patient care as their primary goals, but their definitions differ. How nursing is viewed, and the disparity between administrators' and nurses' goals, determines the extent to which nurses must accommodate interference from structural components.

Some administrators view nurses simply as a group of employees to be managed (just as housekeeping or kitchen personnel must be managed) and consider nursing directors to be their agents, employed to implement their policies and to achieve their goals. In such settings, nurses can be required to emphasize activities that do not enhance effective nursing care. They may be required to perform administrative tasks that simplify the jobs of administrative personnel, although the welfare of patients might call for a reversal of these roles. While nurses are gathering data or filling out forms for the administrator, the administrator is making decisions about patient needs. Whenever administrators decide how funds will be allocated, whose projects will be given the highest priorities, and how nurses—particularly those in leadership roles—will spend their time, they are rendering judgments about patient needs.

Fortunately, in other institutions, administrators view nursing as a professional service and expect directors of nursing to provide them with expert guidance for meeting the nursing departments needs. Needless to say, nursing directors in such settings are more likely to influence the components that make up nursing departments' structures.

3. Generally, nurses are not secure in their knowledge of nursing as a discipline. Nor are they confident when they musι distinguish between content specifically pertinent to achieving patient outcome goals and that concerned with the systems established to facilitate such achievement. This distinction is important. Nursing content consists of skills and knowledge that are relatively constant; the individual who has mastered a particular segment (such as postoperative care) while working in one setting can immediately and appropriately put the skill to work in another setting.

In contrast, nurses must learn a good deal about other less constant content. For example, a nurse working in hospital A learns that hospital policy mandates the routine checking of vital signs at stipulated times during each 24-hour period. On moving to hospital B, she finds a different system to which she must, of course, adapt. In my view, the knowledge that hospital A has one system and hospital B another—even the knowledge that most hospitals have some kind of system for monitoring physical signs—is not part of the *basic content* of nursing.

Nonetheless, such content, because it may significantly facilitate the nurse's work, should not necessarily be regarded as unimportant. But the knowledge ought to be acquired on the job, not in the context of basic nursing courses. The challenge to the

young nurse is to recognize what comprises basic nursing content (and, hence, is important) and what does not (but nevertheless is important in some job settings).

Paradoxically, many young graduates come to their first jobs trained to focus on certain peripheral aspects of nursing but without any clear picture of the role played by those factors. For example, the new graduate may have been given experience in team or in primary nursing. She is likely to believe that this distinction forms a crucial part of the basic content of nursing, yet she has no genuine understanding of the strengths and weaknesses of these alternative approaches, or no appreciation of the fact that such strengths and weaknesses vary, depending on the hospital setting. Unfortunately, many nursing trainees learn that only one particular method or approach is "right," regardless of the circumstances surrounding its use.

The fact that a new graduate has taken "management" courses as part of her basic training reflects the confusion that plagues nurses about what constitutes significant content for the practice of nursing. If basic students are taught management, their teachers presumably believe that management content forms part of the discipline of nursing. A reasonable analogy might be the first-year curriculum of a medical school inclusion of a course on clinical administration. Such knowledge will eventually be necessary for a doctor who is going to administer a clinic. But one would hardly expect to find a *course* on clinic administration in the basic medical school curriculum and required of all students enrolled in the school.

Even experienced nurses may find it difficult to understand that the routine practice of admitting a patient to a unit—a practice that includes, say, weighing him and taking his temperature, pulse, and blood pressure—does not constitute *basic content* of nursing. Rather, the practice should be viewed as part of a *system* established to make certain that particular information is always available, in the event that medical or nursing decisions will require them. An admission blood pressure may be used as a baseline for assessing a patient's progress after surgery or after some course of treatment. The use of blood pressure readings in this fashion does constitute a part of nursing content. But the practice of obtaining the information routinely when the patient is admitted forms part of the facilitative structure in use in that particular system at that particular time. The same purpose might be served in different ways in other settings or other times.

Perhaps the major reason why nurses have difficulty separating nursing content from system content is because they do not tend to be well versed in the scientific content of their own discipline.

4. Content relevant to developing the structural components of the nursing care delivery system is elusive. The scientific basis for organizing a nursing department is not as easily available as is the scientific basis for coping with the patient's physiological and anatomical problems. Some nurses have studied organizational theory and are familiar with the relevant research, but most nurses must accept the word of authorities who maintain that a particular approach would be most appropriate for their departments.

Consequently, the beliefs and principles of business are adopted in developing a nursing department, whether or not such principles have proven valid when applied to nursing. Perhaps nurses with expertise in organizational systems can adapt management principles to develop an efficient and effective professional service, but many nurses attempt to apply such principles without determining how such methods achieve their professional objectives. Even nurses with administrative knowledge in decision making seem unable to identify specific information needed to assess the feasibility of a particular mode of operation.

Nurses often select the approach to an administrative problem before they have identified the problem and without specifying the structural outcomes that the method should bring about. For example, the prob-lem-oriented medical record is often recommended to nurse administrators who are not aware of any difficulties in this method and with no more justification than that it provides a systematic way to plan a patient's care and document his progress. The recommendation is made as a solution to a problem that is not well defined.

The problem-oriented record might very well be an efficient and effective way to organize the content of the medical record, but if the underlying problem exists because of lack of knowledge about patient care, its use will not guarantee effective planning or the desired patient progress. Successful outcomes could include the substantive content of the records, the ability to identify significant problems in the patient, and knowledge of the treatment or care procedures those problems require; these generalizations hold regardless of the particular medical record chosen.

One might argue that it is better to be efficient and systematic, even if the care provided is not optimally effective—that time-consuming, inefficient mediocrity is worse than efficient mediocrity. This premise might be acceptable if the use of a method does not substitute for an attempt to solve the problems that actually interfere with achieving the desired goal. The danger always exists that implementation of a process or procedure will itself become the goal, rather than using the mission of the system and one's knowledge of how that mission might best be served to determine what procedures are adopted.

Characteristics of Institutional Nursing Care Delivery Systems

The four major reasons that account for the difficulties inherent in applying the goal-directed model to the structural elements of the nursing care delivery system have certain implications about the characteristics of such institutional systems themselves.

1. Confusion is likely regarding the purpose of a given structural element in the system.

2. In developing the system, individuals will be trying to satisfy various peoples' objectives, some of which will conflict with one another and will either conflict with, or be unrelated to, the ultimate mission of providing high-quality nursing care.

3. Various systems will be developed independently of other systems. Thus, for example, the staffing program will be developed without considering how that program will relate to the quality assurance program, the staff development program, or the personnel evaluation program, even though the way each functions will affect the others.

4. Criteria not integrally involved in the department's goal will be used to assess the quality of the various systems. Thus, the individuals who judge a given system's effectiveness might have no knowledge of that particular element's intended role in the provision of care to patients. An administrator might like a particular staffing program because it is less expensive. Another might pour money into a patient-education program because it draws compliments from physicians and patients, even though the program is doing little to effect the intended changes in patient behavior.

5. Decisions about whether to adopt a particular approach to meeting an existing structural need may be based on what personnel in nursing departments in other institutions do. That is, decision making occurs by consensus rather than by validation of the approach.

6. Individuals in charge of various programs (such as personnel, evaluation, staffing, patient education, or staff development) tend to engage in empire-building activities. Their personal goals are allowed to supersede those related to patient care.

For the most part, these deficiencies do not reflect a lack of interest in effective and efficient patient care on the part of nurses developing the structure. But the situation makes it easier to adopt a prefabricated design than to tailor a system meeting the needs of a particular hospital—needs that may be difficult to identify in the complexity of the overall hospital operation. This is particularly true when a prefabricated system has acquired a degree of respectability by virtue of its use or its endorsement by authorities in the field.

Identifying Structural Components

The components needed to facilitate the achievement of high-quality nursing care can be identified by starting with the relevant clinical content. Such content should suggest what problems currently exist. Merely identifying some of the structural components should not be difficult. The average young staff member could doubtless do so, once she has been provided with a definition of the term "structural component" through a number of examples (including those she may consider parts of the nursing process—such as a system of nursing care planning). She is more likely to have difficulty knowing what outcomes should be in evidence if the system is serving its purpose, what factors must be operative if those outcomes are to be realized, and what information must be gathered before competent planning of the system can be initiated.

Identification and mastery of the knowledge needed to determine the structural requirements in a given situation constitute the area of greatest difficulty for most nurses. Such determinations are likely to require the following information:

1. *Clinical information regarding the activities and resources needed to achieve projected outcomes.* This information can be obtained from the nursing procedures and the programs of care, if these documents spell out the specifics of an activity in sufficient detail.

2. *Information regarding resources and constraints.* This category includes information about patient populations, the frequencies with which certain conditions occur on various areas, when and under what conditions patients are admitted, the physical setting involved, the kinds of restrictions imposed, the sorts of flexibilities permitted, the numbers and kinds of staff available, the type and amount of turnover that typically occurs, sickness patterns among staff, the availability of back-up personnel, service requirements and resources, scheduling controlled by other services.

3. *Information that identifies variables (factors) associated with the kinds of systems being contemplated.* This area might include information about learning and motivation (to be used in developing a staff education program), labor laws and practices (pertinent to the establishment of personnel policies), or the balance between work capacity and effectiveness (as applied to the establishment of staffing systems).

The third category is perhaps the most difficult of the three to obtain, because relatively unsophisticated individuals have difficulty recognizing that such content is pertinent to planning a system. Identifying the content area is not sufficient. One must proceed to identify the information most directly pertinent to the problem and then interpret that information appropriately.

As pointed out in chapter 2, one can start the development of the structural components using two different approaches. One can identify all the nursing activities required by the programs of care and from these ascertain what structural components are needed to facilitate the staff's involvement. Or, in contrast, one can start with a particular structural component for which precedents exist and analyze it for the characteristics necessary to facilitate participation in sound nursing care activities.

DESIGNING THE SYSTEM FROM PROGRAMS OF CARE

If one were attempting to redesign the total structure of a new unit, it would be useful to start with the programs of care designed for the patient population to be served by that unit. From those programs of care, one could identify the general patient care objectives and the performance standards that have to be met. This analysis should make it possible to identify structural objectives that would stipulate the conditions that must be present if appropriate nursing activities can be guaranteed. One can then arrive at realistic designs of the various structural components required to assure the establishment of whatever care standards the programs of care indicate should be in effect.

General Design

Again, consider an objective related to the provision of emergency care. Such an objective might be worded: "Emergency conditions are kept to the lowest possible level of threat to the patient by virtue of the occurrence of timely and effective intervention on the nurse's part." General nursing activities (see chapter 8) can be used as guides in specifying more circumscribed activities designed for coping with specific emergencies. Additional information is needed, as well, to determine the structural elements (and the characteristics of those structural elements) required to meet the objective.

Emergencies vary somewhat in the immediacy of action required and in the seriousness of their consequences to the patient. If all the factors (biological, psychological, and environmental) likely to be associated with a given emergency are considered, a plan can be laid out for a general design consisting of the needed structural elements. Such considerations pertinent to preventing death or irreversible damage include those discussed below.

1. In most emergency situations, irreparable damage or death can occur if the process is not reversed or blocked immediately. Although emergencies

differ in the exact amount of time required for definitive action, in general time will *not* be available to contemplate different courses of action or study procedure manuals.

2. Any emergency situation is associated with high stress. High stress, in turn, tends to be associated with lowered performance levels, particularly when the task is difficult[2]. These relationships have implications for any training program to prepare individuals to cope with emergency situations, as well as for any policy formulations that set performance standards or prescribe particular activities for certain emergencies. One might characterize a given job designation partly on the basis of the difficulties in providing sufficient education to guarantee safe performance under stipulated stress conditions.

3. Emergencies do not occur frequently enough for staff members to benefit from daily practice. If provision is not made for practice beyond the time required to acquire the skill, then the skill (depending on its complexity) may deteriorate with time[3]. This relationship has obvious implications for the training process and the time the staff member invests in assuring the maintenance of such skills. Like high stress, lack of practice opportunities also carries implications for policies stipulating which types of employees should be prepared to perform which kinds of tasks and under what circumstances.

4. Most emergencies require definitive therapeutic procedures that require the services of a physician, even when the nurse has taken initial therapeutic steps. Systems for obtaining the required services of the physician must be provided.

5. Most emergencies require the administration of medications or intravenous solutions. Many medications present potential dangers related to both dosage and the manner of administration.

Policies, procedures, and methods must be established to make certain that medications necessary for emergencies are available and are administered safely.

6. Other equipment and supplies may be needed immediately (for example, to assess vital signs and maintain airways). Systems for assuring that these materials are *immediately* available for *safe* and *effective* use must be established.

7. Emergencies absorb the attention of at least one, and usually more, health worker, possibly for an extended period. Such individuals are not available to attend to other duties or to other patients during the emergency, which has implications for staffing, systems governing patient care assignments, and policies concerned with the allocation of responsibility and accountability for patient care.

The structural components required to ascertain that all emergencies are handled adequately would include:

1. A statement of philosophy that specifies a commitment on the part of the nursing department and the hospital to saving patients experiencing emergencies and that clearly indicates the degree of investment in this goal expected from staff members.

2. A set of policies, procedures, and statements of standards that clearly communicate the level of functioning expected of staff, together with the responsibilities they must assume and the restrictions under which they must function.

3. An administrative structure that makes explicit which levels of staff bear the responsibility for given types of functioning and who will be held accountable for particular deficiencies in the system.

4. A staffing program assuring that staff members will be available in the necessary numbers, in the appropriate loca-

tions, and with the skills required to assure that immediate emergency care will be provided.

5. An education system that prepares staff to provide effective and efficient emergency care, and ensures that no unprepared staff member will deliver emergency care.

6. A system of patient care assignment assuring that someone will assume responsibility for any emergency that occurs, while at the same time other existing patient care needs are met by additional competent personnel.

7. Systems of communication assuring that any health workers involved in emergency actions are provided the information they need to perform adequately at the time of the emergency, to provide competent follow-up care to the patient, to help prevent unnecessary occurrences of such emergencies in the future, and to correct any deficiencies in current emergency care procedures.

8. A system that makes the equipment, supplies, and materials needed for adequate emergency care immediately available for safe utilization at all times.

If the references to emergency care were eliminated from this list, the resulting components would be generally applicable to the achievement of patient care objectives. To set up systems to achieve all such objectives, it would be necessary to identify specific information relevant to the particular patient results to be achieved. Emergency care requires information regarding the emergencies likely to occur on a given unit and the methods for successfully coping with them.

Specific Information and Variables

For example, consider the necessity of establishing a system to implement a program of care for patients suffering cardiac arrest while in a minimal care unit. Suppose the population in this unit consists of patients who have been hospitalized for diagnostic tests, patients being prepared for discharge, and patients undergoing long-term therapy that cannot be provided on an outpatient basis. Assume that all these individuals can take care of most of their physical needs most of the time.

Cardiac arrest would not occur frequently on such a unit, but nonetheless it could strike any patient at any time. To ensure that the patient goals are achieved in the case of cardiac arrest, the variables or factors likely in this situation must be assessed. Because those factors are interrelated in complex ways, staffing will be determined by, and also may influence, the philosophical position taken by the hospital with regard to saving patients experiencing cardiac arrest. Both factors will be influenced by the staff education program in force.

An appropriate first step would involve summarizing the relevant clinical information for planning facilitative systems needed to cope with the problem. In the case of cardiac arrest, irreversible brain damage can occur after four to six minutes of oxygen deprivation[4]. Basic life support processes must be initiated within four minutes of the onset of the arrest. The procedures for instigating immediate ventilation and circulation can be taught to individuals with minimal backgrounds, although mastery of the skill does take practice and time. The procedure can be carried out by one person, but is more effectively handled by two. In addition, the basic life support procedure must be supplemented by more definitive care procedures within the next few minutes to maximize the patient's chances for survival and recovery. Definitive treatment requires knowledge about and skill in intravenous administration, intubation, and defibrillation, as well as the appropriate use and administration of such drugs as sodium bicarbonate, epinephrine, lidocaine, and the like. Adequate patient care requires that appropriate procedures be instigated as soon as possible and that the equipment required be immediately available.

Factors specific to a given hospital and to a particular unit within that hospital determine how the relevant clinical considerations are considered in the planning. Consider different units within a hospital. One reason for establishing a minimal care unit is to reduce the costs of providing patient services. If all units were staffed in the same fashion as an intensive care unit (low nurse-patient ratio, highly trained staff members present on a 24-hour basis), immediate and effective care could be guaranteed all patients in the institution. But such an approach would obviously constitute a gross misuse and waste of talent, as well as an indefensible financial investment.

A reasonable compromise is needed between two extremes; (1) having more staff members available than are needed, and (2) losing patients because of inadequate staffing. The concept of the *intelligent* or *reasonable compromise* must be emphasized in planning the structural components of a nursing care delivery system. Seldom is one able to achieve a goal without also sacrificing to a degree other legitimate goals. Such choices call for skill in being able to weigh the alternatives, taking all factors into account to make wise judgments about the cost-benefit ratios involved.

In the case of the minimal care unit and its plans to cope with cardiac arrest, one must determine a reasonable investment that is also substantial enough to give the unit's patients a good chance of surviving. If two qualified staff members were available at all times to provide basic support, one could start the basic resuscitation procedures while the other requested assistance and then returned to assist her colleague. This approach would mandate that a minimum of two individuals competent in basic life support procedures would staff the unit on each shift.

However, if the two were the entire staff on duty in the unit, their focus on the cardiac arrest victim would of course preclude the provision of care to the remaining unit patients. Under the assumption that the latter patients would need concentrated care only at certain times (such as after a special test involving anesthesia or heavy sedation or while receiving chemotherapy), the problem could perhaps be solved by scheduling one additional individual with the necessary skills to provide care for those patients at those times. To make such an arrangement, one would need information indicating when these sorts of needs would arise. If the patients' tests or treatments were always completed by noon, it might be possible to get by adequately with just two nurses on duty during the evening and night shifts. If the patients returned from tests or treatments later in the day, then three staff members might be needed for the evening shift, as well. A system for providing supplementary help during periods of staff shortages would also have to be arranged.

All three nurses on duty in the minimal care unit should be competent in basic life support procedures because one cannot predict who will be close enough to a victim at the time of a cardiac arrest to provide prompt assistance. Thus, an educational program must be developed to ensure that all such staff members possess the necessary skills and knowledge.

Because basic life support measures would not be used very frequently in a minimal care unit, the skills in such staff members would have to be maintained over time. Information about skill acquisition, retention, and performance under stress would be important in this context. To ensure continuous competency in CPR performance, a sizable investment in training, review, and practice time will be necessary to ensure not only high-level acquisition of the skills involved, but also long-term retention. A study carried out at the University of Iowa Hospitals and Clinics indicated that staff did not maintain CPR skills (as applied on the manikin) for any substantial period if they were not given early and frequent practice reviews[5].

Setting up a program that provides adequate training and sufficient review is one matter. Making certain that staff members return for reviews frequently enough to ensure their continued competence is a more serious problem. It is not always easy to see that staff are released from work to attend CPR review sessions, particularly when their units have pressing patient care problems.

The philosophical position adopted by the department is important. If the department and the unit are committed to a total and constant effort to protect patients to the greatest extent possible, then the system will have to include: (1) an intensive training and review program for all staff working on the area; (2) provision for constant checks to ascertain that staff members have retained the pertinent information and the ability to perform; and (3) a method for assuring that back-up personnel in the unit only at times of staff shortages also have the necessary competencies.

If one examines only the elements of structure involving staffing and educational programs and the investment required to make certain that the system is fail-proof, one might conclude that the investment required is too great, given the commitments already made to other efforts. For example, there is a low probability of a cardiac arrest at a time when there are not at least two staff members trained in CPR immediately available. Thus, rather than investing strongly in preparations for a contingency with such a low probability, one might deliberately choose to take the chance of losing a patient to cardiac arrest. Therefore, one might not attempt to assure that qualified supplementary help is always on hand, and restrict training or review to regular staff members. An alternative is to prescribe CPR training and review for all personnel, but on a sharply limited basis (restricted, for example, to one training and one six-month review session). Such decisions should be made with full realization of the nature and scope of the benefits, the costs, and the risks involved.

Similar reasoning can be applied to other aspects of the system designed to implement the cardiac arrest program of care. To make certain the definitive care will be initiated promptly, properly trained individuals must be available not more than a few minutes from where the arrest occurs. A system for summoning them is a necessity. Many hospitals have CPR teams of physicians and nurses. However, other institutions may not always have physicians as CPR team members. Planning nursing activities will necessarily differ considerably in each institution. Policies and procedures must be established in accordance with the skill levels of the individuals responsible for instigating the definitive care.

Other Structures of the System

To return to the hypothetical minimal care unit, it would be highly unlikely that the CPR team in this hospital, if one exists, would be made up of staff members based in the minimal care unit itself. Thus, a team would probably have to come from another part of the hospital. To be certain a team was always available, one might decide to constitute at least two such groups in the hospital. If this is not feasible, qualified individuals whose major responsibilities might scatter them throughout the hospital might form a back-up team to all be alerted (using the same communication system that alerts the primary CPR team) when their CPR skills are needed. The contingency in this case, of course, would be two cardiac arrests occurring at the same time.

An emergency cart to organize all the equipment needed to cope with a cardiac arrest is a necessary part of the system. If, in addition, a trained team attended every cardiac arrest, one would not have to be concerned with some issues. But one would have to consider others. If more than one cart were used, standardizing the locations of the various pieces of equipment would be desirable, to facilitate the team member's ability to find them quickly under stress conditions. One would have to decide whether to maintain two sets of supplies on one cart at all times or to depend on inoperative time for replenishing used supplies. In areas in which carts are not often used, a system that provides for frequent, regular checks of the defibrillating or monitor equipment should be established and should make the regularity of the checking mandatory, regardless of existing work pressures.

Administrative structures must also be considered if effective implementation of a basic life support procedure program is to be realized. A head nurse not held accountable for her unit's achievement of departmental or hospital goals might establish her own standards of practice simply by neglecting to enforce those policies essential to the success of the systems adopted by the institution. She may not consciously conclude she is willing to risk that her staff, when called on, will not perform basic life support procedures effectively. But she will in effect be operating with such a philosophy if she fails to insist that her staff members attend review sessions and to require that their competence be periodically verified. An administrative structure should clearly delineate where accountability exists at the various levels and insist that each level hold the one below it accountable for its functioning to generate a uniformly high degree of striving to achieve patient outcome goals.

The Resulting Standards

The final set of standards regarding cardiac arrest cases might take the following form for our hypothetical minimal care unit:

Philosophy. The hospital staff believe that every patient has the right to receive whatever supportive treatment is required to maximize his potential for recovery from cardiac arrest. It is the duty of every nursing unit to commit itself in full to administering CPR procedures to cardiac arrest cases calling for such procedures.

Goals. Every patient suffering cardiac arrest will have basic life support procedures initiated within four minutes of arrest and definitive care initiated within five minutes of discovery of the arrest. (This statement of goals could become a statement of purposes by preceding it with the words, "To make certain that. . . .")

Ultimate Objectives for Structure
(Criteria for evaluating effectiveness of the structure design.)

1. Basic life support procedure is instigated competently by two individuals immediately on discovery of the arrest.

2. Individuals trained in definitive care are available and functioning within five minutes of discovery of the arrest.

3. All the equipment and supplies needed for definitive care are present, easily identified, and ready for use when definitive care is begun.

Minimal Care Unit Structure Objectives

1. At least two individuals competent in basic life support procedures are on the unit at all times. At least three are on the unit from 10 A.M. until 5 P.M.
   a. All staff will be required to attend the initial training session and to return to staff development for basic life support training until they perform perfectly on the first try after a lapse of one day. This requirement will be met every three months thereafter.
   b. Supplementary staff will be required to meet the same criteria for competency in basic life support as regular staff before being eligible to be hired.
   c. All staff will be tested for knowledge of the location of the crash cart and the procedure for summoning the CPR team as part of the competency verification procedure.

2. Cart will be kept in the alcove next to room ____ when not in use.
   a. The night nurse will be responsible for checking all equipment and supplies once a week by use of the checking system outlined in the department manual.
   b. The nurse in charge on the shift during which a cardiac arrest occurs is responsible for seeing that the cart is resupplied and ready for use immediately after the CPR team has finished with it.

3. The nurse in charge on the shift during which a cardiac arrest occurs is responsible for making a complete report before the shift is over, using form ____.

The specific content included in the standard adopted and the explicit philosophy that governs its functioning may, of course, differ substantially in another hospital setting. The intent here is simply to illustrate how one could develop a standard to serve as a reasonably sound basis for evaluating a system and determining its deficiencies.

ADAPTING A SYSTEM TO FACILITATE THE IMPLEMENTATION OF PROGRAMS OF CARE

In most cases in which the design of structures is being undertaken, nurses are actually *redesigning* existing programs or systems. Making the various elements of a structure effectively achieve their intended purposes is definitely possible, even in the case of pre-existing structures with considerable tradition and a history of long use.

Nursing departments periodically reconstruct or revise their performance evaluation systems, staffing methods, audit systems, staff development programs, nursing care plans, policy statements, and so on. At virtually any time, a nursing department will be redesigning at least one of its programs or policies. Some of these come up for complete overhauling as often as once a year. Sometimes the need to rework a program comes from the emergence of new information or a new philosophy of care. But frequently the constant demand for changes in a system arises because it was not adequately designed to meet its purpose in the first place because the appropriate information was not obtained or its purpose and outcomes were not first clearly delineated.

Identifying the Problems

The method used to develop a program of care can also be employed to design a structure element. One identifies the general area of concern, specifies the problems involved, projects the end results that are both desirable and achievable, and then selects an approach that is likely to solve the problems and achieve the desired outcomes. This method is far from being new or original. But its efficacy depends heavily on the validity of the *information* used at each stage of its development.

One of the first and most serious mistakes made when attempting to overhaul or improve a system is to focus from the start on solutions rather than on problems. Given their choice of a solution, individuals proceed to search for a problem to which the solution will apply. The individual who correctly begins with a focus on a problem inherent in the situation is likely to find that, in fact, more than one problem exists and therefore more than just one solution is called for.

The following description illustrates a focus on a solution rather than on a problem. Suppose a supervisor new to a clinical division is concerned about the haphazard manner in which staff assignments are made in some of her units. She believes that the "treatment list" approach being used, whereby everyone pitches in, performing the various treatments, and checking them off until they are all completed, is too function-oriented and not sufficiently patient-oriented to provide the quality of care she desires (not, in the process, having very clear ideas about what she means by "quality of care").

She thus decides that a written assignment be made out each day, specifying the staff member's name and the patient's name as well as the treatment to be administered. As she has analyzed the situation, the problem involves the lack of written assignments in the existing routine. The solution in her mind is the institution of a written assignment procedure, which could result in a more structured method of preparing daily assignments but not in *the quality of the care provided the patients involved*. The ineffectiveness of the previous assignment method was very likely only a symptom of an existing problem with the quality of patient care being provided which is not likely to be altered by her action.

In a problem situation in which the daily patient care assignments are made casually and indiscriminately, the major problem probably is the whole conceptualization of patient care by that department's personnel. The nursing care plans in use are probably skimpy and include superficial notations indicating only those routines that have been ordered by the physician (such as B.P. q. day, up ad lib.). Retrospective audits will probably reveal charting deficiencies. Discharge planning will be spotty, depending on who is on duty. Correcting or improving any of these elements will at best produce only temporary changes; little effect on the overall quality of the care provided within the unit is likely to result.

In contrast, if a unit has used the programming of care approach, in which *the results achieved in patients* become the focus in assessing the effectiveness of care, the redesign of a system can ensure that the system meets patient care needs and is not regarded as a goal to be achieved for its own sake.

In following this approach, the purpose of the system and the problems it is intended to solve will be clearly delineated, because they provided the impetus for first designing the system. The purpose is to make certain that each patient's plan of care is capably implemented and its goals are achieved, with appropriate information being used to evaluate the effectiveness of the care and to modify it when indicated. Obviously, this purpose requires a great deal more thoughtful planning and use of information than one that merely focuses on the certainty that everyone knows her assignment for the day. A concern with assignments can result in a focus on such matters as who is to be designated the "charge person" or when each individual is to take a lunch break. In contrast, a concern with skilled implementation of high-quality nursing plans will lead to concentration on the specific needs of individual patients, the availability of personnel with the various required nursing skills, and the kind of directions to give to ensure that the patients in the area are receiving the best care the hospital and its employees can provide.

If one were redesigning a system for daily patient care assignment to achieve improved implementation of the programs of care in a unit, the first step should be identifying the problems that indicate a redesign was necessary, such as those in the following list:

1. Important signs and symptoms in patients are being overlooked and patients are developing problems that could have been prevented by better surveillance by the nurses on the unit.

2. Because nursing care plans are not modified as patients progress or as their conditions change, inappropriate treatments and approaches continue to be used.

3. Individuals who have cared for certain patients discover belatedly that information pertinent to those patients' needs was available but never communicated to them during the time they provided such care.

4. In chart audits, documentation indicating whether relevant nursing care criteria have been met is inconsistent and in some cases totally lacking.

5. Discharge planning for patients is of variable quality, its occurrence and its effectiveness depends on who is on duty, the time of day at which the patient is discharged, or the amount of notice that is given regarding the impending discharge.

Projecting the Outcome

Projecting to the results that would signify a superior quality of nursing care, one might specify that the following characteristics be in effect:

1. Concurrent audits reveal that references to patient nursing care criteria are identifiable in the medical records; follow-up information has been included wherever notations have been entered regarding the occurrence of significant signs or symptoms.

2. Audits of the records of discharged patients reveal the inclusion of complete discharge notes, with the information supplied being consistent with the programs of care appropriate to the patients in question.

3. Nursing care plans are up-to-date, incorporating information that is present in

the clinical and nursing notes of the medical record and that can be verified by observations of or interviews with the patient.

4. Information pertinent to the patient's discharge has been included in the nursing care plans of patients who have been in the unit no more than 72 hours.

5. Information pertaining to the individual patient and needed for planning or implementing his care is written into the nursing care plan or in the medical record.

6. Individuals responsible for direct care to patients, as well as the immediate superiors of such individuals, can either satisfactorily answer questions raised about the nursing care needs of those patients or can find the answers in the various records kept in the unit.

As one obtains information pertinent to the solution of existing problems, to the achievement of clearly delineated goals, and to an assessment of the potential effectiveness of alternative approaches, it is unlikely that simply establishing a better system of patient assignments will be viewed as effecting the necessary problem solutions and goal achievements. Rather, it is likely that one will see the necessity for building in policies, training programs, and supervisory practices designed to ensure that the system functions as it should.

Recognizing Variables

As an initial step, one should identify at least some of the variables (factors) that might be causing the problems that are identified. Information should be obtained regarding those aspects of the setting most likely to have a bearing on the choice of the approach to be adopted.

In designing a method of patient assignment, one should know what kinds of patient care will be required and the lowest skill level that would make effective implementation of such care possible. In particular, it is important to know *how many individuals are available who can assess patient needs, evaluate the effectiveness of the care currently being provided patients,*

and modify the plans for any given shift when the need for modification is apparent. In my view, such knowledge most frequently is lacking when personnel are faced with serious nursing care problems in their units.

Given the existence of such problems, the staff members involved are probably not oriented to the quality assurance concept of providing nursing care and do not feel responsible for keeping meaningful records about patient progress and the effects of particular treatments or elements of care. They very likely have not assumed responsibility for communicating pertinent information to one another as a means of assuring continuity in a patient's care. One might want to learn about the educational programs that have been provided such individuals, but only to avoid repeating unsuccessful methods.

Suppose that examination of the conditions existing in a given unit has revealed that nursing assistants provide much of the patient care and that, for any given day shift, there are seldom more than two registered nurses on hand in addition to the head nurse. Often, the head nurse may be one of the two registered nurses on duty. Only one registered nurse would be on duty in evening and night shifts, as well as weekends. In addition, assume that two licensed practical nurses are on duty on week days and one on evenings and weekends. The night shift might consist of a single registered nurse and one nursing assistant.

An Approach to the Problem

With this kind of staffing mix, many might conclude that the problem is too few registered nurses on the staff. This may be the case, but, until new staff are added, the leadership on the unit must deal with the present realities to alleviate existing problems. Some standards for patient care assignments could be derived that might be effective, if supporting structures were established, such as those in the following list:

1. Every patient will be assigned to a registered nurse on every shift. The RN in each case must possess demonstrated ability to organize and evaluate plans of care for patients on the unit for both assessment and planning. This individual will be designated as the nurse coordinator.

2. LPNs, nursing assistants, and inexperienced RNs will be under the supervision of a nurse coordinator who will make out the individual assignments according to the needs of the patients and the skills of the available staff members.

3. Written assignments for each staff member will include information regarding the aspects of care, the observations, and the record keeping for which that individual will be held responsible. Also indicated will be any specific observing or charting activities in which she will be asked to engage.

4. Nurse coordinators will be accountable to the head nurse*. The head nurse will be responsible for the following:

   a. Assessing the patient's status at the beginning and at the end of the shift to determine his response to the nursing care currently being provided him.

   b. Arranging for all staff members assigned to an individual patient to participate in evaluations of his condition.

   c. Assigning duties in terms of the level of skill required for the task at hand.

   d. Making certain each staff member is provided the information and direction needed to carry out her assignments capably.

   e. Making certain that staff members are able to capably perform the tasks required by their assignments.

   f. Setting priorities of care and determining what constitutes the best use of available time and resources that result in skilled achievement of the essentials of care.

   g. Determining the extent to which patients are progressing toward the criteria set for them by the applicable programs of care; modifying the nursing care plan as directed by the physician and by the patient's response to the current regimen.

   h. Making certain that nursing care plans are kept in phase with the patient's progress; incorporating appropriate new information about the patient into the nursing care plan.

   i. Making certain that accurate and meaningful recordings are made of any information relevant to the patient's progress or needed to make informed decisions about the patient's nursing care.

   j. Making certain that the regimens spelled out in the plans of care are implemented in the prescribed manner or are modified if unfeasible.

   k. Making certain that information needed for care of the patient in other settings—such as, other inpatient units, public health nursing agencies, or homes—has been clearly and duly transmitted to the appropriate individuals.

   l. Making certain that any information needed by the physician is provided.

   m. Making certain that new orders given by the physician and any changes in the physician's treatment plan are incorporated into the nursing plan.

The approach used to establish a method of making out daily assignments has in this case consisted of the establishment of certain standards. One might instead formulate a policy that incorporates the same ideas and accomplishes the same ends. In any event, it is important that ways be established to evaluate the enterprise by focusing on *patient outcome goals*.

---

* At times, the head nurse may have to serve as the nurse coordinator for a particular group of patients and assume the associated responsibilities involved.

Relation to Organizational Structure

The approach described does not depend on a particular kind of organizational structure, such as team nursing, primary nursing, or the like. The term "nurse coordinator" is not particularly appealing to me, but it was selected because its connotations are fairly neutral. The same responsibilities could be shouldered by someone designated as the "primary nurse" or the "team leader." The responsibilities previously listed were in some cases intentionally introduced by use of the words, "Making certain that. . . ." This wording suggests that the same level of care should be achievable in any setting, regardless of the individuals involved, if the necessary skill levels are represented in the personnel.

In some cases, registered nurses constitute the largest group of employees. In such instances, the staff members may do most of the actual nursing care, as well as the planning and evaluating work, with nursing assistants assigned to make beds, fill water pitchers, and clean. Other settings may have only one registered nurse on duty. She would not be able to tie herself up with a patient care assignment and at the same time be available to evaluate and supervise the care provided by other staff members.

Thus, she would have to determine which tasks only she could perform and which ones could be delegated to others. When the basic philosophy focuses on *tasks to be done* rather than on *results to be achieved with patients*, the transition that the nurse is asked to make—that is, from *doer to programmer and evaluator*—is demanding.

Some might argue, given one RN and two nursing assistants working on the evening shift, that the RN would not have time to evaluate all the patients on the area. The nurse in charge must engage in too many other activities during a shift to ensure that the remaining staff members are doing their jobs acceptably. But the alternative chances what might happen to the patient and accepts the fact that achievement of patient

outcome criteria is likely to be spotty, at best.

The nurse coordinator's task of making certain her staff members are functioning effectively will differ from instance to instance. On the one hand, for example, she might give considerable responsibility (such as charting without surveillance) to an LPN who has learned what is significant and who has demonstrated an ability to make effective use of programs of care and nursing care plans. Similarly, the nursing coordinator might feel completely confident that her nursing assistants could handle any problems certain patients are likely to have. On the other hand, in the case of certain other patients, the coordinator might spend a great deal of time with some of her staff members, pointing out significant findings and helping with the implementation of care.

The coordinator might very profitably examine the duties and activities she has taken on herself to determine if they actually require the level of knowledge that she (and perhaps she alone among the staff) possesses. A similar examination could be made of the duties allocated to others on her staff. She might conclude, for example, that it would be preferable if a nursing assistant, rather than a registered nurse, were to take over the duties of the unit clerk, when the unit clerk is not on duty. She also might conclude that she herself should be involved in implementing the discharge of certain patients (a task previously performed by, say, an LPN) to make certain those patients can cope successfully with a complicated regimen that they must follow at home.

The nurse coordinator, and the other leaders on the area, may have to reconceptualize their thinking about the provision of patient care. They may have to accept the fact that their own behaviors will have to change if the processes and structures essential for high-quality nursing care are to be adopted and made to work effectively. The maintenance of optimal standards of care for the patient cannot be assured unless the system within which it is provided is organized with that goal in mind. If a process or structure has not achieved desired patient-outcome results, it must be judged ineffective, regardless of how many individuals are committed to it. A corollary to that axiom is any structural element or process, no matter how useful it may seem to be or how effective it is in other settings, will not provide a solution to one's problems if conditions within her particular setting prevent its appropriate use or implementation.

Structural considerations cannot, of course, be limited to questions of effectiveness. Efficiency and economy are also of great importance. The challenge is to simultaneously consider all the integrated aspects of a system's components and their significance for nursing practice. An efficient method may not be the most effective or economical in the long run. Cost does not always correlate positively (or at least highly) with effectiveness.

To make certain that any structural component is worth preserving, one must: (1) study the component's role in facilitating high-quality patient care, as well as the variables that affect it; (2) specify what constitutes successful functioning on the part of the component; (3) monitor its functioning; and (4) modify those aspects of the component that are interfering with achievement of the goals for which it was designed.

If the groundwork is established when the system is set up and if systematic, regular evaluations of it are made, defects in the system can be identified and corrected without a need for a major overhauling or periodic adoptions of new systems or approaches.

REFERENCES

1. Donabedian, A. Quality of care; problems of management, Part II, Some issues in evaluating the quality of nursing care. *American Journal of Public Health,* 59: 1833–1836, October 1969.
2. Levitt, E. E. *The Psychology of Anxiety.* New York: Bobbs Merrill Company, Inc., 1967, pp. 116–122.
3. Underwood, B. J. *Experimental Psychology, an Introduction.* New York: Appleton-Century-Crofts, Inc., 1949, pp. 525–527.
4. Grant, H. and Murray, R. *Emergency Care.* Bowie, Maryland: Robert J. Bradey Company, 1971, p. 72.
5. Moore, M. A. Training schedules for cardiopulmonary resuscitation procedure for registered nurses, practical nurses, aides and orderlies. *The Journal of Continuing Education,* 3: 4: 17–26, July–August 1972.

Incorporating Externally Imposed Standards Into Structural Organization

CHAPTER 10

Standards imposed from outside a hospital are enforceable within it only to the extent that those in the institution responsible for establishing them choose to be governed by them. If an agency or organization advocating standards has no power to reward compliance or punish noncompliance, it must rely on the persuasiveness of its personnel to bring about conformity. If an organization enjoys some prestige in the field and elicits feelings of commitment from its members, those members will probably embrace its standards and attempt to ensure their adoption in their own institutions. Their success will of course depend to a great extent on their power in those institutions. Typically, members of the American Medical Association and the American Hospital Association have the greatest power in a hospital and therefore can best introduce standards.

Members of other professional groups—such as dietitians, pharmacists, nurses, and physical therapists—have less influence and less ability to effect changes. Although they may find it possible to meet the standards of their own professions within their own departments, they tend to have considerable difficulty in attempts to use those standards to change the behaviors or performances of other professionals in the institution.

The organizations or agencies that do have a penalty-reward system can effectively impose standards on an institution only if its personnel wish to avoid the penalties or want to obtain the rewards, or genuinely believe in the validity of those standards. In some cases, the penalty could be maximally severe—for example, closing a hospital because of its failure to adhere to state regulations. The fact that some institutions fail to comply with state standards even though such severe penalties exist highlights the difficulties of forcing compliance. If the hospital personnel responsible for meeting externally imposed standards fail to do their jobs satisfactorily, noncompliance will continue. Noncompliance, even in cases in which extreme measures are eventually taken, can persist for long periods of time, exposing patients to dangerous conditions and unsafe practices.

In an institution as complex as the modern hospital, there are varying degrees and kinds of commitments to attaining the benefits accruing from meeting external standards. Among those most influential in shaping hospital policies and practices one might find the following attitudinal patterns: (1) a desire to achieve the *status* afforded by meeting external standards, but unaccompanied by a sincere interest in actually meeting them; (2) a commitment to achieving the standards, but without understanding the relationship between the standards and the quality of care their achievement is supposed to bring about; (3) a commitment to high-quality care, accompanied by a conviction that externally imposed standards are unrelated to such care; and (4) a commitment to high-quality care, with the belief that external standards should be considered *minimal requirements* for effective health care delivery. Needless to say, reconciling these viewpoints to achieve compliance when penalties for noncompliance have been threatened is likely to be a frustrating process.

Nursing department members genuinely interested in meeting standards recognize that the external standards designated "mandatory" and "truly voluntary" cannot be considered in the same light. When the standards *must* be met, under threat of penalties for noncompliance, the question is *how* to do so in ways that will enhance the quality of the nursing care provided patients. In contrast, a question arises whether voluntary standards should be adopted. Thus, mandatory standards call for designing the relevant department structures so that achievement of the standards does not detract from but, rather, enhances the effectiveness and efficiency of the care provided within the institution without raising costs unnecessarily. In contrast, voluntary standards call for determining compatibility with the philosophy, objectives, and resources of the department in which they would be adopted and implemented. Neither mandatory nor voluntary standards can be expected to benefit patients through the delivery of improved health care unless the nurses understand the *reason* for its adoption. It is essential that one know what implementation of a standard is supposed to achieve and how the mechanism set up for such implementation is related to quality of care outcomes.

Most nursing departments are influenced in one way or another by two organizations that have formulated standards for nursing practice in hospitals—the Joint Commission on Accreditation for Hospitals and the American Nurses' Association. Unquestionably, most of what is said about standards put forth by the Joint Commission applies to those formulated by other agencies that impose mandatory standards; similarly, what is said about the ANA's standards applies in large measure to voluntary standards that are adopted by nursing departments.

The ANA does not have input into the Joint Commission as a member agency, in contrast to the American Hospital Association and various physician groups (the American Medical Association, the American College of Surgeons, and the American College of Physicians). Therefore, the ANA lacks a mechanism for requiring nurses and nursing departments to maintain the standards they advocate. Although nurses do have input into the development and evaluation processes of the Joint Commission, such inclusion is subject to the approval of the other groups.

The Joint Commission is concerned with the hospital as a whole, with the role and functioning of nurses comprising just one small part. In contrast, the ANA focuses exclusively on nursing. Understandably, some of the ANA's activities involve attempts to promote nursing as a profession with status and significant input in matters pertaining to the health delivery system. In contrast, the Joint Commission has no such investment in nursing; to the Commission, nursing is just one aspect of the hospital's structure and functioning, of no more importance than any other aspect. Although some matters are of mutual concern to both organizations, the ANA advocates standards not dealt with by the Joint Commission.

All of the standards for "Nursing Services"[1] set forth by the Joint Commission are covered in some fashion by the *Standards for Nursing Services in Hospitals, Community Health Agencies, Nursing Homes, Industry, Schools, Ambulatory Services, and Related Health Organizations* of the Commission on Nursing Services of the ANA[2]. The ANA Standards tend to emphasize nursing's maintenance of its own directions and autonomy, whereas the Joint Commission Standards stress the importance of the nursing department making certain its members maintain a level of practice commensurate with the mission of the hospital.

The *Standards for Nursing Services* of the ANA include standards intentionally designed to increase the power of nurses within the agency. Thus, it refers to nurses having "responsibility and authority for the quality of nursing practice"[3], having charge of the nursing department budget[4], and being "integrated into the total program of the health care organization"[5].

No conflict exists between the standards for nursing services advocated by the two organizations. However, their emphases are different and, although both are presumably based on the desire to achieve a common goal, differences do exist in the manner in which the standards are presented and in the amount of detail included in their specifications. The Joint Commission, as behooves an agency that must make evaluations for granting or withholding accreditation, tends to be more explicit. In contrast, the ANA Standards adopt a more general stance that emphasizes the development of the profession as it is practiced within a health agency.

STANDARDS OF THE JOINT COMMISSION ON ACCREDITATION OF HOSPITALS

Most hospital nursing services have been involved in attempts to meet standards that satisfy the accreditation requirements of the JCAH. For some nursing departments, the circumstances surrounding an accreditation visit can be hectic and frustrating, particularly if they are instituting activities and procedures just to satisfy Joint Commission requirements and they fail to see the relationship between the standards and the daily provision of health care to patients. The survey visit may well be perceived as a threatening and potentially punitive occasion by nurses who do not understand the standards or the purpose of

the Joint Commission. Knowing that their hospitals entered into contracts with the Joint Commission voluntarily is of no comfort to such individuals. Once the hospital has become a party to the agreement, complying with the Joint Commission Standards becomes a requirement for the nursing department, whether or not its members approve of them.

The Joint Commission does not view its role as one of indicting noncompliers or standing in judgment of hospitals or nurses. Rather, it views its Standards as a means of helping the hospital staff to identify the factors that facilitate or hinder the institution's efforts to fulfill its mission—the provision of high-quality patient care[6]. In this regard, the Commission does not specify the quality of care that the patient must receive; it delineates the structural mechanisms needed to consistently achieve high level nursing care. The Joint Commission does not, for example, set a standard for the percentage of nosocomial infections allowable within a hospital or the conditions under which the development of a decubitus ulcer is or is not acceptable. They do not indicate that the problem-oriented form provides the only acceptable type of patient medical record or that nursing care must be provided under the primary nursing method. They do not even require hospitals to follow the audit system developed by their Quality Review Center—only that some evaluation system be employed that meets certain stipulated criteria.

The Joint Commission Standards have been established as a means of achieving high-quality patient care and should not be confused with the end product of such care, as revealed in the patient's long-term progress. These standards reflect years of experience with hospital practice, accumulated by professionals who have identified the "basic supporting elements of hospital life" that are compatible with achieving high-quality patient care[7]. The standards represent the elements of structure which those professionals consider the necessary ingredients in an optimal care delivery system. Adherence to the standards will not guarantee high-quality care, but the chances of *consistently* achieving high-quality care without adhering to the Joint Commission Standards would be very low.

The time to deal with these standards is *not* just prior to an accreditation visit. If the standards are to promote "high quality of care . . . to give patients the optimal benefits"[8], they must be used as guidelines for the development of a nursing structure that forms an integral part of the overall health care system.

If the standards are to be used as guidelines to complement the other resources employed to achieve patient goals, they must be studied and understood by the nurses responsible for the development and implementation of the various subsystems and programs that comprise the hospital's total facilitative system. Furthermore, adequately informed nurses must go beyond just the standards pertaining to nursing services. That is, they must comprehend the remaining standards that pertain to their daily activities. For example, the standards governing the handling of medical records are in a section titled "Medical Record Services." Nurses are obviously in a position to handle or mishandle medical records and hence must know what is asserted in the relevant standard and also how the standard is to be interpreted.

The standards devoted to other professional services contain provisions pertaining to nurses. In the section titled "Pharmaceutical Services," for example, several standards refer to nurses as participants in their implementation[9]. Nurses must know this material. They not only must be cognizant of their role in the handling and administration of medications, but also must clearly understand what is *not* their role, so they can consistently avoid assumption of activities that are the responsibilities of others (such as the pharmacist). The nurse must see for herself what the standard states and should not depend solely on interpretations by the

professionals most centrally involved. In short, nurses should be familiar with the standards in *any area* that overlaps with their own.

It is important that nurses accurately distinguish between what a given standard actually requires and what merely constitutes examples or suggestions. Discriminations must also be made between standards advocated by the Joint Commission and mere helpful suggestions provided by an individual survey visitor. The manual is explicit in differentiating between recommendations that are mandatory and those which are not. Interpretations of standards are accompanied by information and that helps the reader distinguish between mandatory and voluntary requirements. For example use of the verbs "shall" or "must" indicates that the item is a *requirement* to which the department, the unit, or the hospital in general will be held. The word "should" occurs when a commonly accepted method is being considered that could be replaced by a justifiable alternative. The verb "may" signals a mere suggestion with no preference expressed by the Commission[10].

When the interpretation of the standard states that "Policies shall include . . . noting diagnostic and therapeutic orders"[11], surveyors will expect to see a policy identifying the individuals responsible for noting orders and stipulating the manner in which the procedure is to be carried out. When it states that nursing care plans "may include: medication, treatment, and other items ordered by individuals granted clinical privileges"[12], it is acceptable for such information to be made available in some other fashion. It would be incorrect to conclude from such a statement that the Joint Commission believes medication treatment ordered by the physician does not constitute information essential to planning for the patient; rather, the statement suggests that other ways of making certain the orders are carried out, besides including them in the nursing care plan, are acceptable.

The survey visitor may also make recommendations about using methods that can help fulfill the requirements contained in a particular standard. In such cases, it is important to distinguish between instances in which the visitor is discussing a standard that constitutes a *requirement* and those in which she is recommending a method as a possible means of meeting a particular standard. These distinctions are important because understanding them will help one avoid two kinds of mistakes: (1) adopting poorly understood measures that have little chance of being enforced; and (2) discarding effective systems in favor of less effective ones that have a superficial relevance to meeting some particular standard.

When accepting a charge to develop or implement a policy or procedure designed to satisfy a Joint Commission requirement, it is essential to clearly understand the purpose of that policy or procedure. One also should be able to specify which standard a contemplated policy or procedure is supposed to achieve, as well as the problem its adoption is supposed to solve. A committee trying to write a policy on safety, as mandated by a Joint Commission standard[13], would probably find it difficult to write a single policy statement covering all the safety issues of concern in a hospital. Such a committee would more likely formulate several different policies covering such diverse matters as the use of side rails on patients' beds or the handling of inflammables. Without specific policies dealing with all the potential sources of danger in the hospital, a single overall safety policy statement would probably be meaningless for genuine protection of patients and hospital staff. Because the Joint Commission's intent is to make certain that hospitals protect patients from accidents, it is unlikely that it would consider a single policy statement sufficient. In fact, the only individual who *would* be satisfied by a single safety statement is probably unconcerned about the intent of the requirement and lacks knowledge about the dangers inherent in the hospital setting and effective procedures that protect patients.

Any hospital staff member assigned to write policy statements on safety who does not either question the individual issuing the directive or read the relevant material in the Joint Commission manual (the nursing care standard pertaining to safety, the interpretive comments accompanying that standard, and safety section in the manual) is not likely to come up with useful or effective formulations.

Nursing supervisors rushing around their services prior to a Joint Commission visit to see whether long- and short-term goals have been entered on the nursing care plan Kardex (as the manual recommends[14]) are not providing the leadership needed to assure high-quality nursing care, either. Even if all the Kardexes have long- and short-term goals entered, if they are not used for planning patient care, then the intent of the standard is still not being realized. Approval would not necessarily be withheld when the goals are stated on the Kardex but not used. The surveyors cannot, after all, be expected to go much beyond the evidence presented. But even if such superficial adherence to a standard passes inspection, the effort does not constitute accomplishment of the nursing department's goal. The head nurse who does not question the requirement that she make certain these statements are entered on the Kardex, who knows that nothing is ever done with them after they have been listed, or who is aware she does not know how to use them, is collaborating in the maintenance of an ineffective nursing structure.

The Joint Commission rarely if ever requires unachievable practices or procedures from nursing departments. When nursing departments organize the content relevant to high-quality patient care and establish the conditions that facilitate the provision of such care, externally imposed standards can generally be met without much difficulty. Problems arise when nurses fail to understand a requirement or its intent, when they listen to rumors about

Joint Commission requirements rather than turning to an authoritative source for verification, or when they create a smoke-screen of superficial attempts to comply with standards. Meeting Joint Commission standards will present no serious problems if members of the nursing department staff are willing to make an honest effort to satisfy the intent of the standards and to use them as a resource in planning and developing programs and systems that are essential to providing high-quality nursing care to patients.

STANDARDS OF THE AMERICAN NURSES' ASSOCIATION

The *Standards for Nursing Services,* published by the Commission on Nursing Services of the ANA, have been written to cover all types of organized nursing settings, including hospitals, community health agencies, nursing homes, industry, schools, ambulatory services, and other related health care organizations. Because the standards are so all-encompassing, they are necessarily broadly stated and limited in the degree to which they can provide concrete examples for a particular department of nursing. However, common features are applicable wherever provision of high quality patient care is the goal.

The standards of the ANA or those of any of the voluntary nursing organizations, are not mandatory. Thus, nurses in a given department can choose to ignore them when they establish the structural foundation for the care their unit is to provide patients. However, other nurses may feel more committed to ANA standards than to those imposed by other agencies with the power to dispense rewards for compliance and punishments for noncompliance. Many will embrace ANA standards because they represent the current thinking of the profession; in such cases, the 12 ANA standards for nursing services may be adhered to with as much enthusiasm as the standards of the JCAH.

However, unlike the Joint Commission standards many nurses may not be able to meet all the standards formulated by the ANA. Mainly because the administrative authorities in their hospitals refuse to give them the necessary power and responsibility, nurses may not be able to comply with such standards as control of the departmental budget, determining the nature of the nursing practices to be adopted, and integrating the nursing program into the institution's total health care program.

Individual nurses must then decide whether these standards are essential to realizing their own and the department's goals. If the answer is yes, they must decide the extent to which they are willing to work toward winning the opportunity to adopt those standards. If one concludes that an acceptable level of nursing practice in her hospital depends on achieving a standard, then it becomes necessary to determine the steps she and her colleagues must take to acquire the requisite authority. But the nurse in a position to exert leadership—whether she is a head nurse, a supervisor, or a director of nursing— probably will not achieve any substantial control over her own practice or that of the department if she depends on others for decisions that determine the manner in which nursing care is practiced. Neither will that control become hers if she neglects the everyday opportunities to insist on her right to exert authority in matters directly concerned with nurses and the nursing function. Regrettably, such neglect can occur without the individual's realization of what she is failing to do.

Nursing department personnel will not acquire the power to which they feel entitled in one grand coup, but they can at a minimum refrain from consistently deferring to others. Such behavior, whether caused by doubts regarding one's own knowledge, ability, and rights, or by the fear of incurring the displeasure of authority figures or fellow professionals, weakens nursing's position in the health care delivery field. Standards that assert nurses' right to exercise control over nursing are not likely to be put into practice in the near future in these circumstances, but it is within the power of nurses to determine whether such standards should be rejected out of hand or used as goals toward which to work.

Because the ANA standards are voluntary, even less reason exists to embrace them without understanding their intent than is the case with mandatory standards. Because they are voluntary and no accreditors will descend on the department for periodic checks, one can take the time needed to make certain that attempts to meet the ANA standards enhance the quality of care given patients.

Stevens has said that, to achieve universality of application, the 1973 ANA standards have been divested of any controversial features[15]. She believes this smoothing out to prevent dissent has removed any elements of "color and flair." I might add that rigor and control over level of practice have also been eliminated. The guidelines added to each standard lack the kind of specifics the user needs to elucidate the relationship between the standards and their ultimate goals. As a consequence, the value of the goals themselves is not given a proper emphasis. Because of the lack of specificity, interpretations of the standards can vary greatly from nurse to nurse and from one nursing service to another.

Standards intended for a diverse range of nursing service departments in a diverse range of administrative control situations can possibly suggest requirements in only the barest of outline forms. Undoubtedly, an industrial nursing unit, within the constraints of an organization with major goals unrelated to the provision of health care, must solve different problems in meeting standards than a nursing service in an acute care hospital or in a nursing home. Available resources and the kinds of pressures they face also undoubtedly differ between large hospitals and small nursing

homes. Standards that are sufficiently broad and nondirective to encompass such diverse nursing services constitute standards only in the roughest sense of the term, because of the latitude that must necessarily be allowed in the manner of achieving any one of them.

It remains for the individual nursing service director or nursing service department to determine how the issues raised by each standard may best be processed and what patient outcomes are to be expected when the department has in its own view successfully complied with a given standard.

Standard IV states "The nursing care program is integrated into the total program of the health care organization"[16]. Rotkovitch calls this standard the "heartbeat of nursing services" because, as she says, it will "depend most heavily upon total commitment of the nursing personnel." She maintains further that, for Standard IV to be implemented, nursing representatives must sit on all the committees or deliberative bodies dealing with the various aspects of the overall hospital program[17]. The guidelines listed under the standard themselves state that nurses should participate on "appropriate committees"[18]. Most nurses doubtless agree that nursing should be involved with any bodies making decisions affecting the goals and standards of nursing practice and, therefore, that this standard is worth adopting and striving to meet. Accepting the standard and working to achieve its adoption and implementation may reveal that the difficulties it actually poses are less obvious than they initially seem. Excluding nurses from decision-making bodies may indeed obstruct the achievement of certain patient outcome goals. But this standard could be adopted and implemented and yet such goals still would not be realized. Nurses could serve on virtually every hospital committee and still have no voice in shaping the directions taken by the various programs (including their own); they may not be perceived by other committee members as having anything to contribute or because they do, in fact, lack the knowledge needed to participate meaningfully in the committee's deliberations.

If they limit themselves to what they feel are the ANA guidelines "appropriate committees," the director of nursing and the other nursing department leaders can possibly exclude themselves from the groups that are most instrumental in determining how care is to be provided hospital patients.

Some directors of nursing see themselves as agents of the chief administrators of their institutions and view nursing as an implementing group obligated to carry out the wishes of the hospital's administrative personnel, its physicians, and any of its other professional groups. Such individuals may believe that they are indeed achieving Standard IV, simply because nurses are represented on all the committees dealing with issues related to the *functional aspects* of nursing's interactions with other departments. But serious questions about the validity of such a belief are justifiable, especially when these individuals take the position that discussions pertaining to *administrative policies* and the *instituting of clinical programs* are *not* regarded as part of the nursing department's concerns.

Meeting standards in a way that has a demonstrable impact on the quality of care provided patients is not easily accomplished. A director of nursing might believe she is achieving a major breakthrough for her department when she has managed to obtain control of her department's budget. But she is not contributing significantly to the welfare of patients if she plans the budget without knowing what is needed to assure that the nursing care problems of her patients will be solved satisfactorily. Nurses participating in committees but providing no more than reaffirmations of the positions taken by the other professionals on those committees are not making vital contributions. Their presence or absence

will be of no significance, insofar as the quality of the hospital's total health care program is concerned. "Written personnel policies which assist in recruiting and maintaining a qualified staff"[19] will prove of little help in improving the quality of patient care, unless the word "qualified" is defined in terms of the knowledge and skills required to meet the nursing care needs of patients.

Apparently nothing in the standards of the ANA, if processed appropriately, would not assist in the development of high-quality nursing programs. But neither is there anything that would guarantee the provision of high-quality nursing care. When one starts more or less from scratch with these standards, she has only taken a modest first step in establishing a nursing program designed to provide the best possible care to patients.

Both mandatory and voluntary standards will change as new knowledge is discovered and as a wide variety of societal influences affect the values, customs, and beliefs of those in the health care industry. Detailed discussion of a particular standard at a given time will eventually lose its utility as the standard itself or its interpretations change. The main concern should not focus on whether one is meeting this or that set of standards. Rather, the focus should be on establishing a nursing care delivery system that achieves desirable patient care goals, that makes possible the assimilation of new knowledge regarding patient-care needs and the structures or mechanisms essential to satisfying those needs, and that can change when evaluative data indicate the need for change. For nursing services that have built their nursing care delivery systems with such a focus, external standards from any source will constitute no more than minimal standards that have already been met or surpassed at the time of their formulation and enactment.

REFERENCES

1. Joint Commission on Accreditation of Hospitals. "Nursing Services," *Accreditation Manual for Hospitals.* Chicago: Joint Commission, 1976 (Revision through April, 1977 included) pp. 121–125.
2. Commission on Nursing Services. *Standards for Nursing Services in Hospitals, Community Health Agencies, Nursing Homes, Industry, Schools, Ambulatory Service and Related Health Organizations.* Kansas City, Missouri: American Nurses' Association, 1973.
3. Commission on Nursing Services 1973.
4. Commission on Nursing Services 1973.
5. Commission on Nursing Services 1973.
6. O'Malley, N. C. JCAH Accreditation Part I. *Supervisor Nurse,* 6: 4: 12–14, 18, March 1975.
7. Joint Commission 1976, p. 9.
8. Joint Commission 1976, p. 7.
9. Joint Commission 1976, pp. 143–148c.
10. Joint Commission 1976, p. 187.
11. Joint Commission 1976, p. 123.
12. Joint Commission 1976, p. 124.
13. Joint Commission 1976, p. 123.
14. Joint Commission 1976, p. 124.
15. Stevens, B. J. ANA's standards for nursing services: how do they measure up? *Journal of Nursing Administration,* 6:4:29–31, May 1976.
16. Commission on Nursing Services 1973.
17. Rotkovitch, R. The heartbeat of nursing services. Standard IV. *Journal of Nursing Administration,* 6:4:32–35, May 1976.
18. Commission on Nursing Service 1973.
19. Commission on Nursing Services 1973.

Index

Date Due

. 4 '94